Pleb's
PROGRESS

To Chris,
in gratitude
and admiration,

Mcartin

Pleb's
PROGRESS

The Many Lives of a Social Climber

MARTIN DUFFELL

BROWN
DOG
BOOKS

Published under licence by Brown Dog Books and
The Self Publishing Partnership
7 Green Park Station, Bath BA1 1JB

www.selfpublishingpartnership.co.uk

ISBN printed book: 978-1-78545-030-3
ISBN e-book: 978-1-78545-031-0

Cover design by Kevin Rylands

Printed and bound by CPI Group (UK) Ltd, Croydon CR0 4YY

To Dawn

The events and people in this book are described exactly as they linger in the memory of an old man, and my account of them is therefore likely to contain many inaccuracies. I welcome their correction by any reader with better recall.

CONTENTS

Foreword 8

1. Arrival 12

2. Flight 23

3. Isolation 39

4. Freedom 53

5. Exile 66

6. Respite 80

7. Escape 92

8. Commerce 104

9. Endgame 118

10. Arcadia 133

11. Ice Cream 150

12. Orders 163

13. Soap 182

14. Space 198

15. Heat 216

16. Dust 236

17. Ascent 255

18. Uplands 272

19. Descent 290

20. Minds 310

21. Words 328

FOREWORD

I began this book with the aim of paying tribute to a woman whom I loved but did not praise enough in her lifetime, and I found that as I did so I was able to trace the origins of my most deeply held beliefs. On completing it, I realised I had told the story of an era that is badly misrepresented in the media. *Pleb's Progress* describes a Britain in which opportunities for ordinary people to rise in the social hierarchy far exceeded those available today. But the words *pleb* and *progress* both require some explanation.

The dictionary definition of the word *pleb* is: 'an ordinary person of low social status'. In Britain the use of this word is almost always derogatory, expressing the speaker's contempt for, and distance from, the common people. For most of the last millennium Britain's ruling elite have despised plebs and made it extremely difficult for them to make social progress; it was easier to imagine a rake or a pilgrim progressing than a pleb. And so it was a shock to the system when, in the third quarter of the twentieth century, thousands of plebs swarmed over social barriers in the greatest class migration since the Black Death, six hundred years earlier.

This uprising had its roots in World War II, when close contact taught British plebs how mediocre and shallow most of their officers were. They led their troops to a succession of defeats from which

Britain had to be rescued by ordinary GI Joes and ruthless Russian comrades. From Norway to Singapore the squirearchy was caught with its union jacks down, and the British army responded by opening its commissions to competition rather than confining them to the privately educated. This was rewarded with vastly improved results, and many plebs returned home with pips instead of chips on their shoulders. For a short while Britain lost its awe of the ruling class, and in 1945 its voters elected a Labour government.

Some Tories, however, had already realised that the benefits of open competition might be extended to civilian life, and in 1944 R. A. Butler had steered an act through parliament that offered a free higher education to anyone able to compete for one. The 1944 Act loosened the grip of the churches on the nation's young, raised the minimum school-leaving age to fifteen, and decreed that all children would in future compete for grammar-school places at the age of eleven (and thus might contest university places at eighteen).

One of its more radical provisions was the inclusion in the eleven-plus exam of IQ tests. These tests measure educational potential, rather than achievement to date, and greatly reduce the advantages of a more privileged upbringing. As a result, by the 1950s most British universities were recruiting a much higher proportion of their students from poor families than ever before (or than they do today). Only Oxford and Cambridge resisted this trend, by making admission dependent upon exams that required special preparation, but poor children could gain access even to these if their grammar schools chose to prepare them, as the biggest and best did.

Paradoxically, it was democracy that killed off the first ever attempt (at least in England) to create an educational meritocracy. The 1944 Act led to about 20 per cent of children entering grammar schools and the remainder being assigned to secondary modern schools. Politicians soon learned that they could win the votes of disgruntled parents by closing grammar schools in most parts of the country. The result was a dramatic fall in the quality of state education, which successive governments tackled with a series of shake-ups that made it worse.

Today, able and ambitious lower-class children face innumerable hazards: the first is that the competition for places at secondary schools with high academic standards is distorted by private tuition (the parents of 14 per cent of British children can afford this). The second is that vast numbers of ordinary state schools no longer teach rigorous subjects like individual sciences and foreign languages. Other hazards include lack of discipline, temporary teachers, unqualified teachers, lack of facilities, squeezed budgets, and classes that have too many pupils, or too many unable to speak English. In future very few plebs will progress, mostly via pop music, football, crime, or selling their physical charms; but the educational route to better jobs is no longer open.

At first sight, the shake-up of higher education in the years following 2010 seems to have increased opportunities: anyone can now open a university, and any eighteen-year-old boy or girl can borrow the money to pay its fees. (If I were fifty years younger, I would open a university myself.) Since the non-fees element of student loans is almost double the rate of unemployment pay, the majority of British youngsters will take one out. But the gap in standards between the best and worst universities is now so wide that most graduates will spend their lives doing low-paid jobs. These youngsters know that they will never have to repay their loans, so millions are punishing the government in this way. The government may deserve it, but in the future few plebs will progress.

This book's subtitle is much easier to explain. My long life seems like many because I have been lucky enough to enjoy many different careers: as labourer, chess player, student, soldier, teacher, salesman, manager, recruiter, editor, writer, and academic researcher. To enjoy this variety I have had to take risks and sacrifice promotions: ; instead of rising steadily in one hierarchy, I have slipped in and out of several, and learned much from the experience. Almost all my career changes were my own decision, and almost all the jobs I have undertaken have been of the most satisfying type: work that is largely autonomous, sufficiently complex, and rewarded on results.

The need to earn a living and the ambition to rise in a hierarchy are strong motivators, but they are not the most powerful forces in life. Our genes insist on going forth and multiplying, and they bribe us with moments of ecstasy that are ten times more pleasurable when shared. Love, and its physical expression, played a big part in all my lives, although social restraints in the 1950s delayed my graduation from private practice to a full relationship. Since the joys of sex are mostly mental, many boys in those days developed vivid imaginations; they could summon to their beds at night the wraiths of the girls with whom they flirted by day. And, if more substantial relations were deferred, this made them all the sweeter when they arrived.

It might be argued that the greater educational and career opportunities enjoyed by poor boys in the 1950s were more than balanced by the shortage of sexual opportunities they suffered. But, although at that time sex was censored in the media, it was still at the centre of people's lives: I remember the 1950s as being full of love as well as hope, and sex as well as socialism. My tale is one of individual survival and unexpected success, and it is also the story of a quest for love that ended in an enduring passion. I have been even luckier in love than I have in my careers.

Although they must be satisfied in different ways, human needs remain the same in every era: food, shelter, sex, companionship, status, and mental stimulation. I sought to satisfy all of these needs in an age that is now regarded as somewhat bleak, but which at the time seemed full of exciting possibilities. Perhaps the most powerful argument in favour of the 1950s, 60s, and '70s is that I have no desire to be young again *now*, but I would dearly wish to be young again *then*. In writing this book that wish has been granted.

1

ARRIVAL

I was born on an island where it mostly used to rain, not in torrents, but in a steady drizzle that greened the countryside and taught its inhabitants not to hope for too much, or rise too high. In winter the rain turned first to sleet and then to snow, and every year ice crusted rivers that have since run dry. The adults carved pathways between the buildings and piled the snow high on either side, so that the children spent the winter in blind valleys, where they ran and slid on the crystals that coated the ground. The children grew by falling, and picking themselves up again, and learned cunning by compacting snow in their hands into missiles, which they hurled at whoever was least likely to retaliate. When the blood in their fingers froze they huddled round smoky fires and nursed chaps and chilblains, and they slept long and deep in beds teeming with microscopic creatures that fed on their dead skin. After Easter they changed their clothes and picked flowers, and marvelled at the insects, birds, and mammals that appeared miraculously from nowhere. The sun gradually crawled up the sky: in August it blazed and burned the fields to gold, in September it filled the hedgerows with fruits; and in October the winds blew and heaped the earth with sunburnt leaves, ripe nuts, and broken branches.

The year's rhythm of birth, growth, decline, and death was mirrored in people's lives, although they magnified the importance of the small details, called events, which marked the paths of individuals, and they lingered over the few choices that led from one event to the next. This book is my last attempt to make sense of the events and choices of my own life before I join the millions who have passed before me, enjoying, suffering, marvelling, forgetting, and ultimately forgotten.

My life began, like all others, with an unravelling of twin helices, an impulsive encounter, months of floating in an enclosed sea, and a blinding collision with the atmosphere that I celebrate each year. But the sponsors of this process, my mother and father, stand at the extremes of the known and the unknown: they are the firmament and the void, the matter and the anti-matter of my universe. How can I mention them in the same breath? How can I account for both in the same ledger? How can I find a place for both on the same page? My mother was one of the virtuous poor, who have always predominated in the world's population, but have slaved only in order to be abused by the privileged and forgotten by history. She was brought up to speak truthfully, work hard, obey her betters, and be loyal to her clan and class: all of these she did exemplarily well, until her hands grew calloused, her back bent, her joints hardened, her eyes watered, and her hope died. She was one of nine children born in the East End of London to a timber salesman and the daughter of a fishmonger; that eight of the siblings survived to old age is a tribute to my grandparents' energy and devotion.

The children's given names demonstrate how assiduously the poor of the capital aped middle-class manners: in my grandfather's family the sons of sons were named Thomas, John, James, and Edward, so that at future funerals I would be bewildered by the sheer number of Uncle Jims, Uncle Jacks, and Uncle Teds. The daughters of sons, on the other hand, were named after their paternal and maternal grandmothers, and if (God forbid!) there were more than two of them, their mother at last had a chance to effect a mutation to the name-pool. The sons and daughters of daughters were, of course, exempt from these rules, because they were absorbed into the naming rituals of their mother's husband's clan.

Such strong traditions of nomenclature ensured that men worked as hard as my grandfather to pay the rent on a large house, and that women lost their figures, like my grandmother, by a process that combined almost continuous pregnancy with cooking (and tasting) the cheap but wholesome food at which so many mouths watered. But these worthy Cockneys were fortunate, and they knew it: the poor of Africa and Asia laboured longer and harder for far less, while suffering humiliation and degradation imposed by their foreign masters. Since empire brought such rich rewards, it was not surprising that many millions of Europeans were prepared to die in order to gain it, or maintain it. And just as my mother came of age in 1914, they did.

Sarah, being the second daughter, was named after her mother, and her maternal grandmother, and like them she left school at the age of thirteen. Notwithstanding the fact that by that age she had read more than the rest of her class combined, she was put to work first in a cigar factory, and then in a clothing workshop. If she had followed her mother's example this would have been a brief interlude before marriage and her chance to play the Victorian name game with a family of her own. But soon after her eighteenth birthday Europe was plunged into war, and far fewer dockyard workers, factory hands, and costermongers returned from it than had left, and their bereaved sweethearts had become enamoured of the freedom and independence that the war had brought them. The skills that a record number of women learned in wartime offered a pool of cheap labour: a woman could produce as much wealth for two pounds a week as a man was willing to contribute for four, and market forces did the rest. For almost two decades men suffered unemployment on an unprecedented scale, while factory girls enjoyed money and freedom such as few English women had ever known.

Although Sarah's face was not exactly designed to make her fortune, she had the skimpy figure required today in Hollywood (but not the matchstick legs), and seems always to have had a boyfriend of some sort. By her late twenties she found that the best men were almost always married, which didn't really matter as long as you didn't want to marry any of them. She was as swift a machinist as she was a reader, so the piecework system and long hours provided enough for her keep, for books, for clothes in which to 'go up West and have a good time', and for little luxuries for her mother. My grandmother had fled the marital home as it emptied of those she loved, bringing her into unwelcome contact with the bad-tempered old man who had fathered them (and whom I suspect I closely resemble). Although her children brokered a number of attempts at reconciliation, she died, as she would have wished (and as I shall relate), in her daughter's home.

The inter-war years were Sarah's 'good time', too good to sacrifice for a fate like her mother's, and too precious to yield to a man's dominion. That most men were 'slower on the uptake' than she was didn't matter as long as she did not have to live with them day in and day out. She satisfied her romantic disposition by reading innumerable novels and dreaming impossible dreams: the fact that the men in both were of a non-existent type hardly bothered her; like any intelligent woman, she preferred the men in books to the tawdry creatures around her.

One such tawdry creature was my father. Simon arrived in Stepney from Russia at the age of twelve, having fled with his family from one of the numerous massacres that European Christians have used as excuses to rob their Jewish neighbours. The family's plans to have this bookish boy trained as a rabbi were abandoned along with most of their possessions, and Simon, as a foreign national, was taught the same trade and found the same work as my mother. Male factory workers earned more and were laid off more often, and this enabled Simon to hone his skills at the card table, where he won more often than he lost, and to read widely. I can imagine that, like me, he was tall and clumsy as a young man and bald and morose as an old one; but since I have never seen a photograph of him, I can't be sure.

After his father's death he lived with his mother, whose parsimony and ruthlessness had allowed her to become, in today's parlance, a provider of financial services to her poorer neighbours. Although her faith demanded that her son go forth and multiply, her life became increasingly devoted to him and to her business, and she can hardly have been prepared for the bombshell he would one day deliver. All this was happening in a world where Germans were fabricating the fantasy that they were Destiny's chosen people, which naturally brought them into conflict with a community that had been making the same claim for thousands of years. British Jews had good reason to be fearful at this time but, while Britain's leaders were almost as racist as their German equivalents, the people of London never allowed the fascists to march, or to burn, or to rob their Jewish neighbours.

The notion of race is one that has wilted under scientific investigation; while one population may, on average, have longer limbs or darker skins, most of the world's six billion are of very mixed race, and none more so than the Jews of Europe. Since they were scattered over thousands of square miles, subject to Christian or Muslim jurisdiction, and provided their fellows with essential services, it was inevitable that Semitic and Indo-European genes became mixed. Such interbreeding had long been recognised by Jewish law, which decreed that the issue of mixed unions are Jewish if the mother is Jewish, and gentile if the father is Jewish. This rule evolved in ancient times when Jews, like all subjugated peoples, were in no position to defend their women from the attention of their conquerors; and this was also their situation in medieval Europe. Thus European Jews (*Ashkenazim*) are white, whereas the Jews of Arabia (*Misrahim*) are brown, like the Muslim refugees who made up most of their neighbours for thirteen hundred years. Europeans as a whole are such a mixed race that it now seems amazing that they ever subscribed to the racist fallacy; nevertheless, it was one of two that characterised the period in which my parents had to live their lives. The other was the fallacy that a man who seizes power in the name of the people will be any less a tyrant than a heaven-born monarch.

In the 1930s the giant shadows of twin tyrants in Moscow and Berlin hung over all the peoples of Europe, and those shadows formed the background to my parents' courtship and marriage, along with the perpetual blight of market forces. Left unchecked, the rich always get richer and the poor poorer, because the rich charge the poor interest on their poverty; and the rich of Britain had gone unchecked for almost a thousand years. Until the end of the 1930s the British poor accepted that malnutrition and tuberculosis should maim their bodies, that the contempt of their betters should break their spirits, and that their children should go without shoes in winter. (It was largely the theft of shoes that populated Australia, whose inhabitants still run barefoot at every opportunity to commemorate their escape.) While starving miners marched and itinerant farm-labourers starved, Sarah and Simon conducted their unlikely courtship in the relative comfort of the East End's filthy streets.

Jew and Gentile, they worked at the same factory, hated the same boss, liked the same things, laughed at the same jokes, and experienced the same rushes of blood to the parts that other fluids cannot reach. In Israel today when a Jew wishes to marry a Gentile they both have to flee the country, but in 1930s London such matches were not unknown, and among progressive Jews there was even a ceremony of conversion that for *shiksas* was no more arduous than a Roman Catholic mass. Trollope said that the greatest hardship in a civilised society lies in having to endure sermons, but being preached at in an unknown, and therefore undemanding, language is surely the lightest of such hardships. Simon's mother was doubtless mortified by the whole situation, but faced with the choice of losing an only son or gaining a Martian daughter-in-law, any woman would have made the same bitter, humiliating choice.

Sarah, by virtue of her phenomenal output and lower rate of pay, had been in continuous employment, but in 1935 Simon, too, had work. Perhaps the key to their union was that their thirty-ninth birthdays fell that year, ushering in a period of madness when biological clocks take precedence over having a good time, and hormones weigh heavier than more logical considerations. In any event, they were able to afford rent and a few sticks of furniture, which is all that is required for people to set up home together. And in the snug, stifling world of the East End their sudden exposure to each other could be relieved by visiting their respective mothers, gossiping with sisters, or playing a hand of poker with friends.

My mother once confessed that she had enjoyed a 'full married life', and I doubt if the role of passion in those two years was different from that in any other new marriage. There used to be a rule that the British did it often (think of the birth rate in the industrial revolution), but never talked about it. This has always puzzled Americans, who talk about nothing else (except money), and has led to the weird convention that in Hollywood's versions of British novels obsessive fornicators have to be written out of the script. But, as their scriptwriter, I must not deny Simon and Sarah a little joy, lying together under the giant shadows of their time, and planning to buy a new sofa, or risk a trip to Southend.

For the first two months of my life my mother thought I was the menopause, which often arrives in the early forties for women with poor nutrition. Discovering the truth provoked in Sarah the usual mixture of ecstasy and blind terror; and, as with all working girls, she had the added problem of how to combine work with a baby, a problem that today is met by working longer hours so as to be able to afford an immigrant nanny. In the 1930s East Enders believed that such a dereliction of duty would lead, at worst, to juvenile crime and, at best, to anti-social behaviour, so Simon prepared to shoulder his new family's economic burden alone. Perhaps it led him to approach his boss for a rise; if so, the move had fatal consequences for his marriage, and thus changed my life.

Had I been raised as a Jew, I doubt whether my mother would have tolerated me wearing a hat indoors, or whether I would have been able to forego the pleasures of pig and prawn. But I would have been able to read Hebrew, and that seems to me an inestimable loss. But one fewer Jew can mean several more Palestinians (each of whom consumes less than one-tenth of the water), so I am resolved to be philosophical about it. Anyway, Sarah's slim frame ballooned, a room in a nursing home was booked, and events took their course.

I once knew a boy who thought it would impress his school friends if he told them he had been born in Wembley stadium, and we all have to draw heavily on our imagination to picture our birthing. The bare facts in my case were: a maternity hospital in the Essex marshes, a first howl at six in the morning after eleven hours' labour, and a birth weight of nine pounds. In view of her advanced age and general health, Sarah had been advised to book an expensive (for her) bed in a hospital and to stay with her mother for a fortnight before the baby was due (an ancient custom among primitive people from the Lea to the Ganges).

Since the difficult birth enforced a further week in hospital afterwards, this left almost a month for Simon's world to collapse, and he chose to embrace its ruins in solitude and silence. The loss of his job, and thus both incomes, and his anxiety and despair were all a godsend to his mother, who saw a chance to reclaim him from that *shiksa* and teach her a thing or two. Hospitality and generosity were her weapons: providing Simon gave up the marital flat and sold off the furniture to pay his debts, she would give the pristine trio rooms in her home and keep them all until Simon was back in work. Simon capitulated, but put off telling Sarah until she was well enough to leave hospital. This was a mistake, because it meant that she was also well enough to leave him.

Women are hard-wired to need a child more than a husband, and to need a live-in mother-in-law least of all. For millennia Indian women have fried one another in ghee over this issue, and women from the East End of London feel just as strongly. But Sarah contained her fires within her and issued an ultimatum: she would return to Simon only when he had replaced the home for which she had slaved and saved, and of which he had robbed her. Otherwise he would never see his son again. The conditions were deliberately impossible to fulfil, and Simon's efforts to get Sarah to reconsider during the weeks that followed were half-hearted; his scriptures had taught him the dangers of living with a hate-filled woman: he could never have closed his eyes again as long as there were a hammer and nail in the house. So he never saw his son again; the courts made an award of ten shillings a week towards the upkeep of the child, to be paid out of the father's unemployment money, and a registered envelope containing that sum became the only link between man and wife for the next sixteen years.

Even when Simon, as a Russian by birth, was carted off to a British concentration camp in 1940, the money continued to arrive: I suspect his mother saw it as a blood-price, a debt witnessed by her god, who had returned her son to her. But at least I have always known that I came from reliable people; the last registered envelope arrived on my sixteenth birthday. Simon was released from the camp after Hitler attacked Stalin and the Russians became the goodies instead of the baddies; war work was plentiful and I imagine him making ill-fitting uniforms for soldiers whose measurements he did not know, until peace came and returned him to his natural state of unemployment.

I know only that some years later Simon had another son, by a Jewish girl, whom he slyly told that Sarah would never divorce him. But that girl's mother was even slyer: her solicitor traced Sarah and offered her cash in return for a single divorce-court appearance, an offer Sarah could not refuse. She asked me whether I wished to go with her and see Simon, or what was left of him, out of curiosity (she kept no photo). But the hearing coincided with a game of football I wanted to play, and fourteen-year-old boys have their priorities. So Simon passed out of my life without ever passing into it.

But to return to the East End in 1937, an economic crisis had to be solved: Sarah had chosen a lifetime of penury rather than humiliation. As a single mother long before they became fashionable, she knew she would now be poor, even compared with the poor. She would have to get up earlier, eat less, dress more shabbily, and fall asleep exhausted more often, but she had her son and her independence. In this fashion many wronged women have faced the spite and terror of the universe ever since our species began, and, miraculously, some have survived.

For survival Sarah had nothing so pretentious as a strategy, only some simple tactics developed over centuries by East End girls with babies (as social scientists first noted in the 1970s). She did a deal with her mother: they set up house together, and Sarah returned to the sweatshop, while my grandmother, who was badly missing her own brood, took me over. I called her 'Nanny', a term often used for mothers' mothers in the East End, who should never be confused with the professionals to whom the rich condemned their offspring, trainee dragons who compensated for their daily humiliations by instilling the fear of hell in their charges. For Sarah and Nanny it really became a house because of another accident of fortune.

Sarah's younger sister Ann had fallen in love with and married Harry, a young bricklayer, who couldn't yet afford a house for the family they had just started. But the four adults (two of whom were wage earners) and three babies could fit into one house, which Harry ingeniously converted into two flats. Harry had a very sunny disposition, perhaps because his looks were a blond version of the film star Clarke Gable's and he was so brilliant with his hands that no physical task had ever defied him for more than five minutes. Harry was to have a long and successful career in the construction industry, a long and happy marriage, and more grandchildren and great-grandchildren than his knees could accommodate. It was my great good fortune to have him as my childhood model of what a man might be, and we were still good friends when he smiled his last at the age of ninety.

In the short term Harry provided the muscle and the three women the care to make for a successful household by East Ham standards. And all around us were other uncles and aunts and cousins, who kept our days filled with chores and chatter. So the short term was good: the depression eased, work became more plentiful, and wages rose slightly. Those years I don't remember were, I think, very happy ones and, if there ever were such a thing as a redundancy of love, I enjoyed it. I may have missed the thrill of being thrown into the air by a father, but I thrived on the intimacy of women and the constant stream of language that surrounded me.

My grandmother had loved talking to her children as they grew up, but her ninth was in her twenties when I became her tenth charge, and my grandmother never recaptured the art of talking down. As a result I was speaking in sentences at ten months old, and ever since my biggest problem has been to stop talking. (Silence is something I am learning only in old age.) My grandmother also taught me numbers, because she was addicted to the football pools, in which every match had a number, and I was entrusted with drawing these out of a mixing bowl placed on the table of my high-chair. She faithfully copied my choices onto her coupon, but all in vain; little did she know that her charge's luck would be restricted to getting away with more in life than anyone deserves. I did not make her rich, but I like to think that at least I helped make her last few years happy.

2

FLIGHT

Happiness does not last, as the Czechs found out in 1938, the Poles in 1939, and the inhabitants of London's East End in 1940. The bombs began to fall and the sky burned at night; we saw it as we hurried to the shelter that my uncles had built in the garden. At first the three toddlers, my cousins Sylvia and Kay, and I, thought sleeping in a hole in the ground was the greatest of adventures, but it was a time of anxiety and terror for the adults, particularly our grandmother, whose lungs were not up to it. The only child she had lost, my namesake, had died of pneumonia in 1918, and now the same rattling killer crept into our shelter and took her by the throat. She did not suffer long.

When I look at my grandmother's image in my photograph album I see a rather fat woman, dressed drably, sitting on a beach at Southend. She has a heavy round face that has not found its smile in time for the photographer, and she has a look in her eye that says she will brook no nonsense. She had not raised nine children by love alone, but she had lived and died for them, and for their children. No woman can do, or has done, more. Nearly forty years later Sarah's last wish was to be buried alongside her mother; and so they will lie, Sarah by Sarah, until some flood or motorway development unearths bones that have become one again.

Wartime funerals were hasty affairs; my earliest memory is of an afternoon spent in a neighbour's garden wondering where my world had gone. When Sarah and Ann returned they descended into the Anderson shelter for the last time; as their neighbours' homes went up in flames around them, the two sisters made an important decision. They were not going to wait for one of their babies to become the bombers', or the rattling killer's, next victim: they would run. The decision was made easy by the fate of fathers. Simon was, as ever, absent, but so was Harry. Although Harry had a reserved wartime occupation, he had tried to enlist in the navy as soon as war broke out. To his horror he discovered that he was completely colour-blind and could serve only as stoker.

The recruitment officer advised him to go and build factory chimneys, where he would be far more valuable; so Harry's coolness and total competence when working hundreds of feet above the ground became the Fleet Air Arm's loss and the munitions industry's gain. His war work took him to the skies of the Midlands and the North of England, which were not entirely free of enemy aircraft. But, unlike the stokers of many, many ships, he did not shovel his way to a death he could not see. Simon, once released, doubtless machined uniforms back in the East End and dreamed of the days when workers were laid off and had time to read books and play cards.

In any event, there was no longer anything in London to keep Sarah, Ann, and their children in their hole in the ground. Without Nanny, Sarah had to give up her job to look after me, and Ann's chances of seeing Harry might improve if she lived further north. So that was the obvious direction to run, although neither had ever ventured further north than Walthamstow. The sisters borrowed a railway timetable and scanned it anxiously: how far could you get from London's bombs without encountering Birmingham's (or, as they were to discover later, Coventry's)? Their sanctuary obviously had to have a railway station and be big enough to have what in those dark days was called a billeting officer (a busybody who lodged refugees in people's spare rooms).

The sisters chose Chipping Norton because the name sounded like a joke; it was ninety miles from London, a market town with a small tweed mill and a population of 4,000. There were other decisions to be made: they could take with them only one suitcase each and the three toddlers had to share two pushchairs. Everything else they possessed was left behind, the furniture to be sold to a dealer for next to nothing, the more portable personal possessions to be brought on by a carrier some weeks later.

My second earliest memory is of the journey to Paddington station, much of it on foot because of the devastation caused by air raids. At this time a large part of the British army, not long rescued from Dunkirk, was waiting for the next disastrous posting. It was our good fortune to meet up with a group of soldiers, briefly on leave in London, with time on their for-once-empty hands. Mopping up two women, three toddlers, two suitcases, and two pushchairs took a matter of seconds. Children and suitcases were mounted on pairs of broad shoulders and escorted into exile like the elephant-borne harem of a disgraced maharajah. They carried us laughing and joking through the gloomy streets, to show us they were still young and strong, and that in this war they were the good guys.

In five years' time even younger soldiers, smarting from even more bitter defeats, would be showing the same brave face all over Germany, but for the time being we Brits could imagine that we were uniquely brave, and that survival was a sufficient reason for living.

The conventional wisdom says that World War II brought out the best in our islands' population: certainly, you stop taking people for granted when you don't know how long they will be there. But wartime also brings out less generous traits: young and old become more anxious to copulate, and to hell with the consequences to their partners; spivs, or entrepreneurs as they now style themselves, become more entrepreneurial; and class differences become more bitter. While the elite make sacrifices for their chums, and the ordinary folk for their mates, chums rarely lift a finger to help mates. In fact, mates seem scarcely human to chums, and were often treated as such during the war. It was for this reason that the most popular generals with the troops were always those who publicly humiliated their officers; and when the war ended the mates took revenge on the chums in the most dramatic manner.

But it gratified those soldiers on the road to Paddington to come to the aid of two working-class girls and their scruffy brats, with nothing more in it for themselves than a laugh, and a joke, and a wave of the hand. It enabled those young men to return in better spirits to their world of mud and blood, bullying and helplessness, and, if they were lucky, five long years of frustration.

The station contained the largest number of people I had ever seen and they crowded every inch of the platforms; you would not have dreamed that war had undone so many. Miraculously we found the right train and just enough space to travel in it; and strange men found us privileged positions in the heaps that spilled over compartments and corridors. These were the days when women were condemned to many things, but not equality. It is, perhaps, a sign of my age that liberation seems to me to have made women as bad as men (they used to be far superior) and men even worse. The old philosophers, of course, knew well that empowering people makes them evil, but the young despise the old if they are not taught to respect them, and nowadays everyone wants empowerment.

But back in the autumn of 1940 Sarah, Ann, and their brood were powerless, borne to their unknown destination, like feathers floating on the wind, by nothing more than the goodwill of their fellow men. The goodwill ran out on Chipping Norton (GWR) station. A handful of refugee families fell out of the train and onto the platform, from which they were marched onto a forecourt by a busybody, who fended them off as if they had lice (some probably had).

The busybody was large (very), female (just), and strident, not in the local tongue, but in posh English, which was doubtless her claim to the position of busybody. She informed us that the town was already swarming with refugees and there was not a square foot of vacant accommodation left. As invariably happens on these occasions, there was no room at the inn; but she had gone to great trouble (she said) to find stables and mangers in the outlying villages. That was when we discovered that Chipping Norton was always called Chippy, and that it was surrounded by even more obscure places with names like Over and Hook Norton, and Great and Little Rollright.

The busybody had requisitioned every spare farmhouse room in them all (to the chagrin of the farmers' wives) and proceeded to post us to them. Sarah and Ann were mercifully allocated the only address with two rooms. The children slept on the lorry journey to Over Norton, missing what in more wakeful hours would have been a great excitement. Their mothers were greeted with a cup of tea by a reluctant, but not unsympathetic, farmer's wife and the refugees were soon soundly asleep in two large but comfortable beds.

The next morning the farmer's wife warmed to us a little, probably because all three toddlers (aged two, three, and four) had been nursery trained and had not soiled her beds. She answered the many questions the sisters had to put: no, there were no shops in the hamlet; yes, there were buses to Chippy, every day except Sunday; yes, she had both running water and electricity; but any attempt to improve our accommodation would be in vain, because no other house in the village had either, or an indoor lavatory. And so on, until the refugee sisters had been thoroughly convinced of their good luck and Sarah had resolved silently to move on at the first possible moment.

The refugees then began to explore their surroundings with all the suspicion that most Cockneys harbour for the countryside. The sisters discovered that Over Norton was on a steep hill a mile above Chippy;

their first problem was how to stop the pushchairs exceeding thirty miles an hour on the way down, and their second how to get them up again. Ann, who always looked on the bright side, pointed out what good exercise it was for small children to get out and push, while Sarah, who didn't, noted the increased risk from passing lorries. To her horror, she had discovered that country lanes have neither pavements nor street-lights, and she never forgave the country for it.

Walking soon became the sisters' chief occupation, but to Sarah's mind it was a hazardous one. First there were the beasts in the fields, which all seemed significantly larger than they had in an East Ham picture book, where they had always been shown in fields, sties, and stables. In real life they had to be taken down lanes at frequent intervals and might even make a brief escape. The children, however, were fascinated by them, and the more obscene the things the animals did, the more intrigued the children were. Being trampled and bitten did not enter their minds, which were filled with curiosity as to what the beasts would feel like to touch.

This was where we first learned to disobey, a lesson of the utmost importance in juvenile development. In the presence of our mothers, we kept away from all animals except cats and dogs; in their absence we learned to explore the fields at will and approach any creature we saw in them. Fortunately wolves and bears had long been extinct in that part of Oxfordshire. Today there is doubtless a lobby to reintroduce them, but children have long ago been shut up indoors for fear of far more vicious beasts, human ones.

This, too, was where we learned that everyone is human and fallible. Philip Roth described how, as a child in the USA, he believed that his mother had supernatural powers, and turned into his schoolteacher on weekdays. But in the country you learned that your mother could be afraid of things that you were not.

Another cause for alarm was the occasional sight of troops on field exercises, swarming over dry-stone walls and pointing guns, which prompted the anxious question 'Are they ours or theirs?' Another was the bombardment from the skies: there were birds everywhere, whose resentment of the Cockney invasion was expressed in the places they chose to defecate, and all the roads were lined with horse chestnut trees, armed with shiny brown nuts (how we children adored them!) that could deliver a stunning blow. Maliciously they lay in wait for refugees to pass below, and women who had endured thousands of tons of HE and incendiary bombs walked in the middle of the country roads all autumn.

A further source of panic was the loud siren-like noise that the sisters sometimes heard. 'Is that the warning or the all-clear?' they asked the first wizened local they met in the lanes. The reply, 'Issurmlootah', was their first encounter with the local language, because the busybody had talked posh, and the farmer's wife spoke what seemed only a countrified version of standard English. When we returned, the farmer's wife explained that the mill's hooter was sounded every day when its workers were free to go home, and that this was what the gaffer had been trying to communicate.

The same language problems beset the refugees when they got to Chippy: Cockney voices still turned some heads, and there was blatant discrimination in the shops, where locals always got served first, something that mattered when every sort of commodity frequently ran out before the queue was satisfied. Much nonsense has been written about how the war brought the people of Britain together, but scarcity often widened the gulfs between them. The TV programme *Dad's Army* accurately included in its ranks a spiv who could obtain anything at a price and a butcher whose sausages bought favours.

In theory, rationing and coupons ensured fairness; in practice a free market for coupons soon developed. Thus most grocers gave their poorer customers free margarine in exchange for their butter coupons, and then offered 'under-the-counter' butter to richer ones at vastly inflated prices. No one was above this sort of corruption: in most villages the lady of the manor traded her cast-off clothes for her tenants' and workers' clothing coupons, and her inferiors had little say in this transaction. Most of all, the exemption of restaurant meals from rationing meant that for those who could afford them rationing never existed. In the post-war years claims were often made in the media that wartime rations had been healthy and that people were living longer as a result. But the same longevity figures showed clearly that members of the class that had escaped rationing were living ten years longer than those who suffered it.

Most of the refugees in wartime Britain had been used to deprivation: they had lived through a long depression, and they now complained remarkably little about shortages and rationing. It was the primitive conditions in rural areas that hurt. The foreign country into which the Great Western Railway had catapulted the sisters revolted and horrified them, and in the short term there was no prospect of a return to civilisation. But the children took it all in their stride: it was just the next step in the process of growing up.

Compared to an East End council estate, rural Oxfordshire was a wonderful place to grow up. For the rest of our lives Sarah's hatred of the countryside contrasted with my own passion for it. Similarly, her love of London is matched by my loathing for the place where I have spent most of my life getting and spending in order to raise a family. To Sarah the fields and woods were an empty wasteland, but to me they are full of exotic life. I was never able to change her mind on this issue, and I am deeply sorrowed by the fact that so much of her life was spent in miserable exile. My only comfort is the knowledge that she did, eventually, get back to civilisation, to things like pavements, and street-lights, and frequent public transport.

The two sisters' flight caused a flutter among their siblings back in blitzed London, and, at different times, two paid them brief visits in their cramped sanctuary. Hester, only a few years younger than Sarah, had borne eight children of her own, the youngest now a teenager, and

Hester had inherited her mother's tendency to obesity. She arrived and was shocked to discover that Chippy station was at the foot of a steep hill and nearly a mile from the town. Her visit was brief and she declared that she would rather be bombed to smithereens than live like a savage in the back of beyond. I did not know where smithereens was, but she never reached it; although she caught the next train back, she survived bombs and doodlebugs to die at a ripe old age.

Edith was the baby of the family and barely out of her teens. She was probably the most affected by her mother's death of any of the siblings, and her new freedom from moral censure combined with the war to make her what today we would term a *tearaway*. Being single, she had either to join the women's services or do war work; she had trained as a tailor (a *tailoress* in those days), but she realised that waitresses met even more handsome officers than girl soldiers did, and under far more relaxed conditions. So instead of becoming a WRNS, WAAF, or ATS girl, she became a waitress, and to escape the blitz she took a job in Oxford, at a posh hotel where the military guests all had pips on their shoulders or rings on their sleeves.

Waitresses are in a privileged position when it comes to sexual opportunity, because no sooner is a man's stomach full, than his erectile tissue becomes his priority. Edith embarked on a series of love affairs across the class divide and, since the first of these was with an army officer named Theo, her sisters referred to each of her partners as the latest Theo. Edith was equally unimpressed with the refugees' lifestyle; Chippy, she declared, was the deadest place on earth, and she formed a plan to rescue at least one of her sisters.

She invited Sarah to join her in Oxford, where Edith's hotel was short of waiting staff and would provide Sarah, and her toddler son, with luxury accommodation: running water, electricity, and an indoor lavatory. Sarah was tempted and fell, and Ann encouraged her to take the opportunity. Ann was encumbered with two children, but she had Harry, who had learned that he could get away to visit his family once a month. He was devoted to Ann, and to his children, and as he laid bricks in the skies to the north of us, he thought only of returning to enjoy them, something impossible under the prevailing arrangements. Now Ann was left in possession of both rooms in the farmhouse and knew some privacy again, while Sarah packed and took me to Oxford. My earliest memories of that city are of shops and traffic beyond belief, and double-decker buses. The place that made the greatest impression on me was Gloucester Green bus station, though I have a vague recollection of ancient buildings, botanic gardens, and a broad river with boats on it. Compared with Chippy, Oxford was paradise.

The serpent it inevitably contained was the work: the two sisters laboured long hours, and their legs and feet grew so swollen that they could barely stand up at the end of the day. This impinged little on Edith's assignments with Theos, but Sarah's parenting was badly affected. Left all day to play in a side scullery, with the antics of the kitchen staff as my chief diversion, I was demanding and difficult when I finally got my mother's attention. It was nice for Sarah to rediscover the comforts of civilisation, and even nicer to have a pay packet again, but she soon had misgivings. She also did not enjoy what Edith found to be the chief perks, because she was much older and less attractive, and rather bitter about men at the time. What was worse, she had little interest in food: diagnosed (probably wrongly) as having an ulcer in her thirties, she ate only the plainest.

The Oxford hotel's greatest attractions were the off-ration food and black-market booze, purchased for the guests and purloined shamelessly by the staff. I remember one hilarious day when a flirtatious army captain asked Sarah, 'Why won't that pretty waitress smile, or talk to me?' Sarah's answer, that Edith always had a hot artichoke in her mouth, seemed to delight him, and eventually the plainer sister had to tell him about me, waiting in the scullery, in order to fend him off.

The curtain came down on the Oxford scene soon after I went into hospital to have my tonsils and adenoids removed. In the 1940s this unnecessary operation was performed on countless children with persistent colds. I went into hospital armed only with a teddy bear, but survived the separation from my mother remarkably well. I remember only being placed in a cot (something I hadn't experienced for years) and sleeping a lot, but no great pain. I think the episode's chief significance was that it reminded Sarah that she had decided to devote her life to her son, and that life in a scullery is not particularly healthy. Somehow she had to find the money to feed, house, and clothe two people, albeit small ones with small appetites.

Simon's contribution to my upkeep was the pound note that still arrived each fortnight in a registered envelope. (Whatever happened to registered envelopes? They were the symbols of a more compassionate society that is gone.) Fortunately, Sarah had been in work for many years and, as a result, was entitled for a limited period to something called UAB money (Unemployment Assistance Benefit, I think). This would give her only twenty-three shillings a week to keep the two of us, but she had a genius for economising, something that would be despised today, but which undoubtedly ensured my survival.

Sarah calculated that the limited period of UAB money would run out in the September after my fourth birthday. If she could get me admitted to school at the age of four, rather than five, she could return to work. So, to make absolutely certain that a school would accept me, she resolved to make me literate and numerate by the following September. After all, if she gave up work, she would have little else to do except teach me to play my part in the economic rescue operation; and mothers are the best teachers.

Oxford rents were unthinkable, and the nearest place to Ann where Sarah could find another farmhouse room was in a more remote village called Lyneham: it was five miles from Chippy and enjoyed only one bus a week (on Fridays). But it boasted a hotel for the motorised classes, which made it the ideal place for dirty weekends (one of the war's boom industries). It was always full and rumour had it that any guest who got out of bed and went to the bathroom would probably have to salute his or her commanding officer. This hotel was usually short of staff because the social facilities and their romantic opportunities were so few, since most of the male guests were too sexually exhausted to make passes at the maids and waitresses.

Each day the children of Lyneham were collected in a bus that took them to a larger village's school, and thus Sarah's twin targets were both in sight. She hated being a parasite: she found living off benefits far more painful than leaving her husband. She hid her shame in the intensity with which she led me, slowly at first, through alphabets, books, sums, and tables. Her own voracious appetite for books was temporarily sublimated and every children's book and comic she could lay her hands on was read and reread during those long summer days.

When it stopped raining, which it does for whole days in Oxfordshire, Sarah walked and, at first, pushed; the road from Lyneham to Chippy was mercifully flat, so she could manage the pushchair without a pavement. As well as making maximum use of the weekly bus, she tackled the five-mile (each way) push to Chippy twice every week. Ann, who had to transport two toddlers and was soon expecting a third, envied Sarah's mobility; but Ann had daily buses, and was usually in the town to meet us when we arrived. Both sisters gradually trained their brood to walk long distances, and the pushchairs were eventually assigned to duties such as collecting sacks of coal. Anyway, that summer I learned to read, write, count, and walk big-time. To this day my leg muscles are by far the heaviest in my body, the only ones that ever pumped iron continuously, thanks to the rolling Cotswold roads.

Thomas à Kempis said that he had spent his whole life searching for happiness, but had only ever found it in a corner with a book. I have been far luckier in life than the author of the *Imitatio Christi*, but I still wonder, like Houellebecq, how people who don't read can bear reality; I suppose they have drugs and religion. Sarah, who abused neither, read assiduously to the end of her life, despite being almost totally lacking in formal education. The most any pupil can ask of a teacher is that she teach you everything she knows, and I am bitterly ashamed that in later years I sometimes felt embarrassed by the fact that Sarah's education had been brutally ruptured at the point where mine really began.

I think Sarah was surprised by the speed at which I learned, and the farmer's wife was amazed. I remember being presented with that ultimate wartime award, a new-laid egg, when that good lady discovered that I could write not only my name, but also hers (which I seem to recall was Beauchamp, and thus broke all the phonetic rules I had just learned). By the time the school bus arrived to pick me up in September all I had to learn from an infant school was how to cope with other children. I am afraid that I left that school, and several others, without having acquired that skill.

School had its pluses and minuses: like all only children, I was hungry for playmates, and found them. My teacher treated my literacy with respect, although the conventional wisdom demanded that she should not try to spread it too rapidly to the rest of the class; she tried to find me books I hadn't read, and she had me read my comics to the class during rainy playtimes. At first Sarah bought me the picture papers *Chicks' Own* and *Tiny Tots* each week from her slender funds, but when she found it took me only minutes to read them those funds stretched to the *Wizard, Hotspur, Rover, Champion,* and *Adventure,* boys' papers that contained many pages of text and no pictures.

All these journals are now extinct as a result of the decline in UK literacy. Although this change has left me one of a dying species, *bookmen,* I don't regret my education: the last tyrannosaur doubtless pitied his successors for the size of their meals (to say nothing of their sexual equipment). In my early school career the reactions of my teachers to the discovery that I found them redundant varied considerably: some resented it fiercely and missed no opportunity to humiliate me, while others seemed to welcome the break, and allowed me to pursue my own path quietly in class.

I received quite a few thumps at infant school, where I spoke a different language to most of the other children, and Sarah had forbidden me to hit back 'like a ruffian'. 'The more you hit back, the more they'll hit you,' she said. Only gradually did I learn that the opposite is true, and that a menace can often be as effective as a blow, and that blows are best aimed where and when they are least expected. But Sarah was ferociously non-violent and believed firmly that one day men would rise to the heights of women in this respect. She would, therefore, have greatly enjoyed seeing her grandson change his baby's nappy; but she would have been appalled at the drunken violence of today's young women. As I have already observed, equal often means worse.

I remember that once, when I had eventually learned to retaliate, a neighbour told Sarah that she had seen me fighting on the way home from school. When I confessed, Sarah didn't speak to me for a week, but she extracted no promises. And afterwards she either failed to notice that I was returning home with fewer bruises or else she decided that the male sex was incorrigible. Nevertheless, as a result of her influence, my aggression has always been more verbal than physical, and my animosity tends to last almost as long as a woman's.

For a while we lived happily and innocently in this haven for illicit lovers. Sarah's feet got used to the work, and having a pay packet again was very welcome. There were also tips, although these were never as large as the chamber maids received for disposing of condoms, sanitary towels, and occasionally foetuses. Sarah put aside the children's books and resumed her diet of romantic novels. So did I: there simply weren't enough comics to satisfy my hunger for the written word. It took me about two years to realise that all Mills & Boon novels are essentially the same, an important first step in the world of literary criticism.

Sarah's working hours also left me loads of time to wander the village, where the local boys, of whom there were too few to be fussy, soon admitted me to their gang. The older boys taught me all sorts of things that Sarah hadn't, and I soon learned not to give her the details, since she didn't seem to want to know. For example, they showed me what fucking was by helping me climb a farmyard wall to watch a bull in action. I remember not fancying the brief, precarious process at all: did women coat their buttocks with excrement especially for the event, and did men have so much trouble mounting them?

Since those older boys slept in their parents' bedrooms, as was the country custom, they were able to reassure me that women on heat were more hygienic, and to describe some alternative positions. But their explanations seemed highly theoretical compared with the vivid experience of watching the bull. It was a relief to pass on to the next lesson of the older boys' curriculum, which was in masturbation, although none of us actually managed to ejaculate.

I returned to Sarah's Mills & Boon novels with renewed interest, but I could find no reference to fucking, or to the parts that performed it. For a while I was firmly convinced that only servicemen and country people copulated, under the influence of war in the first case, and of keeping cattle in the second. But this delusion was soon dispelled by breeding white mice and rabbits, and by the birth of a new cousin, whose provenance his elder sister Sylvia had guessed. For it was Sarah's family, as always, who dominated the next stage of her life.

Ann was expecting a new baby, and was rightly as terrified at the approaching birth as if she had been in the middle of the Sahara. Harry, who was determined to add a boy to his brood, was delighted but also apprehensive, since he was marooned and helpless, high up on a factory chimney hundreds of miles away. Everyone was therefore relieved to discover a vacant cottage in a nearby village that was big enough for two families. Since he was gradually becoming his firm's chief bricklayer in the sky, Harry eagerly agreed to pay all the bills. This enabled Sarah to give up her job and provide Ann with the antenatal care she needed; she would also be able to look after my cousins when Ann was taken into Chippy hospital.

And so we moved again, with some excitement: at the age of five I had already developed a taste for moving that would become a lifelong addiction.

3

ISOLATION

The sisters had been told that the vacant cottage was nearly a mile from Great Rollright, which had a church, a school, a pub, and a shop. This distance was negligible compared with those we were accustomed to walking. But they had not been told that it was also a mile from the nearest road, across two fields. The cottage was known as 'The Buildings', and consisted of living accommodation attached to some barns and a cowshed. Although our mothers were appalled at having horned neighbours, we children were delighted. (When, in time, I told my own children that I used to play cowboys with real cattle, they did not believe me.) Sylvia, Kay, and I thought it was fantastic, and even better was the freedom of walking to school each day on our own.

Our mothers were too terrified (and too busy) to accompany us. One of the reasons they were so busy was that 'The Buildings' had no drinking water. The nearest, at Sour Well, was half a mile in the opposite direction to the village, and half a mile further still was the station, Rollright Halt, which offered an alternative route to Chippy, three miles away. The railway siding was also a dropping-off point for coal, in very short supply, but our only method of heating and cooking. Lighting was from paraffin lamps, which encouraged early nights and required strict parental discipline to prevent the children burning the place down.

Like all children, we needed plenty of discipline, but just beyond the front door we could flout it by chasing cattle; those in the nearest field were bullocks being reared for beef, but we never considered the effect of our whooping and prancing on the wartime economy. Our mothers said that one day the beasts might turn on us, but they never did. They also said that one of the beasts might be a bull; I thought of telling them what any bull would have been doing to the other cattle, but decided against it. I was not sure that either of them was ready for this knowledge; and even though Ann was six months pregnant I had not connected this with bovine behaviour.

Soon Sarah gave up warning us and slipped out to fetch the daily pail of drinking water as we set off for school. She could thus complete her task in safety while we teased the bullocks. In view of Ann's condition, Sarah was left with the rotten jobs: not just carrying water, but also emptying lavatory buckets, and collecting coal from the railway siding in a pushchair. This journey was less hazardous than taking the route to the village, because the fields to the railway line contained sheep, the herding of which we children, like true cowboys, regarded as somewhat below us. But Sarah's task was backbreaking: the loaded pushchair weighed more than half a hundredweight and the grass was usually wet; and our feeble little pushes were less of a help than a hindrance.

Children have a talent for being happy anywhere and, although my mother regarded it as the worst time in her life, I was certainly happy in 'The Buildings'. My cousins were ideal playmates: they were strong, bright, energetic girls who would shirk no challenge a boy was prepared to face. Besides, there was a family tradition that women stood together against men in any sort of confrontation; and in Harry I had a model of a man who was simply too big to bully women. When, at seven, I was sent to a single-sex school, I missed girls and was unimpressed by my rather dull and uncouth schoolmates; but in my cousins I had friends who would endure. Kay, although only four, was also allowed to start at the local school; the locals seemed to think that refugee kids wanted to go to school early because they couldn't feed chickens or do anything useful about the farm.

Great Rollright Infants was a church school, so my cousins and I first encountered debates about whether you would go to hell for dropping your prayer book in a puddle. My cousins never developed the level of interest I found in such questions, but then they never became atheists either. The truth never ceased to fascinate me. How did our mothers know we were lying when we said we hadn't been eating blackberries on the way home? 'Pink mouths,' was the answer, and it was based squarely on evidence. I learned that the truth could be reached by carefully and impartially collecting evidence. But the truths of religion did not seem to have been reached that way; unwittingly I committed myself to testing those truths, until many years later I had reached reliable, evidence-based conclusions.

Sarah had been brought up to believe in God (the process we call 'brainwashing' when that god is someone else's) and she had been taught to pray. All her life she had prayed for prosperity, and had been given poverty; she had prayed for health, and had been given sickness; she had prayed for a good strong man, and had been given a feckless weak one; and, hardest of all, she had prayed for her mother not to die in the shelters. By the time I knew her, Sarah had concluded that if there were a god he was a deaf god: he might have chosen people, but she was certainly not one of them. She was resigned to this disconnection, but not embittered; perhaps most importantly, she thought that I should believe whatever I wanted. She happily sent me to church schools, took me to Sunday school when I wanted to go (because other children went), and stopped taking me when I dismissed its texts as too infantile.

Later in life she supported me in my enduring enthusiasm for bible reading and my temporary fads for the rituals of various denominations. She warned me, of course, that it was dangerous for a young boy to be alone with a man in a skirt, but I never actually encountered that problem. I now realise that the religious freedom I enjoyed is extremely rare, a priceless gift from a woman who had so little materially to give. I used it to the full until my late teens: I tried many new approaches to faith and new preachers, but eventually I gave up my attempts to find the truth by living a lie.

The root of most people's morality is their mother, and Sarah taught me that morality is independent of religion. She had no god but was undoubtedly good – a far better person than the vicars, teachers, and other Christians around me. In the words of the American poet, 'a ship of star by her might steer'. I never knew her to tell an untruth, but she knew immediately I told one: I didn't give up the habit, of course, but I suffered inwardly every time. She was invariably polite and she treated other people's property with a respect that seems quaint, almost comical, today. While she could not love, nor even like, all her fellow humans, she unhesitatingly sacrificed her own best interests to those of her brothers and sisters (not to mention those of her son). If she knew lust and greed, she kept them firmly out of sight, and her aggression (which was verbal and could be scathing) was reserved for the defence of friends and family. I am undoubtedly biased in my views of her character: I, disgracefully, took it for granted that I was the most important thing in her life, and I hope she recognised instinctively that she was the most important in mine.

Sarah knew that her decision to end her marriage had robbed me of a father, so she tried to compensate by being considerably stricter than most mothers. She was very conscious that she had a son to raise and not a daughter, and so she refrained from slobbering over me and equally discouraged me from showing my affection. Our relationship was the diametrical opposite of the typical American family, as shown by Hollywood. There, the actors hug and say. 'I love you,' almost

42

incessantly, but often the parents walk out on the kids, and the kids sometimes take a gun and shoot the parents.

Because I was important to Sarah, I was able to become important to myself; our social position meant that neither of us was important to the world in general, but it did not matter. I have often bridled at posh kids' assumption that they were heaven-born (the chief lesson learned at a 'good' school), but only when this has led them to mistreat others, and I have never wished to be so deluded myself. It has been only gradually, however, that I have discarded the ubiquitous fallacy called variously chauvinism, nationalism, patriotism, or fascism. I am not a class-chauvinist, because I believe that the only thing that stops the rich from being as good as the poor is their wealth. But the belief that the human group you happen to have been born among is superior to other groups is an attractive one, and it has been the cause of much human suffering. Now that humans have the military means to wipe out their species by pressing a button, its survival depends upon discarding this tribal meme.

Most animosities break down unless reinforced by ideology. In wartime Oxfordshire the differences between refugees and locals diminished as Cockney accents weakened and daily contact turned strangers into people. The three children made friends and, because they were bright and cooperative, were well regarded by their teachers. My cousins remained at that school for the next five years and were glittering successes, its first children to win scholarships to Chippy's grammar school.

We had older cousins who had won scholarships, back in the East End before the war, but had not been allowed to take them up because of the cost (of uniforms, extras, and entering employment at least a year later). Although Harry was no scholar himself, he wanted the best for his children. This was not the case with other parents in the village. We had a friend called Frankie who, like many of the village children, had parents who were cousins, and he suffered a congenital defect as a result. Frankie was badly deaf, but on the arrival of the NHS was prescribed a hearing aid, which dramatically improved his academic performance. He was a borderline pass in the same scholarship exam that Sylvia passed. This meant that he was invited to an interview that would decide his educational fate, but his father confiscated his hearing aid on the night before to save the family money and trouble.

Rollright School taught me little, other than that Christians had a god called Jesus and that the Bible is a vast and fascinating text. My most influential mentor became a piece of technology that ended our intellectual isolation. The most important of the effects rescued from London was a radio, designated a *Pye Portable*, a fifteen-inch cube that was far bigger than any modern radio. Its key attribute was that it worked on batteries. Although these were unobtainable during the war, a simple conversion by the local oil-monger made it run on accumulators that we had recharged each week.

From this miraculous device the world poured out into our living room and, as a bonus, the radio probably saved my eyesight, by stopping me from reading by oil-lamp on winter evenings. At the end of each day the two women and three children would gather by the sputtering coal fire to be warmed, informed, and entertained. The news began to get better: we heard the first reports that suggested Georgi Zhukov might win the war; I became familiar with the geography of the Dnieper Bend; then came the news that Hitler had declared war on the USA; then a British victory in North Africa, albeit over a much smaller German force.

The BBC's programmes were extremely varied: we children particularly liked a detective drama with a hero called Paul Temple, and a large number of comedians helped shape our sense of humour. Our tastes differed, just as in comics, where I found Sylvia's *Dandy* and *Beano* rather childish and spiteful, and she dismissed my adventure comics as 'men fighting for lack of women'. The popularity of one type of humour has always mystified me: comedians who get a laugh simply by repeating the same phrase every week. There was a man on wartime radio called Tommy Handley whose show seemed to consist of little else. I much preferred acts like Collinson and Breen, or the team that were 'always happy at the Hippodrome', because their jokes were all different.

Quiz programmes gained their hold on me more slowly: at first I listened because they were there, but I always remembered the answers, and gradually learned that the same questions would come up again. The BBC's children's programmes were also well produced; my particular favourite was about a boy detective called Jennings. And then there was music: Sarah worked through the day to popular music, but she picked up a book as soon as classical music was announced, and my preferences naturally followed hers. Until my voice broke, many years later, I enjoyed singing hymns, but I have almost no musical ability, something my own children have inherited. To their grandmother's delight my grandchildren all play musical instruments.

In the last twenty years an unholy alliance of politicians and media barons has emasculated and now seeks to destroy the BBC. Britain's rulers hate the corporation for not showing sufficient enthusiasm for their lies and wars, and foreign media owners hate it because it is a competitor that will not tailor its news in the interests of the USA. To gain popular support for its licence fee the BBC has been forced to aim almost all its programmes at the masses; that is, make them intelligible to people with IQs well below 100. But in the 1940s, although its German equivalent was the propaganda weapon that our present rulers desire, the BBC was a source of reliable information. Its Director General also believed in education for all, even if it were not to the ruling class's advantage. The days when the BBC's DGs would be political stooges were far off.

So between the ages of four and ten my education was provided by faith schools, private reading, and the BBC, and the sum of my learning in those years can be attributed to each: 5 per cent from schools, 50 per cent from reading, and 45 per cent from the BBC. Today, government and the media pillory schools for failing to educate their pupils; but this is unjust, since schools can offer only a beginning, an opening of minds. Ironically, the latest craze in television entertainment is for programmes in which a well-known face learns to dance, skate, or play the ukulele with one-to-one tuition. The audience always gasps in amazement at how fast the subject learns because he/she is not in a classroom with other people. Then it returns to real life and blames schools for failing children.

Winter in the Cotswolds is bitter and for me was an indoor time: listening to the radio, reading, hearing anecdotes from the East End, and playing eye-spy and memory games. It was also a time of running noses, watering eyes, lost circulation, chaps, and chilblains. I don't know whether I would have been healthier if Sarah hadn't despised sport and any form of physical exercise except work and walking. But I suspect that I would not have been so thin as a child had she given me the appetite that Harry's example gave my cousins, and had she been able to afford to satisfy it. In adulthood I found that I could bulk up to fifteen stone (and beyond) very rapidly on a rich diet. But the medical profession now believe that eating very little fat as a child has a positive effect on longevity, and I know that Sarah's regime kept me free from major illness, and gave more than enough energy to learn. Looking back from senility, it seems to me that my mind then was like a hungry animal, a word-wolf or a number-crunching mantis. Gradually, however, the days lengthened and the temperatures rose, and the allure of the outdoors returned.

'The Buildings' had a large garden surrounded by a dry-stone wall, since even before the war farmhands had grown most of their own food. One weekend Harry planted it with seeds of every sort and in the following weeks we children tended the seedlings and watched them become vegetables. We never got to eat them, because one day we left the gate unlatched and the bullocks got in and ate everything. For once our mothers looked on approvingly as we cut out the corralled beasts in true cowboy fashion and ran them into the fields one by one. The stumps left by the cattle were still attractive to caterpillars, and butterflies were plentiful in those days, so we children gained something from our parents' first agricultural experiment.

But we spent little time inside those dry-stone walls, because we were allowed free run of the fields, free splash of the streams, and free puff of the hills. We made friends among the village kids and they showed us all their games: we learned where to look for nests, how to recognise birds and eggs, and how to pierce the latter with thorns so that their contents ran out. This left the most beautiful, delicate structures that lasted indefinitely when kept in a box lined with sawdust. But we never saw the point of, or followed, the yokels' custom of wringing the necks of any chicks found in the nests; they looked so ugly and pathetic lying on the grass that we preferred to swallow our disappointment and move on to the next hedge.

Sixty years later the same townie squeamishness would rob British country folk of their traditional way of keeping down the fox population. It also kept most of the Spanish-domiciled Britons I knew away from bullfights. But I was present the day that 'our' bullocks were taken off to an abattoir, and I felt the terror inspired by such a protracted and relentless death. I also watched the local butcher kill pigs scientifically, and noted how long it took them to accept the fact that they were dead. The fate of born bulls is to be castrated and slaughtered, or to make one last blood-maddened charge at their mortal enemy. I know which I would prefer. There were many other encounters with death for children in rural Oxfordshire; there were numerous stoats and foxes, hawks and owls; but for mass killing none of these could match the villagers.

At harvest time all the local children gathered round the horses and carts in the hope of a ride or a kill. The centre of each field was left until last, and the locals armed themselves with stout sticks and large stones, and formed a tight circle around it. As the last of the standing crop fell, a horde of rabbits, hares, rats, and mice would break from it. At five, my coordination and reflexes were not good enough to kill anything, but many older boys went home with rabbits for the pot. It struck me at the time that these creatures were just like refugees, who cowered in their shelters until the last moment and then took their chances in flight.

At the opposite end of the DNA saga, Ann's time was approaching, and soon she left for Chippy hospital and returned with my cousin Paul. Paul was even blonder than his father: at school he was nicknamed 'Snowball'. It was later discovered that he had been born with a heart murmur, but with love and care he has lived to a ripe age; he married a schoolmistress, fathered three daughters, and built a very successful business in the Midlands. He was just a little too young to be my ideal playmate, and our adult paths rarely crossed, but we have remained good friends nevertheless. Paul's birth brought an important change: Ann's doctor backed a submission to the council that 'The Buildings', being without drinking water, were totally unsuitable for bringing up a newborn baby, and to her joy she was found a rather dilapidated cottage in the village. She felt guilty at leaving Sarah, who reassured her she would find it easier to cope without her. So joyfully Ann moved.

Nothing within reach of Harry's hands was ever dilapidated for long, and soon the cottage in the village was bright, clean, and fragrant with the aroma of baking. Ann continued to live in it until Paul left school, by which time the war was a distant memory and Harry was motorised, returning every weekend. Missing her children, at that time spread to the far corners of the earth, she moved home in order to be with Harry every day; and so she spent the rest of her life. Eventually they returned to live in the area, but in a modern house close to the centre of the market town of Banbury. Just before she died of cancer, Ann wrote and asked me to visit her for one last time. We talked at length of Nanny and Sarah, and of the war years we had shared, and we rediscovered so many comic episodes that we laughed until we cried. Ann always laughed easily and I think she died easily, just as Harry did more than a decade later.

The next summer I had to wrangle cattle alone, but saw my cousins every day at school and visited them often in their new home. I was a great fan of Ann's cooking: she made cakes and pastries whenever she could get the ingredients, and when she couldn't, bread pudding, which I am sure was the best in the world. I was even grateful for my skinny stature, because it made Ann think that I needed fattening up. This was a concept with which she was familiar because her cottage had a pigsty and all her neighbours actually kept pigs; and the government allowed them to keep half of each animal for themselves. Although pig-breeding was nothing like as scientific as it is today, we suspected one old man of having found the secret of producing pigs that were far heavier on one side than the other. The cottage also had an allotment for growing fruit and vegetables, so many of the war's shortages were held at bay. It may have lacked an indoor toilet and bathroom, but these were things for Harry to plan while he chivvied the council into supplying tap water and drainage.

Sarah, meanwhile, lugged buckets from Sour Well; I badly wanted to help, but had to accept that the heaviest weight I could carry was less than half a bucket, which Sarah called a waste of shoe leather. I became rather more help with a pushchair full of coal. Soon we had a new housemate. One of Hester's children, whom Sarah had been very fond of when he was small, had been convicted of black marketing, and was jailed for six months to teach him an important lesson (how to avoid being caught again). His young wife, who was pregnant, wanted to escape the London scene until his release, so Hester suggested that she follow Ann's example and use 'The Buildings' as a prenatal sanctuary.

Sarah, of course, with fond memories of the little boy she had nursed, who was now behind bars, welcomed the pregnant stranger with open arms. More than that, she waited on her hand and foot, which at least kept her busy while I was at school. Her guest, however, filled her idle hours by writing endless letters to everyone in her family and her husband's, describing the hard labour she too was serving, fetching water and pushing coal in the back of beyond. But Hester could keep few secrets from her sister, and this misrepresentation eventually reached Sarah's ears. Since our guest had scarcely lifted a finger during her stay, Sarah was livid. Forgiveness was never her strong (or, rather, weak) point, and the guest's suitcase was placed on the pushchair, and she was escorted across the fields to Rollright Halt, and thence to civilisation.

Sarah's own yearning for civilisation was heightened by this incident, but various busybodies told her they could not help her find better accommodation because she did not have enough children. She retorted that, at fifty, and having dumped her husband six years earlier, there was nothing she could do about that. Since dumping a husband did not have the cachet it has now, the authorities were unimpressed. So Sarah resolved to take desperate action in order to get to Chippy, pavements, and running water. She learned of a middle-class family who had encouraged the wife's aged father to remain in his own home when he became a widower. But he was unwell and unable to care for himself, and Sarah agreed to become his carer for a small stipend and two rent-free rooms.

The deal was that, since she was not a nurse, she would move on when he became bedridden. He owned a limestone-walled house not far from the centre of the town, and so, more than three years after being tipped out onto its station, we got to Chippy. The change in Sarah's life was dramatic: there were not only pavements, but she could use them to go to the lending library every day, recharge her accumulators more easily, and mix with people instead of cattle. She could even get a part-time job. For me the gains were more modest: a bigger school and a shorter walk to reach it; more kids, both in and out of school; two cinemas, two fish-and-chip shops, and a playground with swings and roundabouts. On the whole, I concluded, civilisation was a good thing.

The old man was a new experience: I had not known that people could be so slow in their movements, or so rambling in their speech, or so unaware of the dewdrops at the end of their noses. But he was harmless and benevolent, and Sarah had taken the job because she had guessed, correctly, that he was no longer bothered by sex and would not bother her. Her alternative offer had come from the local butcher's father, a sprightly old man who always wore a shiny black suit. He had offered to provide her with a place of her own if she would let him help her make the bed. Since Sarah was always asking me to do the same thing, it took me a couple of years to appreciate the significance of her choice. The things I remember best from that period are Rupert Bear, who was rather juvenile but rhymed, and the arrival of 10,000 black US soldiers, who spoke a new language. Since its wartime ratio of women to men was thirteen to one, the second of these made Chippy's streets, and the lanes of all the surrounding villages, hum with sexual excitement.

I also remember having to run the gauntlet of bigger boys on the way to school. Unlike oxen, they wouldn't budge when you said 'Shoo,' but they inflicted relatively little damage, and I was prepared to take a few cuffs and a Chinese burn for the privilege of being allowed to play with them. I learned that there are many ways to deflect bullies: some other victim will usually make the mistake of giving them more satisfaction. The worst of these bullies changed from being my tormentor to my ally after a day when a group of us were playing on a roof fifteen feet above the ground; he threatened to throw me off, so I jumped. This enabled me to land on my feet and, as I limped slowly away, I heard another boy of my size screaming for ten minutes until he was thrown off, when he screamed some more. That, of course, was exactly what the big kid was after; but his first-choice victim was henceforth regarded as a trickier proposition: you couldn't tell what he might do. And, if you ever wanted something really crazy done, he could very well be the one to do it. So I gradually developed ways of using guile rather than confrontation, and this became vital when I found myself in a world where everyone was considerably larger than I was.

When the old man became bedridden and had to go into a nursing home, Sarah's contract was over; but by then she had found a place of her own, with the unconscious aid of the US army. When a tiny hovel that had once been a stable (and later became a garage) became vacant, no younger woman wanted it. It had only one bedroom and, while most country wives were used to servicing their husbands with their children sleeping in the same room, the GIs expected a more enthusiastic and private performance. And so the refugees won the key to the castle unopposed, and we moved into our new home, Number 3, King's Head Yard.

The King's Head was a former coaching inn that had entertained Charles I en route to his final defeat, but was now a rabbit warren of flats. The inn's stables, which ran down a gradual slope, had been converted into cottages of which ours was the first (the former inn was Number 1). Each had its own tiny, gated garden, and the accommodation was basically one-up and one-down; the only door opened into the living room and above it was a bedroom. Both had a small window and an alcove, the downstairs one serving for food preparation and the upstairs one just large enough for a child's bed. The floor was of stone and icy in winter, and the ceilings were exactly six feet above it, which greatly inconvenienced visiting uncles, but seemed plenty high enough to me. Oil lamps provided the only artificial light, an open fire the only heating, and an oven beside it the only means of cooking. Our other amenities were an outside tap with drinking water that jutted from the wall opposite Number 3, and an outdoor toilet, in a communal block, sixty yards down the hill.

All this was Sarah's for three shillings a week, and I sensed that things were getting better, because she sang along to the radio as she cleaned and black-leaded the filthy hearth.

4

FREEDOM

The King's Head stood on New Street, a steep hill lined by conker trees that led down to the station and beyond it to what has become the tourist village of Broadway. At the top of the hill, about two hundred yards away, was the broad, sloping market place, the Town Hall and most of the shops. One of the cinemas was off New Street and the other was at the opposite end of the town, to the south east, on Rock Hill, an area dominated by a Catholic church and school, which to me was foreign territory. Halfway between our cottage and the station was a *common* large enough to accommodate a slide, swings, roundabouts and a football pitch. Beyond it stretched sloping fields, coppices, and a series of brooks that were called the *Everflow* until they trickled into the *Thames* many miles away. If I were a billionaire with children between the ages of seven and twelve, I would build them a playground with identical specifications. But my territory for the next five years also included most of the town; at first the lanes I most frequented were those that ran from New Street to St Mary's Church and its school; later I prowled the roads that led up to the council estates and the grammar school on the south-west edge of the town. And as an only child, I knew how many children each house contained and what they would do at my approach.

This gift of the freedom of Chippy was made mine by economic necessity. Now that Sarah had a place of her own that had to be heated, furnished, and maintained, she had to earn enough to keep it. She had always hated borrowing: the few items she bought on 'tick' (as she called credit) troubled her conscience until they had been paid for, which was usually significantly earlier than the agreement stipulated. Had she lived to see the debts her grandchildren and their generation were happy to amass, she would have been deeply mortified. Since there was no work to be had in Chippy that involved a sewing machine, she had to settle for less skilled jobs, mostly cooking and cleaning. The best-paid work available was at a munitions factory, wrapping explosives, but the hours were antisocial (like so many jobs today), and Sarah had to give it up. Her priority was providing me with a warm bed and hearth, and three meals a day, and such mental sustenance as I required. She provided the same things for herself only because she realised that she was more vital to me than any of them.

When poor people's marriages broke up, a rare event in those days, their children officially became orphans and were placed in something called a 'home'. (Some of these orphans in 'homes' were transported to Australia later.) There was one such 'home' off New Street, a sombre, silent place with a long drive and no sign of life inside. I had a schoolmate who lived there. He and his brother were toughs whom no blows could make cry, but they rarely laughed, and never came out to play after school. When driven to the last stage of exasperation by my naughtiness, Sarah would threaten me with a 'home'; that worked when nothing else did. Other children in the same situation are threatened with hell, which I suspect may be why they believe in gods and I don't. Sarah needed some overpowering sanction because she had to do something that is illegal today: she gave her seven-year-old son a door-key, taught him how to maintain a coal fire, and told him he would often be left alone in the house. This required a strict set of rules: for example, I could never admit other children, light the oil lamps, or meddle with the oven (and, even today, I still prefer cold midday meals).

I already knew how to tune the wireless, which was essential company, because my winter overcoat, which had been bought several sizes too big for me so that it would last, had to be saved for school and special occasions. From spring to autumn, however, I could roam during the hours of daylight; I had to watch the declining sun and calculate when I should retrace my steps so as to be home by nightfall. The penalty for being home even a minute after dark was a week (at least) of being confined to barracks, and this instilled in me a lifelong habit of punctuality that my own children find ridiculous. But I found that by obeying Sarah's rules I could enjoy a freedom such as any child today can only envy. It is, perhaps, because my mother's presence was never a burden to me that I yearn for it so much now.

Because the jobs that Sarah could find were very badly paid she often did two, and sometimes three, at a time. The one that fitted best with school holidays was as a school-dinner lady (9 a.m. to 2.30 p.m.); this could be combined with being a hospital night cleaner (6 p.m. to 9 p.m. on weekdays), and cleaning the school kitchens (2.30 p.m. to 4. 30 p.m.). In this way Sarah could earn fifty-five hours' money and still have weekends free for housework and leisure. To save me embarrassment she never worked at the school I attended; so she was delighted when I went to the grammar school, because the secondary modern offered more jobs and longer hours.

One of the big advantages of living in Chippy itself was access to the cinema: visits were no longer dictated by bus timetables. The New Street cinema was almost next door to the King's Head and it became an essential part of my territory. Now that she was working Sarah could afford to take me every week, and we saw more than one film on each visit, because in those days there was always a second feature and a news programme. The prudery of the times meant that most films were suitable for an eight-year-old boy who had outgrown pixies and wizards but not cowboys and Indians. Today, the reverse seems to be the case: adults flock to films that are patently aimed at children and consist mainly of special effects passed off as magic. In the 1940s films aimed specially at children were shown on Saturday mornings and, in the school holidays, on weekday afternoons. As a child, I could get into the cinema for three old pence (just over 1p today), and Sarah counted the cinema an essential expenditure, like reading matter, because mind-food is more important than gut-food.

I soon began keeping a film diary, a book in which I listed every film I saw, summarised its plot, added my critical comment, and gave it points out of ten. I wish I had kept it, but it was abandoned for lack of space on one of our many house moves. Those films are repeated endlessly on TV today, where they are called 'classics', because the writing and acting is of a higher standard than in modern films, where the action must be frantic, the dialogue minimal, and the close-ups of body fluids realistic. I was particularly fond of comedies; and my favourite stars, the Marx Brothers, the Three Stooges, Abbot & Costello, George Formby, and Bob Hope, still make me, and my grandchildren, laugh today.

Now that I had the key of the door my life at home was perfect, but that at school was full of challenges, none of them educational. Since the lanes on my route were very quiet, I was able to continue going to school unaccompanied except by the friends I met on the way. Nowadays, when I see columns of giant Jeeps parked on the roads and pavements outside schools, I can't help noticing how embarrassed the children look, and how stressed and angry the mothers. I am sure that if kids could only walk to school their mums would be better mothers and human beings. Of course, I took a few punches on the way, and at school; I was small, new, and spoke a different language. But I kept very quiet about it lest my non-violent mother confront either boys and/or their parents, something to be dreaded far more than schoolboy fists.

At school my position improved considerably when we found out that one of my classmates was the teacher's son; thereafter we saved all our punches and teasing for him. His mother did not know what to make of me: she realised I didn't fit educationally into her class, for which she had scrupulously prepared her own son by making him average at everything. Indeed, had we not punched and teased him so much, he might well have grown up into the most balanced and well-adjusted child in the school. In my case she resolved her dilemma by getting me promoted rapidly to the year above, and the teacher she duped solved his problem in exactly the same way.

Thus it was that I came at age eight to sit among ten-year-olds. Chipping Norton C of E Boys' Primary School had fewer than 100 pupils, who were distributed between three un-streamed classes. The headmaster himself instructed the top class in all subjects except religious knowledge, which the vicar came in to teach on Tuesday mornings, so as to give the head half a day for his administrative duties. Mr Smith the headmaster, known to the boys as Gaffer, was a short man with a round red face that twenty years in his post had turned into a permanent scowl. We knew he was married, but his wife kept well away from the school lest her presence undermine his iron discipline, which he enforced with a loud voice and a slim cane. That most of the men in the town could read, write, and count he regarded as his personal achievement. He could not therefore adjust to the concepts of external influence and natural aptitude, and for three years he was my worst enemy.

Looking back, I suspect that anti-Semitism played some part in this, since I still bore Simon's Jewish name. In the 1930s this form of racism was as common as all the others in Britain; thus much ink has been wasted on a few passing references to Jews in the poetry of T. S. Eliot, whose attitudes simply reflected those of most people around him. Today most Britons would deny the historical fact that Israel was our 'final solution to the Jewish problem', yet the Balfour Declaration is based entirely on the belief that people of the Jewish faith cannot live alongside other people. While the behaviour of modern Israel has done much to support this belief, the people of London have been proving it false for centuries. But until 1945 most people in Britain, and particularly its ruling classes, did not care about the fate of Europe's Jews, and the Allies repeatedly refused to bomb the railway lines that carried them to their fate. The Allied priority was revenge on the ordinary people of Germany, thinly disguised as economic attrition, and many brave airmen gave their lives to the fallacy that they were affecting the German war effort. Most Londoners, however, must have suspected that the bombing would only strengthen the German resolve to fight on.

For whatever reason, I represented some sort of threat to Gaffer Smith, and he was as relentless as Bomber Harris. In three years he did me only two favours; the first was trivial: he allowed his wife to give me a kitten she had advertised; I named it *Miff* (a mutilation of *Smith*) and became very fond of it. The second was important: when the eleven-plus exam was introduced he glimpsed a final solution and put me in for it two years early. There are, however, disadvantages to over-promotion, and my presence in a class of ten-year-old boys soon revealed them to me. The first was that, already undersized for my age, I was a flyweight among heavyweights. But I soon learned how to refuse to fight with my classmates; some were pleased to have their superiority acknowledged in this way, and others vented their frustration at not getting blows back from me by turning on someone else. Torture was not as glamorised then as it is today (it was regarded chauvinistically as something Japanese or German), and few bigger boys wasted their time on torturing a shrimp who didn't resist. There were also educational favours I could do them: the boys in my class knew that I had the answers to most of the questions with which Gaffer persecuted them, and they knew that I would help if I could.

At first being in a higher class attracted the aggression of boys of my own size, but I found that if I hit them back we would soon have a crowd of my classmates around us, cheering on their mascot, who refused to fight with them, but did not show the same respect for outsiders. I was doubtless protected from greater bullying by the fact that Britons used to pride themselves on not having a 'kick-ass' culture. Even recently, the same experiment in this field gave very different results in the USA and Britain.

The experiment had groups of students acting out the roles of prisoners and guards in a jail; on the West Coast the American guards bullied the prisoners until their lives were in danger and the experiment was halted; in Exeter the two groups developed a working relationship. So strong is US influence on modern Britain that academics drew every conclusion from this experiment but the obvious one: that the difference was due to the 'kick-ass' culture of the USA, with its love of guns, chains, and executions. The USA, however, has suffered centuries of genocide, slavery, and religious fanaticism that Europe has not. Many Americans, from all latitudes, despise Europeans for being *gentler* (the events of World War II forfeited our right to be credited as more *civilised*); but if we volunteer for the wimps' parts in their movies, or their wars, it is entirely our own fault.

A much more enduring disadvantage of over-promotion was sporting, and sport is to boys what money is to men, the chief source of status, power, and self-respect. I naturally wanted to compete with the boys I knew best, my classmates, both in the playground and down the common. But, in addition to their great advantage in size, their eye and muscle coordination was far better developed than mine. So I became the outfielder who was put in to bat last and never allowed to bowl; and, once my team realised that I was useless as a goalkeeper because I couldn't reach the crossbar, I became the winger to whom nobody passed. As a result I developed little skill at the team games that are the English staples and the cheapest for children to play.

It was only in my late teens that I discovered some ball games I could play with reasonable proficiency, ones where my opponents had not already built an enormous skills gap. But my lack of proficiency in football and cricket did not curb my enthusiasm; and, if nothing else, the neglected winger got plenty of exercise, running the length of the pitch a dozen times for every ball that reached him. Like all my schoolmates, I also became a fervent supporter of the professional game. The nearest top-class clubs to Chippy were Aston Villa and Wolverhampton Wanderers: boys living at the top of the town tended to support Villa, boys living at the bottom Wolves. But, although I can't remember a time when my favourite colours were not old gold and black, in those days I could never afford the pilgrimage to Molyneux.

In class my disadvantages over the illiterate Chippy boys should have been reversed, but Gaffer Smith worked hard to see that they weren't. Because my hands could not keep up with my mind, both my handwriting and my figures were extremely untidy. The first was a scrawl that made readers work hard and the second consisted of columns of hasty symbols that leaned in all directions. When Gaffer deducted half my marks for untidiness, I retaliated by persisting in it; this battle continued for the next three years, and neither of us would give way. So in tests and exams marked by Gaffer I became a solid 50 per cent performer, and this gave me the recognition and satisfaction I needed. At least I always finished my work first, and with 50 per cent I was never far down the class.

Reading proved a far bigger problem, but one where the solution stood me in very good stead later. Gaffer taught reading by having each boy in turn read a paragraph, and by prompting and correcting him as he stuttered through the ordeal. In my case Gaffer was limited to 'Don't go so fast!' He didn't even correct what remained of my Cockney accent. As his least satisfying victim, he would have left me alone entirely, but when he realised that I was always reading ahead or under the desk he found a new torment. He would wait until my mind was far distant and then pounce triumphantly on me to read the next paragraph. He also confiscated many comics, which he tore up, and books, which he did not return to me for at least a week. Fortunately for me, he had never needed to make reading a caning offence and he did not do so now.

Very soon I was reduced to completing the book with which the class was struggling (I remember reading *Black Beauty* four times), and to reading furtively the only schoolbook in my desk. Since interesting subjects like history and geography were taught in church schools without the luxury of textbooks, that book was the Holy Bible (Authorised Version). And the Anglican Church cannot contemplate depriving a boy of his Bible; thus it was that I became a lifelong theology student. At first the only difference between detection when reading the Bible and any other text was indemnity from confiscation, but then the vicar improved the situation even further.

The vicar, who was taller and greyer than Gaffer, wore a shiny cassock and spoke slowly in a posh voice. His Tuesday-morning sessions were short on hymns because, unlike Gaffer, who conducted morning assembly, he did not play the piano. Prayers were also few, since he did not trust the boys for long with his eyes shut. So most of our time was spent reading aloud from the Bible, and learning selected passages from the New Testament, like the Beatitudes. The vicar encountered the same problems as Gaffer with the boys' reading; it took some of them five minutes to get out the word 'blessed'. Naturally, I slipped into the same furtive reading habit I practised with the headmaster. The vicar saw this and for some reason decided to say nothing; either he considered that no harm could come from reading the good book, or he thought that, since I was a boy with a Jewish name, some sort of conversion was taking place. Had he looked more closely he would have seen that I had logically started at the beginning, and was therefore reading an English translation of the *Torah*.

Once I realised that I was going to get away with this indefinitely, I became more critical of Gaffer's attitude. So I plucked up courage and told him that the vicar permitted the very thing that he punished. Bullies often have an almost quaint respect for authority, and though Gaffer never acknowledged my right to read, he interrupted me very rarely after that. In fact the interruptions were no more frequent than anyone else's turn to read, but Gaffer enjoyed seeing me panic and search desperately for the page the class were reading; only after a long pause and a hate-filled glower would he tell me the page, and he revealed it as if he were giving me the key to all human wisdom. On the other hand, Gaffer taught me many types of sum that Sarah hadn't, and he seemed genuinely impressed by my speed and accuracy at mental arithmetic. Only much later did he reveal that he had not been as blind to my abilities as he had appeared.

I did not complete all thirty-nine Books of the Old Testament: I skipped the minor prophets in order to reach the twenty-seven Books of the New, where the vicar spent all the class's time. At first I read the AV more slowly than Mills & Boon novels but, by persevering, guessing, and checking, I increased my knowledge of the fascinating seventeenth-century lexicon and learned to love the marvellous cadences of its English. To my delight and instruction I found that Old Testament characters, unlike those in my mother's novels, did quite a lot of what bulls and cows did, and they gave it all sorts of interesting names like 'knowing'. Moreover, David did it with other people's wives, Solomon with all his slave-girls, and Lot did it with his daughters. Lot even recommended his daughters to his neighbours, saying that they were better for it than angels. Nor was there any shortage of violence: the Old Testament is an excellent read for a boy raised in wartime. It was soon clear to me who were the baddies: the Children of Israel burned, looted, raped, tortured, and slaughtered their way through Canaan, just as the Germans had through Poland and Russia. The Israelites were merciless and there was no Red Army to stop them, because their Fuehrer, whom they weren't even allowed to call by name, was both immortal and invisible.

It was a relief to turn to the New Testament, where a sort of Red, or Roman, Army had more or less put a stop to the slaughter. Jesus Christ was a rare exception, but the Fuehrer had marked him down for sacrifice from the beginning. Then the Greeks and Romans stole Jesus from the Jews, whom they blamed for his death. By this time Jesus had risen from the dead and promised the resurrection of the flesh to all his followers. It all seemed a little far-fetched to someone who had seen what happened to pig's flesh; but, if anyone had told me that in three years' time the Christian powers were about to resurrect Israel, I could have told them exactly what would follow.

I spent many more years trying to link up with the people around me by believing these stories, and only when I had studied a great deal of other Iron-Age fiction did I finally leave them behind. But by the age of eight I had met with some of the most brilliant poetry in the English language; I loved best the Book of Ecclesiastes and, after that, the Song of Solomon, Proverbs, and Psalms. I had encountered the superstitions of ancient peoples in the most superb of settings, and they continued to enthral me for the rest of my life.

At this time I had given up Sunday school, because it was too juvenile, and I hadn't become a churchgoer, because the vicar, apart from allowing me to read the Bible, made no grab at my soul. I didn't need the love of God because I had the love of one woman, and I soon began exploring others. One of Milan Kundera's novels is called *Laughable Loves* and one of J. M. Coetzee's recent novels explored the last, laughable love of an old man. But it's important to get your laughable loving in early; men, in particular, need all the practice they can get. And achieving a deep and enduring passion without the experience of such loves is no more likely than hitting your first-ever attempt at a backhand smash for a perfect winner.

I shall try to be honest about my own laughable loves, but they were all decent and amiable girls who do not deserve to have their names dragged across the memoirs of an obscure boy they have long forgotten. The names I shall use preserve only their initials, carved lovingly into the trunk of the past, and a suitable feminine ending. The nine-year-old Sheena was the first and most laughable of these loves, because she loved and I, being too shy to do anything else, laughed. Sheena lived a little further down the Yard, and her father was a burly man who slaughtered pigs, and elicited similar noises from her mother in the bedroom that they all shared. This made their daughter an expert on sex and the anatomical details of pigs, and she was happy to pass her knowledge of both to her friends. One day on the common she was playing with them on the slide as I passed by. 'Oh, that Cockney kid,' she said, 'I've had him, and he's no different to the others.' This filled me with panic, since she might one day impart the same information to Sarah, but fortunately I don't think she ever did.

What bothered me later was whether Sheena was telling the truth, since she was referring to a day when we met by chance in the field below King's Head Yard. I had been wandering alone and was watching the antics of two six-spot ladybirds, wishing I had a magnifying glass. As she appeared from the lavatory block, I recognised Sheena by her shock of untidy ginger hair. She made her way across the field and joined me. When she saw what I was watching she said 'Do you want to fuck too?' She took my embarrassed silence for assent. At first, like any nine-year-old boy, I was more interested in her knickers, but she threw them aside and fumbled with my flies. She pulled me down and, as she lay back on the grass, I caught a glimpse of a white, smooth mound with a cleft below it. I got almost stiff and she got me almost inside, but we couldn't find the correct angle. We were reduced to rubbing one another, and she placed my finger very precisely. She handled me clumsily but eventually, since I was too young to ejaculate, I experienced that dry burning feeling that small boys achieve. When her handful had shrunk she became bored and removed my hand. Once we were on our feet again she shimmied back into her knickers, and soon we were hunting together for ladybirds and other exotic insects, many of which succeeded where we had failed.

But did this count as having me? Did it stop either of us being a virgin? And why hadn't she noticed that I had been circumcised, unlike the other boys? I also resented being described as 'no different to the others'. I suppose I have always wanted a woman's heart and mind as well her inlets, and I am not sure that Sheena had either of those higher organs. Yet I was fortunate to have enjoyed an introduction to sex that was relatively free of guilt. I didn't connect what we had done with any of the long list of *shalt nots* I had found in Exodus. I knew that shepherds heartily approved of rams tupping ewes, and wasn't the Lord some sort of shepherd? Every moving creature I had encountered did the things that the ladybirds and Sheena and I had been trying to do. This included GIs and local women, who seemed to do it more than most. My mother didn't seem to do it, but I figured that this was because she was too old and, as she so often said, 'off' men.

Sarah had caught me masturbating twice around the time I first discovered its (at that point, dry) joys, and I could see she was not exactly pleased. The first time, she told me a story of two mute neighbours who had married back in the East End; they had both contracted TB, as a result, Sarah was sure, of excessive use of the parts I had my hands on; but in their case it was forgivable because they had little else to do. The second time she explained that men and women had separate public lavatories because otherwise some men would do this sort of thing to women who didn't want it.

I did not let Sarah catch me again. But in an earlier age I might have had to suffer a cruel chastity device, or been terrified by claims that masturbation turned you blind, or sent you mad. Instead, I had been given the Cockney equivalent of two maxims I later found among the wisdom of the Ancients: μηδεν 'αγαν and *volente puellā*.[1] But in the short term the problem for me, as for most boys, was finding a *volentem puellam*. I knew that they existed, however, because, although my girl cousins had never shown an interest in anything beyond verbal exploration, Sheena's willingness was clearly 'αγαν. Although her advances had been a surprise, they were not entirely unwelcome, and she had raised something else in me: a curiosity that I would spend many years trying to satisfy.

---

[1] Epicurus gave his followers the advice, 'Nothing to excess,' and Ovid encouraged young lovers to 'do anything provided the girl is willing'.

5

EXILE

The fields and woods that surrounded Chippy were the preserve of the local boys (*tenuerunt locum*, in the words of the Domesday Book). Chippy girls, in contrast, confined their play to the common itself, where knots of them formed to gossip, laugh, and tease. Only the older girls sometimes ventured into the nearest bushes with boys of their choice. Chippy boys knew nothing of 'rights to roam', but none of us had ever encountered gun or gamekeeper, so, like the Native Americans, we assumed that the land on which we hunted and gathered was ours. Although our staple fare was blackberries, sloes, and crab apples, our real quarry was dreams. We rambled, talked, and squabbled as we explored and acted out our fantasies of adventure. Like sperm donors, most boys require props for their imagination, and ours were the texts of films that we had seen and stories we had been told. As the most avid reader, I was welcomed into many different groups because of the endless variety of scenarios I could recall.

We travelled in small bands of up to half a dozen, not in the large gangs that menace much of modern Britain. If some bend in the space-time continuum had folded the fields around Rock Hill so that they abutted ours, there might indeed have been Catholic gangs with whom we could dispute territory; but no such deformity existed in our universe. Since gangs are the products of lack of space, facilities, and imagination, we did not need them. Although there were often more than twenty boys on the football pitch, they dispersed miraculously at the final whistle. In the fields we encountered many creatures, but few humans: drovers and shepherds were rare. Even when one of the older boys, whose nickname was Scruffy, won fame by raping a ewe, there was no guardian to apprehend him. No townie, of course, would have known the right time of year, but Scruffy became a connoisseur and his fame spread. In one of our scenarios we smaller boys pretended to be sheep trying to hide from this 'Terror of the Folds'. Today, I guess, this would be diagnosed as *homophobia*, but in those days we thought the problem was Scruffy's, not ours.

Much has been written about land-girls, but we never met one on our rambles; these conscript peasants became anonymous in the town, where they wore the same clothes as other girls. They doubtless couldn't wait to exchange jodhpurs for skirts and the nylons that the GIs gave them. In the area around Chippy there were 10,000 GIs and barely 2,000 young women. Men who had left their women thousands of miles to the West met women whose men had been posted to the East several years earlier, and nothing could have prevented the frenzy of copulation that ensued.

As in peacetime, most liaisons began in bars, restaurants, or hotels, or at dances, but now they frequently ended in absent husbands' beds. And any woman who was not fussy could earn a fortune in cash or otherwise unobtainable luxury goods by entertaining groups of GIs, either serially or simultaneously. This situation is, of course, one of the universals of military occupation; French women similarly entertained German soldiers throughout the war, and two years later women in the Russian zone of Germany weren't even asked first, and were lucky if they were given a cigarette afterwards. One of the reasons why ordinary men fight wars is to prevent such local humiliations but, when they returned, those of Britain swallowed their pride for fear of the Russians; and many of those of Germany never returned.

In summer some GIs used the same bushes below the common that local lads had used for centuries; one New Street boy took up collecting used sheaths, and one day he proudly exhibited his collection to a group of us. We noted that they were of two very different sizes, which we assumed were tailored to black and white men's dimensions. In fact, the difference was that one size was British-made and the other had been specially imported from the USA. The difference between the sheaths may therefore have been evidence of British masochism, or of the British inability to complain, since they never talked about sex.

Although *condom* has long been in the OED, I never heard it used in my childhood because it wasn't a woman's word; we Chippy boys called sheaths 'rubber johnnies'. The French word *condom* has penetrated the English language twice; the first time was so long ago that the word became completely Anglicized, with initial stress and a reduced vowel (schwa) in its second syllable (by analogy with words like *freedom*). The second time was when the AIDS pandemic arrived in the 1980s, and women used the word for the first time and restored the full vowel in its second syllable. On a woman's lips the word thus sounds quaint and almost Chaucerian to men of my generation.

Sarah and the older Chippy women were, of course, critical of good-time girls, but they had little trouble avoiding the GIs because the Americans were avoiding them. Like most of her generation, Sarah was racist to the extent that she thought that black should keep to black and white to white. But her prejudice was nothing compared with that to which the black GIs were accustomed. Even in war the US Army segregated its units, but most black soldiers had grown up in a society where servicing a white woman could lead to castration, or even lynching, and any white woman caught *in flagrante* had to cry rape. Black US servicemen therefore found doubly exciting the uninhibited enthusiasm of white women in Europe. And those women found the

GIs more attractive than their own men: they were more cheerful and attentive, and, to judge by the prophylactic evidence, they were either more satisfying or in less pain.

My personal involvement in the sexual occupation of Chippy was confined to an episode in the town when a GI gave me a stick of gum and offered me half-a-crown to find him a woman. I knew a Florrie who would do anything with any man (I had heard Sarah say so), and I spent more than an hour searching the streets for her in vain. When I told my mother of this adventure, she became very cross and made me promise not to speak to GIs or take their gum again. Thus an interesting career, one of the few that allowed poor boys to become rich, was nipped in the bud.

These large men with even larger smiles (and in Chippy they had much to smile about) were always popular with the town's children. The GIs were invariably friendly and playful, since they missed the kids on their own streets; nor could they be sure they would ever see them again. Many men did not return home from Europe because of their generals' excessive zeal to beat the Russians in the race to Berlin. But those that did return had glimpsed a world where the black man was at least equal, and they fought an even more bitter war for equality when they got home.

A great hero of my youth was my namesake Martin Luther King who, according to the press, was a man such as many Chippy women would have enjoyed. All my life I have cheered on black American athletes, from Althea and Arthur to Ali, especially when they were competing against white Americans, many of whom I have found self-righteous and arrogant. This, I suspect makes me a racist, too; but I have been rewarded by watching my heroes and heroines win many magnificent victories.

The GIs were not the only human beings I discovered who, at least superficially, were very different from my friends and family. I also encountered the godly, the affluent, and the gifted. One day on the common, two Roman Catholic boys from Rock Hill approached me and made friendly overtures. They wanted to catch fish and tadpoles, they said, and their territory was too far from all the best streams. So I escorted them to Pool Meadow, which held the largest expanse of water in the vicinity.

As we walked, they educated me on the superiority of the Roman religion: on discovering that I was at the C of E school, they explained why I must leave it as soon as possible. The Jews, they told me, were Protestants like me, and they had killed Our Lord; this meant that, as a Protestant, I would be personally responsible for the crime unless I converted with immediate effect. I tried to remonstrate, but they had already developed the deaf and blind spots that all true believers consider the highest virtue. Our disputation was interrupted only when we reached the pool. Here we were treated to a spectacle that was on offer only once a year.

The edges of the pond were teeming with frogs, clinging to everything that moved and ejaculating over it. Some of the amphibious pyramids were six frogs high, with just one female at their base. It struck me that this was how Florrie might have managed when she went off with a group of GIs. But my musing was interrupted when the two boys produced a box of matches and revealed their plan. They found some kindling and started a fire, and then they began to gather frogs. They heaped the pyramids, clusters, and individuals onto the fire, which hissed, and smoked, and spat, and filled the air with the smell of burning fat. All Pool Meadow reeked, and after a half-hearted attempt to join in the labour I shrank back.

The older boys travelled back and forth with handfuls of frogs for what seemed a long time, until there were no more within reach of their zealous hands. This was my first experience of genocide, for which Pool Meadow paid by being infested by insects for several years after. On the way back, the boys explained that God would burn all fornicators in the same way eventually, and that this was the most important reason for immediate conversion. As we said goodbye, I think I promised that they would soon see me on Rock Hill, but they never did, because I knew that Florrie was a Catholic, and imagined their hell as a place she would await me in flames, covered by half a dozen GIs. The Anglican hell seemed preferable.

On another occasion, I was wandering the more affluent streets of Chippy when I met a boy on a scooter. Scooters and bikes were always beyond Sarah's budget and she often pronounced them too dangerous for a town of steep hills. This boy's parents were less risk-averse, and the boy unwisely tried to impress me with the tricks and stunts he could perform on his mount. He was going downhill and so achieved a considerable speed on one leg. Suddenly, he turned a corner, parted company with the scooter, and skidded for several yards along the pavement. I rushed to his aid as he lay there. He checked that he could get up and walk, and then counted his bruises and grazes.

I recovered his mount and, since he wanted both hands free to wipe away his tears, I pushed and rode the scooter back to his home. This was a larger house than any I had ever seen, almost a hotel. His mother, who seemed extremely young and charming, dried his tears and heard his story. I was embarrassed to be treated as some sort of hero, since all I had done was to covet and retrieve the scooter. Having accomplished this, I would have fled, but she produced lemonade and biscuits and suggested the two of us play together indoors for the rest of the afternoon.

I could not believe either the size of his room or the number of toys that spilled from his cupboard: castles and ships, infantry and cavalry, cowboys and guns, tanks and planes, football and horse-racing games, and more puzzles and books than I knew existed. Most of these toys must have been his father's before the war, particularly the Hornby train set that we laid out across his floor and played with longest. We continued happily until his father, who managed the local bank, returned from work to learn of our adventures. At first he seemed as welcoming as his wife, but more inquisitive. He asked me a number of questions, ending with where my home was. 'King's Head Yard,' I said, ready to tell him the story of Charles I's last days if he hadn't already heard it.

This had a strange effect: the father became distinctly uneasy and whispered anxiously to his wife. She said, 'Have another lemonade before you go,' and I thanked her but said I wasn't thirsty. So I returned home, a pedestrian again, with something special to tell my mother. She seemed surprised that I had been invited into the house but, of course, I never was again. I didn't dare to call for the boy, whose name was Keith, but I passed his house as often as I could. Indeed, I never saw him again, so I guess his parents must have sent him away to be bullied and buggered at some boarding school rather than expose him to the contamination of King's Head Yard.

One of my school friends, Terry, was in the class below me, but was the same age and size. He was a terrific athlete and his dad had dreams of his becoming a professional footballer. So good were his shooting, dribbling, and heading that the older boys not only let him play centre forward, they actually passed to him. One day his father, who was a factory worker, came to the common to collect him for tea and was enraged by what he saw. He vowed never to let Terry play with 'that crowd of has-beens' again; he feared that crunching tackles from bigger, less skilful boys would surely lead to injuries that would end Terry's career and shatter his father's dreams. Professional football was not the money-making scam that it is today, but it still brought in twelve pounds a week, plus fame and prestige, and escape from slaving at a factory bench.

After that I saw much less of Terry, but I would have traded a few injuries for just one pass. My only injury was being knocked unconscious by a clearance that hit me in the face from close range, and I didn't remember much pain, only the thrill of being the centre of attention for five minutes. I tried to solve the problem of how to develop some ball skills by buying one of my own. I asked for money as my present for two birthdays and a Christmas, but just as I reached my target I over-wound the only clock that Sarah possessed, when she was out one day, and repairing it took my entire savings.

Even poor boys have toys; and if they don't they beg or steal the boxes in which rich boys' toys arrive and make toys from them. I made most of my toys from cardboard boxes and plasticine, which was what I usually requested from my mother on my birthdays and for Christmas. My aunts gave me *Dinky* cars when they came back on the market, and before that any type of metal vehicle they could find in the shops.

My mothers and aunts had sometimes mentioned their father (they called him 'The Old Boy'), and he died peacefully sleeping beneath his own dining table, where he was sheltering from doodlebugs. This was the only thing he had in common with his wife at the end. His brothers, sons, and daughters gathered for the funeral and I was pleased to discover tube trains and to receive several half-crown avuncular tips. My grandfather left almost nothing, but he had tried opening a toyshop when he retired, and I was given his only memento of that experiment, a red tin double-decker bus. It became one of my treasures and was passed on to a younger cousin when I no longer played with it. Toys were my only companions during winters indoors; that is, apart from comics, books, and the wireless.

I still read, and reread, adventure comics that I bound to make thick, cover-less books so that serialised stories would be accessible in their entirety in a single volume. I reread them so that I could rewrite them in my head, including new episodes, and adding different endings; in this way the same comic could provide endless entertainment. The term *heterotextuality* had not been invented then, but I was well aware of my debt to other stories and the Bible. Genesis and Rockfist Rogan could be combined to make amazing narratives and I still wonder whether my fictions would have sold. I was often tempted to write them down, but Gaffer Smith's assurances that my handwriting was illegible stopped me from showing them to anyone.

Like my outdoor rambles, all my indoor games were also stories; although I had no history or geography textbooks I had a good memory and loved both maps and war reports. The floors of our cottage were of stone and they were covered with linoleum, and rugs that my mother made from rags and canvas. The lino became the sea and the rugs the land; pieces of furniture became mountains, which I mapped using contour lines as Gaffer had taught us. Each room was a different country and on its floors I played out my adaptations of every period of history.

Plasticine, or 'clay' as I mistakenly called it, is by far the best toy: one moment I had Roman and Pictish armies, the next Cavaliers and Roundheads; and then the *Wehrmacht* fled before the wrath of relentless Georgi Zhukov. Monty, Britain's favourite general, also enjoyed victory on the sand-coloured doormat, but with black GIs in his team he could hardly lose. Although wartime plasticine came in only the primary colours and green, I soon learned to blend them into every colour of flesh or uniform. Cardboard castles, pyramids, bunkers, and even skyscrapers fell beneath the furious onslaught of my plasticine legions. And when I was tired of war I would break all my soldiers off at the knees and swap their calves and feet for those of a different colour. Thus kitted out in shorts, they were flown to the dining table for an international football tournament.

In this fashion I solved all the world's political problems, and when the colours of my tiny figures were blurred from mixing, I remoulded them into dinosaurs and began the whole of Earth's story again. Because I played indoors only in winter and restricted most of the action to the iciest parts of the room my figures never collapsed, but provided me with endless entertainment. Market research has shown that today's children, confined to their rooms and plugged in to their electronic toys, pine for the freedom to roam; I can't help feeling that their hands must also yearn for the touch of clay.

As I played, momentous events were taking place in the real world. Germany capitulated and the Russians and Americans divided Europe between them. Russia then turned on Japan and the USA used its temporary nuclear monopoly to ensure that there was no race for Tokyo. British forces returned and voted to replace their former masters with a revolutionary government that made more social progress in the next five years than their predecessors had in the previous 500. Britain finished the war bankrupt, because Churchill had mortgaged his beloved empire to his mother's people, and Truman called in the loan (which was paid off only in 2006). Britain could no longer afford to hold down the Middle and Far East and most of the pink parts were soon to be washed from the atlas.

The GIs departed, leaving only the American Air Force behind. Farmers returned home to contrite or defiant wives and children with skins that tanned easily; the locals nicknamed the latter 'liquorice allsorts'. One Chippy husband, a Chindit newly returned from Burma, found his wife's bed still under allied occupation. When the GI with her was discovered at the foot of the stairs with a broken neck, the court said it was accidental death. But later we learned that the same accident had befallen many Japanese soldiers, silently in the jungle, where it was said to be a Chindit trademark. Readjusting to peace and to each other was clearly difficult for many couples.

Sarah didn't have this problem, but she had others. These events changed life for ordinary people remarkably little in the short term: free health care, competitive education, and state pensions were slow to take effect, and in the meantime rations got smaller and queues longer. As men flooded home a dire new shortage appeared: housing. London suffered worst: many streets were now mostly bomb-sites, and the government, for some reason, demolished as many homes as it built. Sarah and Ann had different attitudes to the country and to getting back to London, because by 1946 Harry was supervising work all over the Midlands and he drove home every weekend. Since Sylvia, the village school's star pupil, was in her eleven-plus year, Ann was happy to remain in Great Rollright for the time being.

Sarah, on the other hand, was desperate to escape. She contacted the Housing Departments of every East End borough but, as a single person with one child, she had no priority and was wasting her time. She realised that her exile was not just for the duration of the war; she never lived in 'the Smoke' again, and eventually stopped trying to get back. I think she came to realise that what she missed was a combination of London and youth, to which she could never return. Most of the places and many of the people she remembered were no longer there.

To escape, even for a week, Sarah took me to spend Christmas with Edith. As the war ended the tearaway had replaced her last Theo with a flight sergeant in the RAF. He had newly returned from assembling and checking aircraft in Russia, and he came from Portsmouth. Moreover, he had marriage in mind despite being, like so many ex-servicemen, recently divorced. I went with Sarah to the register office for their utility wedding, where we were the only guests. Edith, ever ready to relocate for love, joined him in Portsmouth and they invited us to spend Christmas by the seaside. The new bridegroom took me for a walk along the promenade where he found a bar full of his pals. I sat outside with a glass of lemonade and, since my overcoat had been stolen from the school cloakroom a fortnight earlier, I shivered inside two jerseys. The sea looked icy cold and menacing; thrilled by stories of the Russian convoys, I scanned the horizon for U-boats. I was torpedoed a few days later by pneumonia.

I was very lucky with my timing: penicillin was already on the market, but there was scarcely enough to treat the GIs' syphilis, which took first priority. This was serendipitous because I am allergic to penicillin, and I probably owe my survival to its non-availability in 1946. Sarah, who had prayed in vain for brother and mother, did not pray for me. But she was constantly by my side until the crisis had passed, and I slowly recovered: care, she said, beats prayer. She had another chance to prove it when we returned to Chippy (probably too soon), because I went down with mastoiditis. Her care prevailed again and I recovered without either hospitalisation or an operation. But our exile continued and a whole year passed. I continued to play happily in the fields and streets of Chippy and study theology furtively in class. Sarah continued to scrub and cook and read, but her hopes of escape gradually turned to despair.

That despair deepened in the months between Christmas and Easter 1947, Britain's coldest winter of the century. The snow began to fall soon after Christmas in the Cotswolds and it did not melt until Easter. The country was almost smothered by this blanket, which brought agriculture and industry to a halt, so that the nation was nearer to starvation than at any time during the war. In hilly areas the roads were blocked and villages cut off: Great Rollright was one of many that received parachute drops of bread and other essentials. In Chippy the snow was shovelled into banks on either side of the street, forming walls of dirty white higher than my head. The icicles on the cottage windows never melted; jugs of drinking water froze overnight, and coal, which was in short supply, had to be used sparingly. To reach school and work we picked our way carefully through the icy streets, and even the children tired of sliding and playing snowballs. Nothing made Sarah more determined than that dreadful winter to escape the Cotswolds, but for the present she was helpless.

In the midst of the great freeze something happened that I took little account of at the time. Gaffer Smith invited Sarah to the school and told her that he was entering me for the eleven-plus exam almost two years early. She expressed her surprise since, as she pointed out, I had never topped the class. Gaffer's reply was that the examiners wouldn't deduct 50 per cent for untidiness and that he thought I would pass with ease. Sarah reported this to me, but I forgot about it among more important things, and so I was surprised when one day my class was confronted by exam papers instead of lessons.

I enjoyed answering the questions much more than lessons or reading the Bible, but forgot to tell Sarah about it. She was only slightly cross when a letter arrived a few weeks later to say that I had passed. But a second letter followed saying that it had been decided that precocious passers would have their grammar-school places deferred for a year. Sarah breathed a sigh of relief, because she would have eighteen months instead of six to save up for a school uniform. She had always been critical of her sisters who had not allowed their sons to take up similar places before the war, and she had no intention of making me work as hard for a living as she had.

The following September there were new faces at the desks around me but nothing else at school changed. When I realised that I was condemned to another year of *Black Beauty*, the Beatitudes, and furtive theology, my heart sank. By the end of 1947 I had all the symptoms of depression, although I don't think it had yet been invented. My physical symptoms were those of severe gastroenteritis, and when they went on for weeks I was admitted to the local hospital.

Since there was no children's ward I was quartered with the men, and forty-eight hours of stimulating adult conversation cured me before my condition could be diagnosed or treated. The doctor discharged me in puzzlement and the matron labelled me a fraud, but I am sure that the cause of my ill health was frustration. For the third year running I sat in the same place, doing the same lessons. I returned, without enthusiasm, to the Minor Prophets, and each day walked to school with what Spaniards call *pies de lomo*.[1]

I was rescued from this plight, as Sarah was rescued from exile, by events beyond our control. It is human to attribute any good fortune that comes our way to our own merits, but that is vanity, all vanity. The race is not to the swift, nor the battle to the strong, and wisdom is learning to love the random universe we inhabit. Some of

[1] 'Feet of lead'.

my schoolmates doubtless lived in Chippy for the rest of their lives; married there, raised children there, and enjoy grandchildren there. Today they may be mowing the lawns and mucking out the stables of the new elite that dwells in Chipping Norton. Their grandchildren will not have the opportunity of escape that I had, nor indeed any of my opportunities. Chained in the basement of society by the Iron Law of Oligarchy, they can only look up in awe at their masters, or perhaps, if they chance on this volume, they will look back to the golden age of which I tell.

The story of Sarah's and my escape from Chippy and from grinding poverty is not a dramatic one. It relied upon a series of strokes of good fortune: Sarah's escape was possible because of her devotion to her family; mine was possible because of the social opportunities that existed in Britain during the period that the French call *Les trente glorieuses,* the years between 1945 and 1975, when Europe was remaking itself. I shall relate how an East End mother and a Chippy boy fared in that Golden Age in the chapters that follow.

6

RESPITE

Sarah's nostalgia was for youth, as well as London, and the steps that lead from the former no one can retrace; as the great Italian poet said, *no spero di tornar giammai.* Sarah, like ET, yearned for home, and home, until the twenty-first century, was the family (and woe betide anyone who did not have one). Today there are a number of alternative arrangements to the family on trial, but none looks capable of lasting even one thousand years, never mind over a million. Geographically, Sarah never returned to the East End, but emotionally she never left it. She escaped from Chippy by returning to her family, her seven siblings who had survived two world wars, and a plague, and a long depression. She had shared a home with her sister Ann before the War, and after it she shared homes at different times with her brothers, Jack and Teddy, and her younger sister, Edith. Having no brothers or sisters, I was envious of her, but my compensation was having a plethora of uncles and aunts.

Sarah's first saviour from the horrors of the countryside was Jack. Like all her brothers he had gone to night school when he left school and by it had secured a white-collar job. He sold things and was quite successful at it; like many East End successes he moved out to Essex, to a place called Upminster, where he had a house almost as grand as the Chippy bank manager who had once cast me out of his. When war broke out Jack exchanged his job as a commercial traveller for one in the Ministry of Food. There he rose rapidly to the top of the Executive grade, which was as far as the middle classes were allowed to go. This gave him an office, a car (an economic Morris Eight), and petrol coupons; and every food producer and distributor in East Anglia sought his favour. Jack had married a girl called Florence, whom he met at night school, and they had two children who were a few years older than I was.

Jack loved Florence passionately, and the war, the power he now enjoyed, and the example of the GIs rutting around them led the couple to produce two further children, who were mere babes when Jack came back into Sarah's life. But Florence had produced her second daughter and second son in her forties, and this triggered one of the most rapid and vicious of cancers, leaving Jack a widower in 1948. There was an obvious (at least to East End families) solution to Jack's short-term problems and that was Sarah, the proverbial poor relation, whose own child was now ten years old and remarkably independent (an urchin who roamed the streets, everyone said). So Sarah gave up her three jobs and took on the task of raising two toddlers and two grieving teenagers as well as her own son. All this at the age of fifty, when the menopause was beginning to give her a bad time.

Jack paid our rent (three shillings a week) on the cottage in King's Head Yard and fed and clothed this very extended family, and Sarah, the two toddlers, and I shuttled between Upminster and Chippy. Thus it was that I experienced a bathroom and an indoor toilet, and a school with girls. Upminster Junior School even had a school field and a sports day, and I learned that I could run and jump better than I could control a football. In the extended family I learned to cope with both older and younger siblings, and I became familiar with a wider variety of food than I had ever experienced. My elder cousins teased me that I had been raised on bread and jam and preferred it to the fancy fare to which a Food-Ministry family had become accustomed.

I learned many useful things in Upminster: how to make the most of the hot water and do mountains of washing up, how to clear the garden of dog's mess, how to jump on a running train, and how to masturbate like a teenager (which meant hiding evidence). But I continued to roam the streets on fine evenings and the town had a huge park where I played with new friends until the sun went down. On wet days I read as usual and, to my delight, I discovered that Jack owned a set of encyclopaedias. I read every volume from cover to cover that year, and I concluded that they were far better ordered than the Bible, and far freer of contradictions.

Sarah struggled with her housekeeping and child-rearing duties in our two homes, and the stress involved sometimes gave her bad headaches. So she was more than happy to relinquish her roles of housekeeping and child-minding after just over a year. Jack was a good catch and he met many women from his hobbies of golf and bridge; so by the end of his second year as a widower one known as Dee had become his mistress, and she rashly offered to take over his home and four children. Dee lasted for a few years before the magic went, and she soon followed. But Jack sent his children to good schools and they grew up bold and independent; and when he took a second wife some years later the younger children slowly, but relentlessly, drove her out. Jack eventually went to live in Cornwall, close to his eldest son Michael, where he continued to enjoy his bridge and his golf (when arthritis let him) until a ripe old age.

From Jack I learned how important luck is in life (because his was so mixed), and how to enjoy both the good luck and the bad. Jack and I remained on good terms to the end; when we lived near enough we met across a bridge table, and he tried unsuccessfully to convert me from tennis to golf. In the 1970s Sarah met him a few times, in my home, but when Jack moved to Cornwall we all lost touch. Sarah remained fond of all her nephews and nieces and always sought news of them, and she never lost her sense of being a member of a large family. I did not gain that sense in Upminster, because my cousins were either too old or too young. I could amuse the younger ones by telling them stories, but the older ones regarded me as a bit of a nuisance, especially my nineteen-year-old cousin Doreen, who laid claim to the sofa every evening with her boyfriend, and who made a priority of driving me off to the park or my encyclopaedias.

My elder boy cousin, Michael, was sports mad and became a PT instructor during national service. Back in civilian life, he became a very successful businessman, owning factories and making millions. Michael showed his entrepreneurial flair as a teenager: for example, he perfected his skills in order to win all his schoolmates' marbles and then sold them back to them. Michael went to a public school, as private schools are known in Britain, and affected a scorn of girls, but he gave me the impression that masturbation played a big part in his schoolmates' lives (but not in his: to Michael other boys were just a source of income). Michael vowed that he would not marry until he had made his first million, and he did both in his thirties. He also became a good golfer, which pleased Jack immensely.

School for me at that time was heaven, partly because my new form master, a moustachioed Mr Cole, didn't deduct 50 per cent of my marks for untidiness. I repaid him by endeavouring to be a little tidier and rising to the top of the class, a position I shared with my first real love. I was placed in a class where some of the children read books and were interested in ideas, and the brightest of them was a girl called Jana (according to my convention of naming laughable loves). She was exactly the same height as I was, and her face was pleasant, her eyes lively, and her smile enchanting. But it was Jana's figure that first transfixed me: her blouse bulged ominously towards my eager eyes and its contents danced to the music of her shapely legs when she ran. Her conversation completed my downfall: she was interested in everything;

she was even interested in me.

Jana and I soon became inseparable; we sat together at the back of the class, because Mr Cole insisted that the dullards and delinquents sat at the front where he could give them more attention. But his questions were a race for Jana and me to see who could raise a hand first. Mr Cole treated our attachment with amused tolerance (perhaps he too had had a childhood sweetheart), and our classmates treated it with a teasing acceptance. Our romance blossomed still further on the playing field, because the one team game a mixed class can play happily, and at ten years old evenly, is rounders. Jana and I shone at this game because she had a good eye for a ball and I had rapid reflexes. Jana could out-hit most boys, and I could gain a base while the ball was travelling between the pitcher and bat (and two or three bases if the person with the bat actually hit the ball). So Jana and I were almost impossible to get out and our team always won.

The only time our bodies ever lay together, however, was when we sprawled on the grass, waiting for our turn to bat. Jana's parents did not let her have the run of the streets, so evening meetings were out and we had to be satisfied with daytime romance. Although we never missed a chance to touch one another, ours was mainly a mental alliance: Jana had a beautiful mind, to which I had free access, and that made up for the frustrations of the flesh, which were many. In those days girls played rounders in their blouses and navy-blue knickers (the last line of defence for their virginity), and Jana filled both beautifully. But I removed them and held her only in bed at night, when her wraith snuggled in beside me and I dutifully poured my first libations in her worship.

These were the early days of the eleven-plus exam and educationalists were arguing how big a role intelligence tests (as against English and maths) should play in it. Mr Cole's class was among those chosen by the county's education department to carry out trials of new matrices at the end of term. Afterwards each child was told his or her own score (but nobody else's), and I was flattered by mine. In later life it ensured that I never joined MENSA and slummed it with people's whose only achievement was an IQ in the 140s or 150s. When Mr Cole gave me my score he said that he was sure I would pass the eleven-plus exam easily next year (since I would soon be eleven). I shall never forget the look on his face when I told him I had passed the exam eighteen months earlier, or on Jana's when I told her of the teacher's dumbfounding. But my success left me heartbroken: Jana was to stay on at Upminster Junior School, no doubt to pass her eleven-plus exam with flying colours, but I had to go to a grammar school, whatever that might be.

Jack, as head of our new joint family, was keen to get me into what he called 'a good school' and Sarah, who had been denied an education herself, followed his advice. Our target was a direct-grant grammar school in nearby Grays, one that was halfway in status between Michael's minor public school in Brentwood, and the County Grammar School in Romford. Jack believed that my problems with Chippy's Church of England school had been that I carried Simon's Jewish name. In those days many Christians were openly anti-Jewish and many Jews anti-Christian, so this made sense. To Sarah's surprise she discovered that Jack could simply get our names changed on her ration books and identity cards (which were being phased out) and she reverted to her maiden name and it became mine too. This seemed only just, since Sarah's family were my family, and Simon's name was just a relic pressed by medieval Christian masters on Jewish families who would have preferred to name me Moysha bar-Shimon.

Jack's ruse worked, and thus it was that I spent a term travelling to Grays every morning by train and hurrying a mile uphill to its oldest boys' school. I remember little of that school (which has long-since closed), because I was numb with the loss of Jana. I begged for news of her life when her wraith climbed into my bed every night, but wraiths know little of life. What I remember of the school at Grays consists mainly of my first lessons in swimming and languages, and the school lavatories. I failed to learn to swim in my only term of lessons, but managed to join the rest of the class in athlete's foot. The instructor tried to teach us to swim by numbers, but they weren't the numbers I loved.

French lessons consisted of trying to make alien noises when reading a book about a girl called Bobette who, despite her beautiful name, wasn't a patch on Jana (or perhaps the illustrations didn't do the French girl justice). My Latin lessons, however, were riveting, partly because they were taught by our rather eccentric headmaster, Dr Jordan. He refused to use the cane (which Gaffer Smith had wielded like a magician's wand) and delegated discipline to the senior maths master, a burly thug whose features better fitted a mortician than a mathematician. Dr Jordan's other eccentricity was that he regarded learning Latin as one of life's great privileges, and he refused to teach new boys one word of the language until they had earned it. This they did by mastering English grammar. By the end of my first term I had learned to dissect every type of English utterance and identify the function of every word in it. When I did come to learn my first word of Latin in my next school I was the only one who understood why it had twelve forms in Latin and knew exactly how to use each. This was a head start in a heavily inflected language, one that Bobette had failed to give us in French.

My final memory of my last all-boys school is of the 'bogs', as the lavatories were called. Each lunchtime older boys would shut themselves in cubicles with younger boys and produce unmistakeable noises. The older boys always emerged first, and sometimes the younger boys appeared with wet hair, which could only have come from immersion in the lavatory pan. I was never a victim of this activity, partly because I was not good-looking (as the younger boys usually were), and partly because I didn't linger hopefully in the bogs, as some of them did. Although buggery was made legal in my lifetime, I am happy to say that I always avoided situations where it became compulsory. I suspect that, if I had been initiated, I might have picked up the habit (just as I picked up smoking from other boys a few years later), but I think it made my life infinitely less complicated to have escaped it. And I bless the fact that the escape was girls, however besotted I became with them, and however much pain that brought.

When Sarah returned to Chippy and her three jobs, her headaches soon disappeared, but her sense of exile grew deeper and more bitter. Her sojourn in Upminster had reminded her of the existence of modern plumbing and the cottage seemed more primitive than ever, even though Jack had arranged for electricity to be installed. She planned tirelessly and hopelessly to end her exile. Meanwhile I, for the most part, enjoyed myself, transferring to Chippy's grammar school and meeting lots more girls.

Although this grammar school served dozens of small towns and villages it was rather small. Since an eleven-plus pass by a pupil from the C of E boys school was a rare bird I was not embarrassed by my new name. Most of the Chippy boys in my year were from the Catholic school, where they were beaten harder and more often and learned more (*sine disciplina discipuli non discent* [1]). Chippy Grammar School's academic standards were lower than those in Grays and for two years I maintained my position at the top of the fast stream in most subjects. Allowed to learn Latin at last, it took me just a week to catch up with the term's work I had missed. But there were problems elsewhere on the curriculum: staff shortages meant there was no chemistry teacher for first or second years, so we simply didn't study it. This ruined any chances that the class would produce a scientist, but most of the pupils were happy enough to be escaping the fates of farm labourers and shop girls, so there were no complaints.

The only cloud in my academic sky was that boys had to waste half a day every week doing woodwork and another messing about in the art room; I had no talent for either subject, or for music, which

---

[1] Like the Scots, the Romans believed that pupils don't learn without discipline.

occupied another double period. The woodwork teacher, known as Tarzan because he looked like a gorilla, became my chief enemy: he thought anyone who couldn't plane flat or saw straight was an idiot, and I thought likewise of anyone who wanted to waste good schooltime doing those things. He carried a thin lath of wood that he used to tap the boys he labelled idiots on the head, but it was his talent for sarcasm and abuse that was most cruel. This would have mattered little had we not lost a maths teacher, and Tarzan took over first-year maths. He used this opportunity to humiliate the idiot boys verbally before the girls, although he never dared to wield his lath with girls in the room; some girl's father would doubtless have put him to the test as to whether he really was Tarzan. Maths had been my best subject until then, but Tarzan never noticed, and soon I was deliberately going slow in class and skimping my maths homework in favour of subjects where my efforts were appreciated.

With my old friends now at a different school, I made new friends, the closest of whom was called Alan. He came from a large family living on the council estate, and his father was a skilled factory worker, so Alan owned a bicycle, something well beyond Sarah's means. Alan taught me how to ride his bike, and in return I he taught him chess (which I had picked up during my short stay in hospital). Soon we spent rainy days and evenings over a board and I found that I read less. At school we were oddballs in that neither excelled at football or cricket, but we found that we were intensely competitive mentally, and fiercely loyal. Any larger boy who tried to bully one of us had to deal with both, and we were largely left alone to our oddball interests.

My love life at Chippy was messy because I was greatly smitten by a girl who didn't reciprocate, and pursued by one that I didn't fancy at all. The first was the daughter of one of the workers on a vast aristocratic estate. Sasha (by my naming convention) was dark-haired and petite with cat-like features, and she was a bright and well-behaved pupil. All the boys in the class were in love with her, but she treated us all with equal politeness and indifference. Her home was nearer to Oxford than to Chippy, and she never spoke about her private life, so none of her admirers got any closer to her. Boys who tried to charm her in school hours would find she could be charming back, but she refused even to flirt. Her wraith gradually replaced Jana's in my bed at night, but she must have had many wraiths in many beds, and it was a wonder that she always looked so fresh and beautiful each morning.

Rosa was the daughter of a farmer in a nearby village: she had mid-brown hair and pink cheeks; she was plain, but healthy-looking rather than attractive. She had nice blue eyes and more promise of a figure than Sasha, but Rosa wasn't the brightest button in the box. She was, however, one of the boldest, and for some reason she chose me as the boyfriend she wanted to be linked with at school. She had her friends tell me this when they had cornered me in the school field at mid-morning break one day. She proposed that we walked together in the lunch hour so as to get to know one another better. This was the first stage of courting at the school, and the stages that followed culminated in lying together in the bushes on the field's furthest edge. I wasn't attracted to Rosa, but was flattered by the invitation and getting nowhere with Sasha. So in a moment of weakness I said yes.

We walked and talked, and with some persuasion and a little embarrassment we held hands as we walked. Rosa let me do most of the talking, and I told her of many of the strange things in encyclopaedias. She spoke mostly about her family and our schoolmates, and she kept suggesting that we sit down 'for a rest'. I remembered sprawling on the grass with Jana and I didn't feel like doing it with Rosa, or kissing her, which she clearly wanted. This curious courtship went on for weeks and I had no idea how to end it. Even the weather didn't help: on wet days Rosa wanted us to huddle in a corner together and talk, which was even more embarrassing.

I solved the Rosa problem as best I could. I spent as much of the lunchtime as possible with Alan or with groups of boys, and I struck up a lively but platonic friendship with Cora, the girl who was my chief rival in class. She was much more interesting to talk to than Rosa, because she also had read a lot, and she had interesting things to say about the ideas I came up with. As I sought out Cora's company more and more, I could see that Rosa was unhappy, but I was cruel and cowardly. Eventually Rosa gave up hope and looked elsewhere for a boyfriend; so we never finished up in the bushes, where I might have learned to appreciate what she wanted.

Throughout my school days I continued to have the problem that the girls I desired were not the girls who desired me. It was partly the result of the fact that I wanted girls' bodies, while the ones who were interested in me wanted my mind. Like most men I was too concerned with looks; I didn't follow the advice of the poet Ghalib, who wrote:

Pay no heed to pretty faces;
They deserve a handsome lover;
Lose your interest in faces;
Go look in a mirror.

In my youth I was thin as a Vice's dagger, and my otherwise not exceptional face was marred by what Americans call English teeth. The front ones were crooked and uneven, and they repelled more than my sensual lips attracted. I waited years for orthodontistry to arrive in Britain and then lost patience. In my first year at university I met several rugby players who had sacrificed their front teeth to their sport. They now wore gum shields on the pitch and small plates containing a few perfect false teeth off it. This gave me the confidence to pay a young dentist to kick out my front teeth with his drill, and I joined the scrum. After that I had no trouble getting dates with pretty girls, so the rest of my face must have passed muster.

Some ugly men are very successful with women, most of whom are less deceived by looks. Most women like to laugh, and they warm to men who make them laugh; and many have a streak of masochism: as book sales show, millions dream of being tortured to orgasm by a handsome millionaire. Although I noted how many girls fell for men who treated them badly, I never tried that route to a woman's heart. Instead I tried to keep my dates entertained and I took an interest in their interests; and I tried to make them feel good about themselves. I also think I showed that I really liked women, which is a pleasure that some men miss.

The length a childhood romance lasts depends largely on chance and often on parents. Only in a minority of cases do two people gel, when both find they are happier together than apart; but even in those cases circumstances frequently dictate how long this lasts. Throughout my school days I had many laughable loves, all as female as possible. I continued to desire the unattainable, but learned not to reject the plain girls who desired me, as I had rejected Rosa. Some of those plain girls were very intelligent and had lovely personalities. In this way I learned more about women's minds and bodies, and I practised my courtship skills for the day when I would meet a girl who was beautiful inside and out.

7

ESCAPE

By the middle of 1951 I was settled comfortably into life at Chippy Grammar School: I was top of the class, or near to it, in all the subjects I enjoyed; I liked the teachers who taught those subjects and they seemed to value me. Alan and Cora were two of the closest friends I had ever had; Rosa had given up on me, and Sasha at least showed no preference for any other boy. At football I still ran along the wing hoping for a pass that never came, and I still waited on the boundary for the 1-in-360 chance that a cricket ball would come my way. But I had chess, and schoolmates with whom I could discuss books and ideas. In maths Tarzan had been replaced by a supply teacher who was even worse at his job, but who bore me no personal antagonism. And I was looking forward to starting chemistry next year (physics bored me because I had learned most of the elementary stages from encyclopaedias). In Latin I now had all the declensions and conjugations, in French I was making more convincing noises, and in English, history, and geography I was being encouraged to read better books. So life was good.

In contrast, Sarah hated life in Chippy more than ever; Upminster had given her a renewed appetite for running water, bathrooms, and indoor toilets, to say nothing of regular buses and decent shops. She pined for all these things as she scrubbed floors, scoured pans, and peeled vegetables for a pittance. And when she returned to good health she resolved to do something drastic. When the schools closed that summer, just before my thirteenth birthday, she did not take on extra hours at the hospital, as she had done in earlier years. Instead she accepted her sister Edith's invitation to join her for six weeks on the South coast. Because her husband managed the Hayling Island branch of an estate agent, Edith, who was childless, lived in a roomy flat above a grocery store, with spare bedrooms. She was working as a waitress in a seasonal restaurant and, since the tips were good and the restaurant needed another waitress, Sarah joined her. They worked long hours and bathed their feet in methylated spirit each night to harden them, but Sarah was earning much more money than from her three jobs in Chippy.

Hayling Island was the first Norman possession in Britain (it had been a wedding present for Queen Emma, Ethelred's, and later Canute's, Norman bride more than a thousand years ago)[2]. Hayling is one of three islands projecting from the South Downs towards the Isle of Wight. To its west lies Portsea Island, home to a great dockyard, the city of Portsmouth, and the holiday resort of Southsea, which between them held a quarter of a million people. To Hayling's west lies Thorney Island, which held an RAF base. Hayling was sparsely populated even in 1951 because during the war it had been covered in artificial lights so that the pilots of the Luftwaffe would mistake it for Portsmouth. In the 1950s Hayling attracted thousands of holidaymakers and was the place where the rich of Portsmouth went to die.

Hayling had four miles of sand and pebble beach, backed by a common strewn with gorse bushes, a yacht club, a golf club, a funfair, a large park, a council-house estate, and a bungalow town that was flooded most winters. In those days it also had a railway station, and its buses, though regular, could cross to the mainland only if

---

[2] Canute (Knut) married Ethelred's widow in 1017.

their passengers alighted and walked across a rickety-rackety bridge. For Sarah it had everything that Chippy lacked, and for me it had everything. In summer it was full of holiday kids, separated from their friends and looking for companions in mischief. In winter the island's secondary modern school provided me with friends, who pitied me for having to go to school by bus every day. My life there revolved around the beach and funfair in summer, and the park and the winding lanes in winter.

I was soon suntanned almost all over, which was good, because a tan makes thin children look healthy, and both Sarah and I enjoyed remarkably good health in our years on the island. Hayling offered no work in winter, so in August Edith went job-hunting in Portsmouth and found two jobs (one for her, one for Sarah) in their own tailoring trade. When Sarah agreed to move home, Edith's husband found us a place of our own. This was a flat in a dilapidated building on the seafront; we guessed it would be bitterly cold in winter (we found that two people were required to close the front door when a gale was blowing), but the flat shared a bathroom with the flat next door, and Sarah couldn't resist it. The flat was necessarily tiny, because otherwise holidaymakers would have paid more for it in the summer than Sarah paid all year round. It consisted of a living room, a minute kitchen, and one small bedroom. So I lost the alcove in King's Head Yard that contained my bed and the precious space beneath it, which contained my few possessions. For most of my remaining school years I slept on a collapsible bed in the living room; I folded it up like a concertina each morning, and opened and made it up each evening.

Having no bedroom and little storage space proved a boon later when I went off to do my national service: in basic training the NCOs forced everyone to be obsessively tidy: we folded our bedclothes and spare kit, polished our brasses and floor space, and pressed everything from our battledress to our boots. It was hell for untidy people, but I slipped effortlessly into this routine. The locker the army provided for my kit and rifle was larger than any drawer or cupboard that Sarah could ever allow me, so, while other conscripts complained bitterly about what we called 'bull', I thought barrack life was rather luxurious. And later I considered life in an officer's mess like living in a palace.

The flat was a mile from Hayling station, so when Sarah resumed her skilled trade she had a very long day (leaving home at 6.30 a.m. and returning at 6.30 p.m.). The sweatshop and clothing store below it were owned by a Polish immigrant in his forties, and his business consisted almost entirely of selling made-to-measure civilian suits to sailors. This was known as the *allotment* business, because the Navy paid for these up front and the matelots had a sum deducted from their pay each week. The business was gained by three 'travellers', who used to sell the suits on board ship, measure the customers, and supervise fittings.

The travellers were colourful characters and all homosexuals: their perks started with measuring a matelot's inside leg and often finished with the slipping of two lengths. The custom of allowing them aboard was an ancient one: in the centuries when Britain was great, pressed men were not allowed ashore until old age had robbed them of their value. So, when the fleet was in, sundry pedlars were allowed aboard and, of course, the sailors' women. Thus all pressed men's children were conceived on the gun deck, which was cleared in port, because making love in a hammock is a very rare skill. This gave rise to the expression 'you son of a gun'. In the 1950s Portsmouth people still spoke with a vaguely Cockney accent, because they were largely descended from generations of East End girls, who in earlier centuries had flocked there when the fleet was in, and had been prepared to wait until it came in again.

Because matelots are rough trade, all three of the sweatshop's travellers were pretty thuggish individuals. One of them lived with a policeman, and he once broke this young constable's nose during a domestic tiff. Another married a girl for her money and when they returned from their honeymoon she got an annulment because she was still a virgin and had acute haemorrhoids. The bridegroom made a pretty penny from the wedding presents, which the bride's family didn't dare reclaim. This case got into all the Portsmouth papers and made the bridegroom something of a celebrity: he got many a sip of rum, and much more, on the strength of it. Edith sometimes flirted with this man behind the boss's back, but she knew on which side her bread was buttered, as the saying goes, and it went no further.

Sarah and Edith worked from 8 until 5 with an hour for lunch, which they spent shopping, because the workroom was above a shop in a busy street. The sweatshop staff consisted of a male master tailor and two female seamstresses (one of whom was Edith), a (male) presser who wielded a flat-iron weighing several kilos, a (male) cutter who wielded a giant pair of shears, and two (female) machinists. Sarah was taken on because one of these had left. The other struggled to produce thirty pairs of trousers a week, partly because she spent much of her time on the floor of the boss's office. When Edith became the boss's mistress and Sarah showed that she could produce nearly seventy pairs of trousers a week, the other woman became redundant and was given her cards.

Sarah and Edith worked in that sweatshop until they retired; in Sarah's case this was until she was nearly seventy. Her job was never in jeopardy, because two replacements would have cost her boss twice as much in national insurance and holiday pay. He always treated Sarah well, even though she was too old for his harem, and he increased her rate of pay as the years went by and inflation crept in. He was also generous to me: when I grew tall he gave Sarah clothes that sailors hadn't collected (usually because they were in custody), so that she could alter them to fit me. Sarah equipped me for university in that way, and none of the middle-class students I met there were better kitted out. They all also envied my stock of jerseys, because Sarah's knitting was of the same high standard, and no fancy pattern could defeat her.

Her work place was a major part of Sarah's social life, as indeed it was of Edith's, who was furiously compensating for an unhappy marriage. While machining Sarah could listen to the radio and chat happily to her fellow workers: her capacity for multi-tasking was amazing. On her journey to and from work she always got a seat (because men were polite in those days) and she read and knitted for a couple of hours. And in the evenings and at weekends she would sit for hours reading a novel, knitting a jumper, and listening to the radio, all at the same time. On Saturday she cleaned the flat thoroughly and in the evening went to the cinema, either Hayling's small theatre or a larger one on the mainland. At first I went with her, but at fifteen years old children develop a mortal terror of their friends seeing them with their parents, so Edith usually accompanied her and Edith's husband at least knew where she was.

On sunny Sundays Sarah would sit on the seafront and read; in her annual holidays she would visit or entertain her brothers and sisters; and at Christmas her brother Tommy usually brought the young family of his second marriage to Hayling to join us. So Edith had a full house and cooked a large roast fowl, and we all sipped gin or ginger beer, and we played cards and yarned about the good old days that I couldn't remember. Edith wanted no children of her own but was great with her nieces and nephews. Since I was the nearest one, she often spoilt me; for example, she gave me a shilling (5p) a week pocket money because Sarah, who had rent to pay, couldn't afford to.

Once she had returned to her own craft, Sarah enjoyed work again. I remember being incredulous when I first read Robert Graves's statement that work is much more fun than play, but with experience I have come to agree with him. Certainly, Sarah's work had the three ingredients that make work a pleasure: (1) autonomy: it was her choice of work, and she decided how it would be done; (2) complexity: music and conversation made machining challenging enough; and (3) reward for extra effort: every pair of trousers brought an extra one shilling and sixpence. And at the end of each week her pay packet was three times what she had been paid to do three menial jobs in Chippy.

Once Sarah had decided to move to the south coast she had to sort out my schooling; she applied to the county's education officer to find me a place at a local grammar school, but unfortunately there were no vacancies until January, and so in 1950 I had six months off school. I dealt with this by making friends with boys from Hayling's council estate and secondary modern school, probably the worst boys, the ones who played truant regularly. I would meet them at the park or on the beach once the school day had started and we would go off to find all sorts of mischief. For example, when it was open we robbed the funfair, using a table knife to get pennies out of slot machines; and we found ways of getting into the cinema without paying, and of leaving Woolworths in Havant with sweets in our pockets we hadn't paid for. We often met up across the toll bridge in Havant. I walked there, so set out fifty minutes earlier on the five-mile journey. They had fathers and therefore bicycles and caught me up in the town's centre. Since I enjoyed walking I didn't resent their wheels; I saw all their black eyes and bruises, and occasionally an overenthusiastic father broke a boy's limb, so I wasn't envious.

Throughout my time in Hayling I had two sets of friends because only one pupil from my grammar school lived on the island. She was an attractive but stand-offish girl called Lisa. The other Hayling kids divided into rich ones who went to private schools off the island and poor ones who went to the island's secondary modern school. I naturally made my friends among the latter, and so I had one set of home friends and another of school friends – mostly lower-middle-class children whose fathers had white-collar jobs and didn't beat them up. This dichotomy was awkward because the secondary modern school gave no homework, and when I at last resumed school my home friends still expected me to join them in the park or on the seafront every evening. But that wasn't a problem during my early school-free months.

There were two schools in South-East Hampshire for boys who had passed the eleven-plus exam, a posh school (Churcher's College) and an ordinary one (Purbrook County High). Churcher's was a boys' school that played rugby and prepared its brightest pupils for Oxbridge; Purbrook was coeducational and played soccer and hockey, and its brightest pupils had no special preparation, so went only to red-brick universities. Since records of my passing the eleven-plus exam at nine years old lay in Oxfordshire, and my scores in the IQ-test trials lay in Essex, Hampshire decided to allot me a school on the only basis they had: Sarah's application for free school dinners and a school uniform allowance. So Purbrook became the last of my many schools. When I discovered that it held twice as many girls as boys, because the area had no posh girls' school, I was delighted.

Since nobody in my family had ever attended university, Sarah wasn't bothered either. The chief purpose of education in England has always been to ensure that the children of the rich get the best jobs (from bishops in the Middle Ages to media stars and politicians today). Britain's two oldest universities are more important as a conduit to power than they are to academic standards (which are now set by the USA's top dozen institutions). The British system is no doubt wasteful, since barely one in three of the nation's brightest go to Oxbridge; but this is a blessing to Britain's other universities, who share most of the rest. In my old age I don't regret not having had the opportunity to become a diplomat, politician, banker, publisher, or media announcer; but I do resent the fact that the decision was made for me by a stranger on the basis of class prejudice.

In the1950s I was more concerned with another divide in class-ridden Britain, that between my very lower-class home friends and my mostly middle-class school friends. I made many social gaffs because behaviour ingrained in one set of kids was not acceptable to the other. The most important was homework, which I always completed on the bus so as not to alienate myself from the Hayling friends. I had two hours travelling each day in total and used it frantically, producing an almost illegible scribble. Another danger was language: I had to be careful of my vocabulary in the park and on the seafront, and I had the wrong accent for school (East End Cockney, shading to Pompey-Lil Cockney). Its compensation was that when reciting a poem I could have the whole class in hysterics.

So I soon became one of my class's clowns, competing with another boy, nicknamed Sticky, for the class's, and the teacher's, laughs.

The Purbrook headmaster interviewed me with Sarah when I joined. When he saw my last Chippy school report, and learned that I had spent much of my six-month break from school reading, he placed me in the fast stream. And there I stayed until streaming was replaced by small classes specialising in each subject. For two years circumstances kept me near the foot of that class: my combined woodwork, art, and music marks never totalled more than 50 (out of 300); in other subjects my exam marks were around 70 per cent, but my term work earned me on average nearer 30 per cent, so when combined the result was mediocre. I am grateful for the understanding that my teachers showed: I was never in danger of relegation to a lower steam for two reasons. The first was their belief that when I stopped clowning my exam marks would be reflected overall.

The second reason for my security was Latin, which was only taught to the fast stream at Purbrook. Its teacher was the most ferocious in the school, and in her lessons no one laughed. Kitty was a small Welsh woman with aggressive spectacles and a beautiful voice with a charming tonic accent. She hated children (although married, she had none) and her acid tongue could make girls weep and boys' eyes sting. Before her displeasure even the most hulking youth felt as small as a *ridiculus mus* and the daintiest girl felt as clumsy as a *horribilis sus*.[4]

---

[4] 'Ridiculous mouse' and 'horrible boar'; oratio recta is 'direct' (with pun upon 'correct') speech..

But, strangely, I loved Kitty and her lessons.

When I started at Purbrook I found that it was a long way ahead of Chippy Grammar School in all subjects, but in Latin it took me only a couple of weeks to catch up. I had always found grammar beautiful, and for Kitty I made my ablatives the most absolute, my accusatives the most infinite, and my *orationem maxime rectam*. I even took special care with my Latin homework, correcting my school-bus errors at home or before assembly in the morning. I think, in retrospect, that, having no father, I found a substitute in Kitty. Although I excelled at her subject, she showed me few favours, and she slapped me down when I crossed the line she set for familiarity. But we built up a mutual respect for one another's minds, and she appreciated my achievements in a way that Sarah never could. Kitty always encouraged me to give my best and rewarded me for it with her approval.

It was a good job I had something to love at Purbrook because my love life in the first two years was meagre. Many of my home friends had sisters, and some of them came down to the park in the evenings and went into the bushes with groups of inquisitive boys. Most of these girls settled for having their breasts rubbed and commented upon, and for allowing a favoured few to touch them up below. But one thirteen-year-old, Bella (by my convention), would go the whole way for half-a-crown ($12^{1}/_{2}$ p in decimalised money); she was fearless, partly because she was the daughter of the local abortionist, but not very attractive, and I avoided becoming one of her favourites. I doubt whether she had a wraith to climb into any of our beds and inspire our emissions.

The wraith in my bed was now Lisa: I tried replacing her with Hollywood stars, but I found their embraces lacked realism. Only flesh seen in the flesh could satisfy me. I confess that I sometimes tortured Lisa a little, in revenge for her jibes on the school bus. But I never saw her in the evenings: her parents were Christian extremists (they consigned all other Christians to Hell), and they kept her on a tight rein. I think it was all that kneeling and praying that made her so malicious. At bedtimes I had the wraith of Lisa, and when wandering around during the day I had the wraith of Kitty, who showed me the glory that was Greece and the splendour that was Rome.

For two years I lazed and clowned in class, and on the football field I waited despairingly on the wing for a pass. I waited just as hopelessly on the boundary for a handful of cricket ball, because at number nine or ten in the batting order I hardly ever went in to bat. Afternoon form games were limited to an hour for each innings, and only if the games master picked hopelessly ill-matched teams would I get lucky (and face all the best bowlers). As a batting nonce I was never allowed to bowl; and, since the cricket nets were reserved for boys who played in the school's teams, the skill gap became ever wider. At least it was possible to read while my team-mates batted. I balanced this inactivity by doing somewhat better than average on the athletics track, and by playing chess competitively for the first time.

Purbrook's senior maths master started a chess club in the lunch hour at about the same time as I discovered that there were books on chess. My chess progressed rapidly and by the time we were ready to enter a team in the local schools league I was its captain, and played on first board. The price I had to pay for this was teaching new players and running coaching sessions, both of which I enjoyed. This enabled the senior maths master to spend his lunchtimes in the staff room, chatting up the younger women teachers and showing them his rowing muscles. He was nicknamed 'Bob' and he gradually lost his enthusiasm for chess as more of his pupils were able to beat him. When we reached the stage at which he could never scrape a draw with me, he resented it badly.

It also annoyed Bob that I would never work at maths in the way that I did at my chess. He punished me for this heresy by demoting me to the slower maths set (of which I always came top, but he was unforgiving). So for more than a year I suffered from useless supply teachers whose lessons were riots. Eventually I persuaded the worst and most depressed of the supply teachers to let me miss his lessons and pursue my own studies in the senior pupils' quiet room. There I read my arithmetic, geometry, and algebra books from cover to cover, and I became his only pupil to pass O-level maths. But he was sacked at the end of the term, so his only reward for releasing me was one rioter fewer.

By then I had also come to terms with the teachers whose subjects I hated: I was never there for the art master, who saw only beauty and never found it in my work. And when my voice broke before any of the other boys', the music master allowed me to sit quietly at the back of class and do homework. This meant that at least my Latin translations were neat, and perhaps Kitty heard the music beneath them. The woodwork master had made me plane pieces of wood for two years without their surfaces achieving horizontal adequacy; when I had planed each piece down to a wafer he threw it away and made me start again. Eventually he settled for less, and in my last-ever lesson I finished the tea tray that was the only fruit of my years of labour. When the master asked if I wanted to buy it for one shilling and sixpence, I told him that I might be awful at woodwork but I knew rubbish when I saw it. So the tray went into the bin with all the wafers that were its prototypes.

Those first two years at Purbrook were years of great frustration, relieved by little triumphs on the chess board, signs of approval from Kitty, and moments of exhilaration when I got away with things I should not have. But I was glad that Sarah was much happier now than she had been in Chippy, and I took each day as it came.

8

COMMERCE

Although Sarah was happy at her work, she found her journey to it irksome: before and after settling down on the train she had a mile to walk in all weathers. She was also reminded daily of how much more often the Pompey buses ran, how many more shops there were to choose from, how many more cinemas there were. And she preferred its seafront, which had flower gardens rather than gorse bushes, and paths, and lots of places for an older person to sit down. Most of all, it had crowds of people like the East End of her youth. So she began looking for a flat in Pompey, a task as difficult in 1953 as in 2013; and she had only the saving on rail fares by way of paying a higher rent.

When an opportunity for us to move to the city came, however, it was from an unexpected quarter. Sarah's youngest brother Teddy had gone to night school like his brothers and had obtained a job with London's largest estate agent. He rose through that company's ranks to become a senior negotiator, married a middle-class girl, and lived in a middle-class house in Harrow. Their marriage was ruined by the death of their eldest son at the age of one: of all unlikely things, he choked on a hazelnut at Christmas. At first the couple tried to bury their grief by producing two more sons, but then Teddy's wife Irene got religion and snuggled up to the Roman Church instead.

When Irene began to refuse sex to expiate her sin of allowing her child to die (where was God?), the marriage was over. Teddy tried every form of persuasion, but priests have more practice, and Irene remained obdurate. To compensate, Teddy threw himself into his work and into his hobby; he had served in the RAF during the war and afterwards had obtained a commission with the RAF Reserve. So he spent all his evenings training air cadets and rose to the rank of flight lieutenant. But uniforms are irresistible, and his next step was to find a girlfriend, named Fay.

Fay was mad about Teddy, but came from a posh and straight-laced family, and she promised them to become the last woman in Britain to marry *virgo intacta*. So she and Teddy had to wait for a long and messy divorce. Fay's parents said it would test the couple's love, but it actually frayed the couple's nerves with frustration. When they got to meet Fay, Teddy's sisters liked her. Her manners were perfect, and she and Teddy were obviously having a terrible time trying to keep their hands off one another. I liked her because she treated me like an adult. She also had a sense of humour and could talk intelligently about serious things.

Teddy's senior work colleagues, however, took Irene's side, and he realised that there would be no more promotion at work. Fortunately, the RAF had a long experience of adultery and his reservist's career prospered as his business career stalled. So Teddy decided to change his job and location as well as his woman. He had accumulated enough capital and credit to go into business for himself and the place he chose to do it was Portsmouth, which was just over an hour from London on a fast train. His choice was influenced by there being an estate agency for sale there; it was on a main road and had a large flat above it; and it came with a second business, a greengrocery shop that the previous owner had bought as an investment.

Since Fay wouldn't live with Teddy until they were married, he asked his sister Sarah to go into business with him in the short term.

He knew she was looking for a home in Portsmouth and this was a golden opportunity for her. He also persuaded her to give up her work and run the greengrocer's shop. He was confident that with the aid of his agency he would be able to find Sarah a flat when Fay eventually moved in with him.

Sarah was always unable to resist the appeals of her younger siblings, and when she discovered that I could stay at Purbrook (and just have a different journey to school), the deal was cemented. That neither she nor Teddy knew anything about greengrocery didn't seem to bother them. Thus it was that I spent a year in Pompey that changed my life. I discovered capitalism and customers, Anglo-Catholicism and youth clubs, and a place of excitement and competition that would become my second home. In the flat over Teddy's Copnor office I also had a room of my own in which to read and dream. And since I had lost all my friends from the Hayling council estate, I even began to do a little homework in it.

Sarah ran the shop each day, and I worked there on Saturday mornings and all day during school holidays. Teddy had helped persuade Sarah that I should stay at school until I was almost sixteen in order to sit what were known as 'O levels'. He assured her that going to night school later had been the hard way to get an education, and that it was no longer the only route out of hard manual labour. Those years married to a middle-class girl had changed Teddy's attitudes even as Sarah's remained those of the Old East End. So, although she had been set to work in a factory at thirteen, Sarah agreed to keep me for another year providing I worked on Saturdays and in the holidays; and at first I worked for her.

I served in the shop, helped work out prices, and did lots of heavy labour, and my presence allowed Sarah to take time out for her own shopping. The first surprise that greengrocery had in store for us was that it necessitated a visit to the Commercial Road wholesale market at 6 a.m. on at least two days a week. Fortunately Teddy had a car to transport our purchases to Eastney, where our shop stood close to the Royal Marine barracks. The second surprise was the weight of the sacks and the amount of earth that had to be cleaned off before sale. The third was that as a small business we were obviously paying more per hundredweight than the bigger well-established greengrocers. When we were not busy my job was to monitor prices at these bigger outlets, and our profits were narrow if we matched them.

The one way we could compete with price was to offer a delivery service, and so my Saturdays began with carrying bags laden with veg and fruit for distances up to a mile. My pay was my keep (I was now fifteen and my Hayling friends were at work and paying for theirs) and the tips I received from grateful customers. This was always enough for me to visit Fratton Park once a fortnight to watch professional football and to try to find friends. There I met a crowd of urchins in their last year at school who were football crazy. During the holidays we met in any of the city's parks and improvised a game; someone always had a ball and someone's elder brother would often be off sick from work and act as referee.

I was no longer the smallest and lightest player, and I discovered a new enthusiasm for the game by watching the professionals. I even watched Wolves, my heroes from Chippy days, play once (they lost as most away teams do). But I discovered that at our low level it did not matter much if nobody wanted to pass, providing you played fullback and were quick on the tackle. Good reflexes, long legs, and the willingness to incur (and cause) injury made me an asset in defence, and as I grew taller my head often made vital interceptions in the penalty box. My improvement wasn't enough to get me into my school's elevens, but it earned me a secure place in my house team from then on.

This was when Simon's mistress's mother made Sarah the offer she could not refuse. Sarah invited me to the law court for the hearing, thinking I might be curious as to what Simon looked like. But I had a game of football fixed and, as I have noted, teenage boys have their priorities. In the event Simon did not appear; Sarah identified him from a photograph and the uncontested case went through quickly. She said that Simon looked very much the same, but had gone bald. She spent some of her ill-gotten gains on clothes, including a sports jacket and a pair of cavalry-twill trousers for me (Edith made the jacket and her boss gave her the cloth as a bonus). These were my first non-school clothes and made me feel grown-up, as did Teddy when he occasionally offered me a cigarette. He had started smoking at fourteen and it did not kill him until sixty years later.

Teddy's estate agency prospered no more than the greengrocery shop. Copnor Road was only the fourth or fifth best shopping centre in Pompey, and it was the farthest from any railway station. His long-established competitors had more vendors and buyers on their books, and Teddy became the agent of last resort. Since his overheads represented a higher proportion of his turnover, he also made lower profits; and although he survived the first, most difficult, year, prospects for both businesses were bleak when he eventually sold them. The estate agency went to one of his competitors who was foolish enough to open a Copnor branch, and the greengrocery shop to another poor sucker who didn't understand how capitalism worked.

Today there is something close to a Neo-liberal consensus: most people have a naive belief that free markets and competition are the best way to produce economic growth. But free markets rarely produce fair competition: the bigger players, with their lower costs, out-compete, destroy, and take over their rivals. Most markets are rigged (as J. K. Galbraith showed in the 1950s), because size brings power and power includes the power to rig them; and cartels, bullying, and bribery offer the fastest routes to wealth. The only way to beat bigger rivals is to fight dirtier; thus no one in the USA can compete with the Mafia, and in Britain the individual who sails closest to the wind legally has an enormous advantage. Politicians now urge us to admire entrepreneurs (who fund their parties), but entrepreneurism is only crime with capital (and crime is just entrepreneurism without it).

Most important of all today, the competitor who doesn't pay tax will always beat the one who does. Twenty-first-century media (owned by some of the world's worst tax pirates) paint the maximisation of growth and profits as the ultimate good. But 2 per cent growth that is widely distributed is far more desirable than 4 per cent growth, all of which is piled up in tax havens by a small number of secret owners. Similarly, the only way to maximise profits (having taken all other measures to improve it) is to overcharge customers and cut staff wages. Capitalism is essential to economic growth but, as Keynes remarked, it is a wild beast that needs to be kept chained. And, as Warren Buffet correctly pointed out, Neo-liberalism actually makes a nation poorer: if workers in the USA were paid more, they would spend more, and every industry (to say nothing of governments) would be richer for it. But today's politicians are a craven crew and the rewards of corruption at national level are great.

So Pompey introduced me to the world of work just when I was ready for it. But Teddy was very aware that I had lost all my home friends by the move and he encouraged me to be more outgoing. One of my solitary pursuits in my newly won room was constructing aeroplanes from balsa wood and doped paper. They mostly crashed on their first elastic-propelled flight, but it gave Teddy the idea that I might enjoy becoming one of his air cadets. I did not, however, even at that age, see aircrew as heroic figures; in the conflicts after 1945, when they mostly attacked small, weak countries without air defences, they seemed the opposite of heroic: they bombed helpless civilians, and when they had created hell below they flew home to breakfast. Moreover, I knew that national service was waiting for me, when I would have to move my limbs to other people's commands, and I saw no point in bringing forward that date.

Deprived of a new recruit, Teddy urged me to join a youth club, which I found a much more attractive proposition. My home was 200 yards from the nearest church, which ran a boys' club once a week; it was an Anglo-Catholic church, with coloured vestments, incense, and candles, and by attending a service on Sunday (when there was little else to do anyway) I gained access every Tuesday to a mob of other urchins and some sports equipment. One item of equipment was a table-tennis table, and at last I found a game where I had no experience deficit and where my good reflexes paid dividends. Within weeks I was the boy who gave the organiser the fiercest competition, and so I played a lot. This man was a PT teacher and his coaching improved our reflexes, because he taught us to take the ball off the floor when our opponents missed the table. In later years I demoralised many an opponent at this game by hitting a winner off the floor.

I also grew to admire the curate who officiated at the Sunday service. He was an intelligent and open-minded man: he recognised that I would never reason my way to his god, but persuaded me to give faith a chance. And when he prepared a small group of neophytes for baptism and confirmation, this preparation usually became a meaningful enquiry and discussion. He knew the Vulgate and Greek New Testament as well as the Authorised Version, and this added to my knowledge. Sarah had always taught me to beware of men in skirts, but this curate was planning to marry (which was probably what kept him from the Roman church). Yet I think that had the services been in Latin I might have become hooked. I struggled for several years after to find the curate's faith, but I never lost my conviction that his Holy Writ was the invention of primitive minds.

After confirmation I joined the Christian Union at school, where I was welcome because I was the only person who had read the whole Bible and I was interested in ironing out its contradictions. I was even elected its treasurer and attended a CU conference in Staffordshire, where there was even more serious discussion (but no table tennis), and I went for invigorating walks on Cannock Chase with earnest but not unattractive girls. I didn't find the young curate's faith on the road to Cannock, but I tried to cultivate his open mind, and in later years I gave Christianity (to say nothing of Hinduism, Buddhism, Judaism, and Islam) other chances to close it.

Apart from helping me stay on at school, Teddy did me one other great favour. One of his friends was on the committee of Portsmouth Chess Club and he was invited to a meal, after which he promised to give me a game (mainly to see what standard one of the local schools was producing). When I won it by playing a sound middle game and adopting an efficient end-game strategy, he insisted that I join his club. He promised to speed the acceptance of my membership and Teddy paid the first year's subscription. This opened up a new world, where I spent two evenings a week playing with the best adult players in the town. My game improved dramatically that winter, and (after a summer back in Hayling) even more so in the following one. My results gained me a place in the Hampshire men's team (where I played a modest board thirteen) and the captaincy of Portsmouth's junior team (where I played first board). Eventually chess was to play a key role in my getting to university.

Teddy's finding buyers for his businesses was doubly serendipitous (my favourite word in 1952). When there was yet another delay in his divorce proceedings, he went on a date with married woman named Mary, whom he met in the course of his work. When Mary's husband found out, he beat her very badly. And when Teddy learned from friends that this was a regular occurrence prompted by the husband's drinking, not Mary's behaviour, Teddy confronted him. Like many wife-beaters, the husband proved reluctant to take on a man and the row finished with Teddy packing Mary's bags, and her moving in with us. Teddy was a very compassionate man, but he was also a passionate one, and Mary must have been worth it, because despite her bruises she went straight to bed with Teddy and they didn't emerge for three days. I felt sorry for Fay whom I rather liked, but it just went to prove something the curate always claimed: that virtue is its own reward.

Teddy and Mary eventually had a long marriage: they moved to Brighton where they adopted the sweet little girl that Teddy had always wanted. Teddy kept in touch with his sons, however, who did not share their mother's enthusiasm for the pope, and who both joined the RAF. Teddy was one of life's good guys, but he wasn't always lucky; nevertheless, when he lost one wife he gained another, and though he lost one son he kept the other two and he gained a daughter. Sarah and I kept in contact with him until Mary's death, and I shall always be grateful for Teddy's contribution to my development.

Sarah, who could not find a place in Pompey at such short notice, took me to live for a few months with Edith, and was welcomed back to her sweatshop. I returned to my old school bus, but no longer completed my homework on it. The temptation to spend my evenings with my Hayling friends had gone, and it took time to make new and rather different friends. The old ones had all left school and were earning money, which they spent on girls, cigarettes, and alcohol; they rarely appeared in the park and, when they did, they didn't want the company of a mere schoolboy. But I had discovered work and was about to discover real-life romance, so I didn't care.

My school life had altered, too. In the fifth form I was able to drop woodwork, art, and music, and my overall position in class immediately shot up. And, since a major external exam was on its way, mock exams replaced homework assignments and my position shot up still further. Instead of being in the bottom ten, I found myself in the top five. So I began to take all my subjects as seriously as I had taken Latin, and this established me in the top three. Once I had stopped being the class clown and had become one of its stars (and a County chess player, to boot), this brought other rewards: the first was a plain, but intelligent girl called Anna; she joined the chess club, it seems, for the privilege of my coaching, and soon she was staying behind for inter-school matches. She volunteered to serve the teas and biscuits with which we regaled our visitors, and I was amazed by the amount of attention that players from all-boys schools gave her. I think she was responsible for several opponents' blunders that gave me easy victories, and she went up in my estimation.

Although Anna's middle-class parents thought chess a genteel and harmless occupation, they were strict Roman Catholics and wouldn't allow her out on other dates. Our relationship therefore developed in a most bizarre way: Anna began writing me long and explicit erotic letters. She wrote of entertaining my wraith in her bed, and she described her body's cravings for me in terms that resembled the *Moradas* of St Theresa.

Anna's letters described to me in aching detail how she thought of me last thing at night and first in the morning , and how this made her moist and *concupiscent* (this was her word for 'on heat'), and that she longed to melt in my arms and flow around me. It was from Anna that I learned exactly how badly a girl could itch and where, and I realised that I, too, had a wraith that could serve the needs of a lurid imagination.

This epistolary romance went on until Sarah found one of Anna's letters, and hit the roof. Sarah was convinced that Anna must be much older than I, and perhaps was one of my teachers. I had extreme difficulty in persuading Sarah not to confront Anna in her home the next weekend. Since she didn't believe that Anna was a schoolgirl, Sarah would probably have confronted Anna's mother. But Anna and I had barely touched *en passant*, and this would have led to other unjust accusations and lots of Catholic contrition. So to save Anna from being exposed as a sinner and a lecher, I promised Sarah to give up what I had never had. So I wrote to Anna saying *j'adoube*, and she gradually transferred her attentions to another, perhaps more appreciative, reader. I sometimes wonder how Anna fared in life; she probably grew up to write the most exquisite women's pornography. May her royalties keep flowing!

I had a deal with Sarah, one that I found easy to keep in Hayling: in return for my keep beyond the age of fifteen I was to work at weekends and in school holidays. Each Saturday I worked on a mobile shop operated by Mr Edwards, the local greengrocer. He drove to his customers' homes all over South Hayling delivering fruit and veg. He went into those homes to collect orders, and I carried laden bags down drives and up stairs to their destination. Where he could collect two women's orders in the same parking place, he would deliver the bag to the more attractive of the two; and the more attractive she was the longer he would take. The ladies I served, however, dazzled me with their homes: the décor, the carpets, the furniture, the pictures, the huge bowls of flowers, and the grand pianos. Nothing in Eastney's council houses had prepared me for this.

As I approached my exams I began to carry a school book to revise in these intervals, and Mr Edwards joked that I was becoming a *scholard*, while the only thing he knew was that pig's arse is pork. But he knew all the island's gossip, and to judge from his stories it was a hotbed of lust; as a gangling teenager in a brown overall, however, I never got lucky. When no exam was on the horizon I just ate fruit, since eating as much as I liked was one of the agreed perks of the job. This must have cost Mr Edwards almost as much as the ten shillings (50p) I received at the end of the day, but it was a diet on which I throve. Today everyone is urged to eat five portions of fruit and veg every day, but I consumed a whole week's portions on a Saturday. I didn't get fat on it, but it helped me recognise that Mr Edwards was a good employer, and I left him only when I was offered a job that would fill six days a week.

That summer I also worked on Sundays at the local funfair, where I had found a legal way of fleecing holidaymakers. In those days a very popular type of slot machine consisted of columns of pennies, and unwary visitors poured their pennies into these machines in attempts to win a column, which looked easy, but was very difficult. When the visitor gave up in frustration, a crafty teenager who had perfected the technique could step in and clean up. On a good Sunday I would win fifteen shillings in this way and, while Sarah accepted my ten shillings Saturday pay, I kept most of my Sunday winnings. Thus my churchgoing habit was broken, but I sometimes pondered theological questions as I waited for visitors to weary of losing their money. And it became clear to me that its creator had made a world where predators prospered.

I now had a new way of spending my ill-gotten gains. At this stage I travelled the first half of my journey to school with a boy called Michael, the son of a rich builder, who attended a private school in Portsmouth (as posh people called Pompey). Michael was my age and height but broader, and very good-looking: he tried his luck with Lisa on the bus, but met with the same Arctic reception that had long since frozen me. When we met one evening in Hayling Park, Michael pointed out two girls who were sitting on the swings idly talking about films and make-up. He told me they attended a girls' private school on the island, named the *Priory* (and known to the local lads as the *Proary*), and he suggested we approach them and chat them up.

Their names were Carla and Tina (by my convention), and this approach was what they were waiting for. Carla was beautiful, like a film star, but said little; and Tina was talkative and looked very much a schoolgirl. But Tina had nice hair, bright eyes, and a pleasant smile, and her figure was as good as Carla's. Our chatting-up led to a double date at the local cinema, where Carla chose Michael and Tina was left with me. This seemed so natural that both couples were soon close enough to make further dates; at least once a week at the cinema (programmes changed on Monday and Thursday) and a couple of times at the park.

Both these posh girls were very reserved in the park, where flirtation prevailed over entering the bushes. (They despised Bella, the abortionist's daughter, whose activities continued unabated when she left school). But Tina was a different woman in the darkness of the cinema: she was soft and warm and fragrant, and as eager to explore and experiment as I was. That the passion was confined to the cinema resulted from Tina's fear of her very strict mother. I learned that Tina's mother was the owner of the most opulent of all the homes to which I delivered greengrocery. Each time I went there after that I hoped desperately to find the mother out and Tina in, but it never happened. Tina's mother always sat there imperiously, looking down her nose at the delivery boy and guarding her daughter's virtue.

Part of my attraction for Tina was that I was her bit of rough and her biggest risk. If her mother had discovered her romance, she would have packed Tina off to boarding school immediately. And Tina didn't want girls, however good fingersmiths they might be; she wanted boys. I could tell how much, as we sat entwined in the back row of the cinema (known as the finger-stalls). We often talked fondly of going away together, to somewhere exciting, for a couple of days (we didn't mention nights). But that couldn't be paid for in pennies, and Tina knew that her mother would have killed her first. Tina was even afraid of spending an evening on the beach with me; since her home was near the seafront, her mother's image loomed larger there. And sand would doubtless have offered clear forensic evidence of Tina's guilt. So we contented ourselves with making love each night to one another's wraiths. But Tina now had a real boyfriend, and I a real girlfriend, and they were roles we both needed to practise.

When the school term ended in July 1953 I said goodbye to my friends there and went to work full-time in Hayling's dairy, which was much busier in the summer holidays than at other times of year. My understanding with Sarah was that if I passed all my O levels I would return to Purbrook's sixth form, and if I didn't I would seek a permanent job (in the dairy, if my work had impressed, or in Pompey if it hadn't). My job was to operate a bottle-washing machine, lugging crates of dirty bottles to it and clean bottles from it. Loading and unloading bottles rapidly was a skill it took me weeks to master. My workmates were friendly, but loved to tease me about my sexual inexperience. I saw one of them lose a finger when a crate he was unloading got hooked on his signet ring, and I have recoiled from wearing jewellery ever since. I don't think my work speed impressed the management, so it was a good job when a postcard arrived saying that I had passed all my exams. But at least I had sampled what my life would have been like if I hadn't.

I was paid three pounds a week at the dairy, all of which I gave to Sarah, because I was still working the slot machines at the fair on Sundays. From the money she received Sarah bought a bolt of cloth for Edith to make me a new school blazer. I can't say that Sarah was proud of me, because I don't think she really understood education, but there were no hard feelings that I would not be continuing to bring in a teenager's wage. The household at that time was too excited about something else: Sarah had at last found a flat in Pompey, and I was to mark my sixteenth year by making my sixteenth move of home.

Tina was fifteen a month later, so we had done everything that was legal for lovers of our age. When I gave up work we enjoyed one last ultra-affectionate evening at the cinema and the long walk home after it (Tina's mother, of course, thought she was with Carla). Our last goodnight kiss was a goodbye kiss, and we separated with a smile; but Tina was my least laughable love so far, and our hearts were full of hope as we straddled the age of consent.

9

ENDGAME

The flat that Sarah had found was in Southsea, a far better suburb of Pompey than Copnor: our new home was 300 yards from the seafront, 200 yards from the hotel where Portsmouth Chess Club met, and 100 yards from the posh school where my future bride was still getting crushes on other girls. The accommodation consisted of a living room (in which I also made up my collapsible bed), the tiniest bedroom on the planet (for Sarah), a small kitchen, and a bathroom in an extension with a corrugated roof. It was the most luxurious place of our own we had ever had, and its higher rent was covered by Sarah's saving on train fares and a rise which her boss gave her for the occasion (he had ideas about future overtime now that Sarah lived locally).

The living room was large enough for a table and four chairs, a sideboard, a settee and a space for my bed. The flat also boasted a large worm-eaten cupboard on the landing outside, which Sarah gave me for my possessions: my first space since that beneath my bed in Chippy. The cupboard had a padlock, so future love letters would be safe from surveillance; and my possessions consisted of some books, a chess set and board, some other board games of my own invention, Lisa's old tennis racquet, which she had given me in a sudden fit of generosity, a table-tennis bat, and two teams for a table-soccer game called *Subbuteo*.

Most of my books were a gift from a retired schoolteacher in Hayling with whom Sarah had become friendly. When this lady discovered I was enamoured of Latin, but that my private reading was detective novels, science fiction, and paperback pornography, she gave me my first non-fiction books. These were grammars of German, Dutch, Danish, Italian, Spanish, and Welsh. She also offered me a French grammar, but I said the language had managed very well without one during my lessons at school. I read these books with great interest and kept them in case I might one day visit these exotic countries. I also begged, borrowed, or stole every book I could find on chess. The cupboard also held some items of stationery, which have always been among my treasured possessions, and the books I chose as school prizes, since I now received them thick and fast on speech days. They varied from a leather-bound King James Bible and an anthology of English poetry to the droll humour of Stephen Potter's *Gamesmanship*.

At school I was now studying only the subjects I liked best: Latin, English and history, and I was no longer the class clown. I also had evenings free: I knew nobody of my own age in Southsea, and so when I wasn't preparing chess openings I did homework in the evenings. My time on the bus to school was now spent in conversation with a schoolmate named Tony, who, by coincidence, had once lived in Chippy and had passed his eleven-plus at nine years old. He had attended the RC school, while I had been at the C of E school. He was studying English, history, and geography, so we spent a lot of time in class together and became rivals with another Tony (whom I shall call Ant) for first place in class. Ant had a habit of getting 100 per cent in maths exams, which put us essay-writers and translators at a disadvantage: no teacher considers giving 90 per cent for an essay, although Kitty came close to giving me this mark for my best translations.

Ant, the scientist who lived miles away, became my closest school friend, despite the fact that Tony and I had so much in common. The barriers between us that Tony never lowered were his religion and his mother. He came from a white-collar Roman Catholic family that lived in the posh suburb of Old Portsmouth, and his mother allowed me into his home just once. She decided that friendship with the son of a divorced factory hand could bring Tony no advantage and she forbade him ever to enter my home. So we were friends only on the bus and in class. Tony was very bright and very competitive: although he had studied Latin and played chess in the middle school, when he realised he would never match me at either he gave up both. But Tony's English and history were better than mine; his parents had always persuaded him to read literature (when I was reading trash), and when I discussed books with him it widened my tastes. His mother would have said that Tony became a good influence on me without my becoming a bad influence on him.

My new wider reading prevented my becoming too obsessed with chess. I spent every hour I could at the city's club, I studied theory assiduously, and I played in numerous competitions, becoming ever more successful. To my regret I had to leave the school chess club, and my old enemy Bob, the senior maths master, was the cause. I had now reached six feet in height and looked so ridiculous in a school cap that I refused to wear it. Since I now travelled on public transport, there was nobody to enforce school rules about uniform (today sixth-formers are excused this humiliation). Bob, however, took a strong objection to my not wearing the cap when he accompanied his team to school chess matches. He stipulated no cap, no captaincy, and threatened to bar me from the school team.

We went before the headmaster, who inevitably backed Bob, and I resigned on the spot. When Bob had marched out triumphantly, the head reassured me that he would continue to pay my travelling expenses to county matches. So I guess he found a way of cutting the baby in half. On my trips to county matches I made friends with adults who treated me as an adult. And the head had showed he harboured no ill-will: he welcomed and debated my doubts in the sixth-form religious education classes he taught, and he made me a prefect when I reached the upper sixth. He kept his word on travelling expenses, insisting I add a sum for lunch, and he congratulated me on my victories. He also urged me strongly to go to university and offered to talk to Sarah about it. So I had heroes and an enemy, things that every boy needs to help him navigate his way towards maturity.

My biggest problem in Pompey was finding work: I scoured the vacancies ads and knocked on many doors, but there were too many sixteen-year-old boys at Portsmouth's own grammar schools for me to stand a chance. I found two ways of making money, in both cases a pittance. Calamitously, the funfair at Clarence Pier had no machines with columns of pennies, but it did have a stall where people raced horses by rolling rubber balls into holes. I discovered the knack to this, and I could soon win three races out of four. The cost of entry was sixpence and the prizes items that retailed for about three shillings (15p). So there was a margin: two shillings won me goods worth nine (from toys to towels and other household items), and Sarah and Edith's friends were happy to choose items in advance and have me win them: since I sold them for half retail value, I could make a few shillings on Saturday and a few more on Sunday.

I soon made friends with the men who ran this stall; and they asked only that I take a break after two consecutive wins, but they welcomed me to roll balls in practice whenever business was slow. Only when the sound of balls rolling reached a certain volume did the last few of the stall's twenty places get taken. I worked out that the stall made at least six shillings for every one that I made, but once again the unwary holidaymaker was being lured into a pretty certain loss. Between races I would walk the promenade and handsome public gardens of Southsea in search of better employment and more congenial friends. There were jobs on the seafront, but the council was able to fill them with older workers, so I remained unemployed.

The other work was tutoring, something rare in those days. In the twenty-first century one in seven British schoolchildren needs it to gain entry to (or remain in) the top stream of a privileged state school aiming to compete with schools in the private sector. My pupil was the son of Sarah's boss, who wanted him to pass the common entry exam set by the public schools. These terms amused me because the entry wasn't common and the schools weren't public. The boss's son badly needed coaching in maths, which he found difficult, but most of all in English, since his family spoke Yiddish at home. I used the boy's school textbooks and explained everything very slowly. His mother always fed me cheesecake after the lessons (two each week) and, when the boy succeeded, his father gave Sarah a length of cloth to make me my first suit. My fee per lesson was almost as much as I could make in three hours on the racetrack at Clarence Pier.

Although I brought in so little, Sarah kept her part of our bargain, and when she learned from my headmaster about grants and scholarships, she backed the idea of my becoming the first member of her wider family to go to university. Today most people go to 'uni' at eighteen; in the 1950s barely 5 per cent did so. Thirty universities then have become nearly 200 now, and if I could raise the capital to start a university that taught only astrology and the art of clairvoyance, I could. But the most important thing that today's undergraduates learn at university is how to live with debt. Most will owe £50,000 after three years, but many are simply gambling that they will never repay it. Obviously, if all British eighteen-year-olds took out student loans, half of them would earn less than the median national wage, and millions would escape repayment.

In 1955 I applied for a county major scholarship, which would pay my tuition fees and give me a living allowance of £6,000 a year in today's money (£300 in 1955 money). That sum can be compared with the £450 a year (1955 money) that Sarah earned as a skilled worker. The living allowance, but not the fee payment, was means-tested: with a father earning £1,000 a year, my grant would have been halved, and with one earning £2,000 I would have received only a quarter. Sarah was amazed by this generosity and signed up for whatever I wanted. I foresaw a problem, however: until my grant cheque arrived in the middle of my first term I would have nothing to live on. Sarah had neither savings nor a bank account and she hated debt (despite her poverty, she had never owed money to her family). So I could only hope to cover that first-term gap by winning enough money at chess, and this governed my priorities in my final year at school.

But before then I had to choose a subject and a university. My history teacher advised me to read history and promised me that I would find world history even more fascinating than the European history I was studying for A level. But it seemed to me that there was a lot of world, and that meant a life of reading, while I wanted something more creative. My English teacher urged me to read English and followed up on his advice: he entered me for a special scholarship paper that covered all English lit, and he gave me a long list of books to read in preparation. It struck me that if I read that list, and more, I wouldn't need to go university at all; but, of course, I was underestimating the difficulty of Old English (which was then compulsory).

When I approached Kitty, however, she warned me not to read Latin under any circumstances: Purbrook did not teach Greek, and she said that if I read Classics I would be in competition with the privately educated. They all started learning Latin at eight and Greek at thirteen, and I would never catch up. Kitty had studied at a Welsh university where she had been able to combine Latin with French, so she advised me to read English. But Kitty overestimated the difficulty of Ancient Greek because she knew none, and I had already bought a book called *Teach Yourself Greek*. I found its beautiful script and luxuriant grammatical forms a delight, so that settled the subject. I looked forward to learning Greek *ab initio*, and I had no fear of posh kids who rode to university on their fathers' wallets.

Kitty grudgingly entered me for the scholarship-level paper in Latin, because she thought it would show me how much further ahead the privately educated were in the subject. But, instead of listing the many authors they would have read, she set me to read Cicero's *De officiis* ('On Moral Imperatives'), a much tougher prospect than our A-level set books. In this work Cicero tried to translate the most complex concepts of Greek moral philosophy into Latin, a language that didn't have words for any of them (the three-letter word *res* being the only abstract noun with which the Romans were comfortable). Although I read and learned from it, it didn't provide me with the vocabulary I could have gleaned from reading a variety of other Latin authors, ones whose writing is much more enjoyable. But if Kitty thought that *De officiis* would deter me she was wrong.

The question of which university was more difficult because I knew of only three: the two oldest ones (which most Americans think are the only ones), and London University, which stood after my headmaster's name on the board outside the school. The first two demanded A-level Greek for entry, while London allowed students to study Greek *ab initio* if any college had enough places for them. As already noted, Purbrook did not send pupils to Oxbridge: its red-brick teachers had no idea how to tackle the complex collegiate entry system, and no time to prepare a few students for special exams. So this helped resolve my problem: London it would be. (I dismissed the possibility of a northern university because I assumed that places north of Chippy were even more cold and uncomfortable).

Because his mother was ambitious, my friend Tony decided to become Purbrook's first (and last) Oxbridge entrant. This meant staying on an extra year at school (something Sarah would never have countenanced) and reading all of Shakespeare's oeuvre by himself. The headmaster made Tony head boy for that year so he could give him interview practice every week and boost his confidence. This may not have been as good as having an Oxbridge teacher coach him, but it worked, and Tony gained a place to read English at Cambridge. The downside of this was that he had to do national service first. Tony, who at that age was attractive but indifferent to women, did not care that the two medieval universities were hotbeds of homosexuality and full of bigger snobs than his mother. But I certainly didn't envy him.

In contrast, Ant argued that London's Imperial College was a better science university than Cambridge, and that London was full of girls. He applied (successfully) for a place to read physics at Imperial, and he urged me to apply to a London college, too, so we could tackle life in the capital together. But London had not impressed me when I visited it for my grandfather's funeral, and it was a very expensive place for students to live. Since places to read Classics were not guaranteed for students without Greek, even at London, I applied to both King's College, in London itself, and the University College of the South West in Exeter, my headmaster's *alma mater*, which also boasted the country's highest proportion of females to males among its undergraduates.

When KCL wrote to me saying that all its places had been offered to students with Greek, I think Ant was more disappointed than I was. UCSW (soon to become the University of Exeter) offered me a place without interview (at which I suspect I would have been terrible). It was conditional upon my gaining a county major scholarship, for which I needed three credits (marks above 60 per cent) at A level, but my marks were always much higher than that. So I was happy and confident with this outcome, and I could now tackle the problem of how to exist at university until my first grant cheque arrived.

My best chance was obviously chess, although there was no money in the professional game in those days; thus former world champion Emmanuel Lasker had recently died in New York of starvation. But each year at Easter an educationally endowed tournament, the Dupree memorial, was held in Portsmouth, and it carried a first prize of seventy-five pounds (£1,500 in today's money). I aimed to win it and prepared carefully. I was getting plenty of match practice: I won the Portsmouth club's senior handicap tournament in 1954, and its junior championship in 1955 (which brought me only a few guineas and a title). And, soon after that, the Portsmouth Junior team, of which I was captain, won promotion to the first division of the local men's league. But the Dupree was open to anyone under twenty-one in full-time education and there were plenty of strong players in the Hampshire schools league from which Bob had barred me.

I tried not to let chess take over my life that year; now that I could play without a board it sometimes kept me awake at night; and only Tina's wraith, growing ever fainter, could help me. My ways of relaxing were simple. I escaped cricket by volunteering for athletic training; the only thing at which I excelled was the triple jump, which wasn't a sports day event, but on summer afternoons I gained a record number of house points by reaching the prescribed standard in every event, from shot-putting to the high jump.

Sixth-form boys enjoyed another privilege at Purbrook: there was a mixed tennis club on Friday evenings, when they were allowed on tennis courts that were the girls' preserve all week. I joined this club and improved rapidly: my table tennis gave me a big advantage, because I was one of the few players at school who had a backhand to match their forehand. My reflexes also helped me: I lost very few points at the net. I was therefore indignant when the games master, who never attended the club, received a challenge from an all-boys school and picked six members of the cricket first eleven to represent us. They were thrashed by boys who had round-the-week access to a court, and afterwards I took pleasure in challenging them, one by one, to a singles match that I won.

But I played best when I had an attractive girl for a partner; the panting proximity of the opposite sex inspired rather than distracted me. My old foil from Hayling, Lisa, joined the tennis club but never played, because she had decided to become the first girl in her class to lose her virginity. She had told her father that she loved tennis and wanted to stay behind on Fridays to play, but she always disappeared into the shrubbery with her boyfriend and emerged two hours later. Her lover was a boy who had been held back a year when he got jaundice and who seemed much older than we were. In any event, he cured Lisa's extreme Christianity, and when her father tried to win her soul back by buying her an expensive new tennis racquet she gave me her old one and lent me the new one a few times to make it look used. Although I suspected it was a form of hush money (I was the only Purbrook boy who knew her father), I found Lisa much sweeter-natured once her soul was lost.

As a general rule at Purbrook, teenage girls dated only older boys; so Lisa was exceptional in becoming involved with a member of her own year. All the other girls in the upper sixth sought boyfriends who had left school and were either at work or college, so I dated none of my tennis partners. This didn't stop the girls in my class from flirting and sharing dirty jokes, but my only physical contact with them was during the dancing lessons we were given on wet games days. I soon knew which girls allowed you to hold them close because they wanted to embarrass you with an erection. But, all in all, my schoolgirl classmates were a friendly bunch who added savour to the day's timetable.

Girls played a large part in my life as a sixth-former: my form held sixteen boys and one girl studying sciences, and nineteen girls and four boys studying arts. The four arts boys were Tony, Patrick who had stayed on an extra year to try for Oxford, a thickset lad called Stan, and myself. And in Latin classes Patrick and I sat with nineteen girls; it was no wonder that I enjoyed every minute of Kitty's lessons. But Patrick did not enjoy them: he had been Kitty's first failure (at any level) the year before, and he was preparing to retake the exam. Kitty uttered not one word to him all year and refused to acknowledge his presence. She marked his work silently and viciously, and Patrick made sure he didn't fail the second time.

When I was in the lower sixth, before Patrick's first humiliation (the second was his rejection by his chosen Oxford college after a hostile interview), the school put on Gilbert and Sullivan's *Iolanthe*. Patrick and Tony had leading roles (probably the cause of Patrick's Latin failure) and, just from hearing rehearsals, I learned all the songs and words. So, in my upper-sixth year, when Tony and Patrick urged me to audition with Stan for the school play, I resolved to confront my shyness and go on stage. The English master producing the play had originally chosen Eliot's *Murder in the Cathedral*, but the girls who formed the majority of our drama club bullied him into changing this to Wilde's *The Importance of Being Earnest*. This had good female roles as well as male ones and proved an excellent choice.

My role was as Tony's butler (I think he had always wanted one), but I was also understudy for Patrick; yet the part whose words remain in my memory is that of Lady Bracknell. From my experience in this minor role I learned that, although I was too introverted to enjoy it at first, I could learn to cope with public speaking. In the event, the play was a huge success, receiving standing ovations on every performance. Sarah attended one of them and thought Tony and Patrick were brilliant. She was surprised to hear me speak in public and thought that I had been quite convincing: butlers, she assumed, would be trying to hide their Cockney accents just as I was.

But I get ahead of myself: the play was in July, and well before that I had a chess tournament to play. I prepared for the Dupree by concentrating on my strength, the endgame. I chose a limited list of openings that all led to middle-game chances for the exchange of pieces, and I looked for variations that would allow me to gain a superior pawn formation, or where my opponent would be tempted to make sacrifices for attacks that I could beat off. Then I settled down to endgame theory with Paul Keres, the most brilliant player of the inter-war generation. Paul won me victories all season; my opponents came to dread my passed pawns, which, after the exchange of queens, drove to the back rank as relentless as Georgi Zhukov's tanks advancing on Berlin. By Easter I was ready: I had finished *De officiis* and had abandoned the English master's list of authors; and instead of revising that holiday I devoted it to chess.

Although a much older boy was the odds-on favourite, I won the Dupree without losing a game. I particularly enjoyed crushing the favourite in an endgame that resembled Alekhine's most famous victory over Capablanca. A local councillor presented me with the seventy-five-pound cheque, which I immediately deposited in my post-office account, and my photo appeared in the local papers. I wore my school blazer for the photo, because I knew my headmaster would like that, but I looked gawky and awkward and very young. When I returned to school I found myself a minor celebrity and everyone except Bob congratulated me. And as April turned into May I at last got down to some revision. But the two months before the exam were not to be all work and no play.

On my first day back at school I was solicited in the lunch hour by a fifth-form girl named Lorna. We had bumped into one another a few times in the previous term and I realised who had done the bumping when she told me that she wanted to get to know me better and demanded a date. She was a tall, slim girl with a nice smile, a bust, and good legs, and she liked to talk and was good at listening. So I decided I wanted to get to know her, too, and we kissed on it.

Lorna also chose the time and place for our dates: since she was only fifteen, her parents would not allow her out in the evenings, but they did let her attend a club at school on Wednesdays, from which she returned home two hours late. Those two hours every Wednesday were mine, and the place she had chosen for us to meet was Portsdown Hill, a vast tree-spattered common that would hide hundreds of courting couples later in the evening. But from four until six the place was ours and we tried out a great many spots in search of comfort and secrecy.

Although my chess exploits had made me her intellectual target, Lorna really wanted to find out about male bodies. So, Wednesday after Wednesday, we lay on the grass, screened by bushes, with our bodies rubbing frenziedly against one another, and our hands and tongues stroking and exploring. But we didn't go the whole way, because Lorna wouldn't remove her knickers and I wasn't inflamed enough to tear them off (even though she changed her school navy-blues for flimsy ones on Wednesdays). When the term ended we parted good friends but made no further dates. I was leaving school and she hoped to join the sixth form if her O-level exams went well. We thanked one another for the pleasure we had shared, and for all we had learned. I respected Lorna for knowing what she wanted and getting it; for what she would want next I would not be available.

In those days there was no such thing as a school prom but the play's cast threw a party at the edge of the school field for the pupils who had come to applaud us. The girls managed some goodbye kisses and left early, and the boys drank themselves silly on beer, gin, and Australian port-type wine. I had borrowed a bicycle to get back home after the buses stopped, and in my inebriation I had one more thrill on Portsdown Hill: I free-wheeled down it without lights. Miraculously, I arrived home safe and sound enough to erect my collapsible bed. I felt that an era was over.

A week after leaving school I reached the age of eighteen, and I applied to the council for a job as a labourer on Southsea's seafront. The work was irregular, depending on the weather: on fine days we sold 12,000 deckchair tickets and spent four hours stacking the chairs up afterwards. The ticket salesmen were almost all students, but casual labourers from the dockyard joined us for stacking. Carrying a minimum of six chairs at a time fifty yards up the shingle soon hardened my muscles, and as my ticket sales increased, so I was given more hours' work. The pay was good because the TGWU allowed the council to employ non-members only on condition that union rates were paid. So, when the weather was reasonable, I could earn twelve pounds to the nine that Sarah received for her skilled work, and I gave her thee pounds each week for my bed and board. Thus it was that when I left the seafront that summer my post-office savings stood at over £100. I felt immensely rich as I kitted myself out for independent adult life.

My friend Tony got the same job with the council at the same time as I did, but when he found that we had to begin at the bottom and stack deckchairs in the evening before we were trusted to collect money, he had a row with the beach inspector and was fired. Tony had always demanded that he be at the top of any hierarchy he joined, which was why he had given up Latin and chess. I wondered how he would get on at Cambridge, where many students would be just as talented and even more spoilt.

I lost touch with Tony as my working hours increased, but I met Ant often, and we went to dances to meet (and hold) girls; unfortunately none of those we met that way lasted more than a couple of dates. We also met on my days off to play tennis before going dancing. In the years that followed, even though he was in London and I in Exeter, Ant and I kept in close touch – that was until he went off to the Middle East to work for an oil company. But that summer I made new friends of both sexes on the seafront and began an exciting new life.

When our A-level results came through, Ant had the three distinctions (marks over 75 per cent) that Imperial demanded, and Tony two, which would help his credibility with a Cambridge college. My teachers had also predicted that I would get three distinctions, but all my marks were between 70 and 75 per cent, and my scholarship papers were equally disappointing. But I had gained my county major scholarship, and Exeter and Greek awaited me. I resolved not to let chess interfere with my university exam results, but I felt that overall I had got my priorities right.

My last laughable love before college was a woman in her mid-twenties who worked in a shop near the seafront. Her real name was the same as Lorna's, so I shall call her Lena. She came to the beach to swim, eat a sandwich, and sunbathe in the lunch hour, when the beach inspector often left me, as one of his more experienced hands, in charge of the bathing compound. Lena was between boyfriends and I was soon chatting her up. She was a warm person, and talking about her many loves was good for her morale; I was an attentive audience. She let me rub her down and massage sun cream into her body when she came out of the water, and she said that I had very sensuous hands. Soon she allowed me liberties in my massaging that made us both laugh and she let me kiss her. I realised that Tina and Lorna had only had beginners' bodies, and I thrilled to the thought that more voluptuous flesh awaited me. Lena often said she thought I was very bright, and I constantly reassured her that she was beautiful. When she found a new boyfriend, however, she said that she would have to give up her lunchtime massage sessions, and I understood and agreed with her. We enjoyed one last affectionate session and a goodbye kiss; and, until I was settled in Exeter, Lena's wraith kept me warm at nights.

When Sarah saw me off to Exeter at Portsmouth Town station I remembered all that she had done for me over the previous eighteen years: her sacrifices and pain, her years of mindless toil, her worries and disappointments. And a sweet sadness was mixed with my excitement. Although she had never been clingy or sloppy about me, I knew that her love had been of the fiercest and purest. And I was determined to repay her by being some sort of success; but of what sort I did not know.

10

ARCADIA

Exeter is a sleepy old town on the lower slopes of the Exe valley, and is surrounded by rolling open countryside that stretches to the sea in one direction and the high Tors of Dartmoor in another. The Romans called it *Isca* of the *Dumnones*, the local tribe, and in 1955 the locals still saw themselves as almost a separate race. Exeter's centre contains a beautiful Cathedral in a picturesque close and the only decent shops for fifty miles in any direction. During my stay the centre also contained the cramped and ramshackle buildings in Gandy Street that housed the University College of the South West. The college's library, science labs, and some halls of residence were already sited on the Streatham Estate, where today's much larger University stands, on a high slope, among handsome trees and the greenest lawns in England. This unique greenness is a gift of the weather (Devon doesn't have a climate).

The *Dumnones* call someone who has lived in Devon for less than five years a *grockle* and, typically, grockles describe Devon's weather as 'mild', while the *Dumnones* call it 'wet'. Nevertheless, thousands of London sixth-formers streamed there in the 1950s because it offered the attractive combination of a London degree and an escape from the parental home (where their grants would be much smaller). It also attracted large numbers of students from Devon itself, who wanted to take their laundry home at weekends, and many home-counties students who thought that is was too grim Up North.

Just over half of the college's students had places in the four men's and five women's halls of residence and the remainder were scattered around the town in digs. I was given a place in a hall of residence called Mardon, which was high on the hill that houses today's university. The building was a mock-Georgian mansion, and I realised as soon as I arrived (in my first ever taxi) and entered its impressive swing doors that I was a bad fit for this place. Mardon was a posh hall: in those days its men wore ties and blazers with the hall crest upon them and carried umbrellas (the only alternative in Devon to a Sou'wester). Many Mardonians were from posh schools, and so they played rugger or rowed, sports I had never encountered. I had left school feeling adult, but their bulky figures, mature faces, and confident voices made me feel very young

The freshers' first contact with these formidable men was to undergo an initiation ceremony in which they were ridiculed and humiliated by the assembled Mardonians. I was one of several who showed too little respect in the interrogation and were given a cold bath in the middle of the night by four hulking figures in balaclava helmets. I remained limp and silent throughout, and this proved to be the final test. I passed it by proving that I could take it, and when I acted normally the next morning, as if the punishment for insolence had been deserved, I soon won acceptance. Within a week I was being taught how to play bridge by one of my assailants, an enormous man called Brian, who rowed as well as playing rugby. In the common room I made many friends and, now that I had been baptised, I became a born-again Mardonian.

In comparison with this initiation, the other events that opened term were pleasurable. I attended a freshers' fair on the Saturday, which was followed by a freshers' hop, where I danced the last waltz with a girl from London called Rhoda. Her hall was a long walk back to Mardon, but we must have gelled because for a whole term she became what Mardonians called my 'big steady'. The following Monday I met my course-mates and the staff of the Classics Department. In those days the staff-to-student ratio at red-brick universities was similar to that at the ancient ones, so there were five staff in this small department to just over twenty undergraduates, seven of whom were freshers.

At London colleges Classics departments offered two courses: one for combined honours in Latin and Greek, and one for Honours Latin and subsidiary Greek. The first course required the study of the vast bulk of surviving Ancient Greek literature (the gift of the Arabs). The second covered only the much more modest body of surviving Classical Latin texts (most having been destroyed by the Roman Church at the start of the Christian Era). The second course was for students without A-level Greek, and three of Exeter's seven freshers fell into that category. But, apart from Greek literature, where we three studied only a few chosen texts, all seven would sit the same exams. Both Latin and Greek literatures were covered by a series of lectures, on a three-year rolling basis, for all the department's students, but everything else was taught in small tutorial groups. The benefit of this was that we got to know our tutors at least as well as we knew one another.

My year-cohort consisted of four women and three men, and most were quiet, scholarly individuals whom I never got to know socially; I think they joined things like choirs and cycle clubs. But although they completed their work promptly, they were subdued in tutorials and rarely disagreed with their tutors. They all finished with undistinguished degrees and enrolled for teacher training, unaware that the classics industry was about to crash. When universities stopped demanding A-level Latin for entry in all arts subjects, most state schools abandoned the subject to private ones. This has ensured that the British public now marvels at the vocabulary and syntax of the ruling class, and cedes to posh boys and girls most jobs that require public speaking.

The final member of my class, however, was very different. Vic was extremely charismatic, and at first I was overawed by his good looks, his social confidence, and his academic and sporting achievements. Vic's father was a civil servant and his mother excelled at sports, and Vic had younger siblings, one of each sex. He had gone to a large and ambitious grammar school in North London where they taught subjects like Greek and Russian. Vic had a talent for languages: he knew five to O level and three to A level. He had gained higher marks in all three of his A-level subjects (Latin, Greek, and French) than I had in any of mine. He was clearly one of the people whom Kitty had warned me about, people with vastly more Latin and Greek than I. But, since he was following the first type of course, he bore, like Atlas, the whole world of Greek literature upon his back. This gave me some hope of overtaking him in Latin.

Vic had also just joined Mardon, where I discovered that he had played both hockey and tennis for his county, and that his intellectual ability and sporting prowess were matched by his social skills. Vic always charmed everyone he met. In today's terms, he had exceptional *emotional intelligence*: an insight into his own strengths and weaknesses and the ability to appreciate and learn from others. Moreover, his personality combined an unassuming modest confidence with natural warmth, and all these qualities made him very popular with both men and women. He had also been at the freshers' hop, where it was clear that he was one of the best ballroom dancers on the floor, and that women flocked to him

I soon learned, however, that Vic had problems of his own. The first was that he was at university without his father's blessing or financial help and that his grant was barely one-third of my own. The second was that he had left behind the love of his life, a girl named Adrienne; he had known her (and her family) from childhood and they were unofficially engaged to marry. Since Adrienne was at art school in London, however, there was no prospect of their being able to afford this step in the foreseeable future. Vic confided in me that he found no girl in Exeter a patch on his childhood sweetheart, but he knew that she was equally attractive to men, which caused him some qualms at their planned three-year separation. I was extremely impressed by the way he was able to discuss his emotional life so calmly and openly.

Vic and I faced the same journey from Mardon to Gandy Street and back again, sometimes twice a day since hall fees included a hot midday meal. The distance was roughly a mile and the first half of our route had a one-in-four gradient; at first Vic did the journey by bike while I walked, but he was surprised by how small the difference between our times was, especially for the return journey when I sometimes overtook cyclists as they lost their battle with the steep slope. We soon became firm friends, bridge partners, and allies against the world. In our second year we shared a room together: it had an equator down the middle, so that he could be untidy in his half and I could be meticulously tidy in the other. Vic used to joke that I folded my socks before I got into bed at night, and he would have found national service (which he missed on medical grounds) a great trial.

Vic and I were very different people, but he influenced me greatly in those Mardon years and helped me mature in many ways. We grew to share many interests and our friendship endured for nearly sixty years. Our wives also became close friends, and we went on hilarious holidays together. We have always followed the fortunes of one another's children and we have been delighted by one another's grandchildren. Vic and I have played every type of racquet game together and I have had to work hard to cope with his natural flair. One of my ambitions in college was to beat Vic at table tennis in the hall championships, something I managed in my final year. Another was to stretch him at tennis, which I achieved only forty years later, when we were both old men restricted to doubles. One of the things that Vic taught me was to revel in my competitiveness.

The ancient universities have an iron grip on Britain's classics industry, so that the best graduates from other universities have to move to Russian or Mandarin if they want an academic career. Thus all my tutors were from Oxbridge, though none was from an aristocratic family, so they were all much brighter than most of Purbrook's teachers. I responded very positively to this by thinking longer and deeper. And at college I adopted a new italic pen that made my handwriting much more legible. It also made it slower and that forced me to be more concise.

The youngest of these five men was John, an Oxonian from an academic family; he tutored us in Greek Art, one of the special subjects that London University offered as an alternative to the Oxford 'Greats' of history and philosophy. He rode a bicycle and he could not afford real leather elbow patches for his sports jackets, which warned me against the lower rungs of an academic career. He was married with two children and had a very attractive and intelligent wife. In his position I would have spent my money on her, too. She treated undergraduates as equals and was able to discuss subjects like birthing pains and contraception in a way that would have left Sarah speechless. John was an excellent teacher, but I never learned how his career progressed later.

Hugh was my ancient history tutor, and the most interesting thing about him was that he had a Yugoslavian wife whose picture stood on his desk. Rumour had it that Yugoslav girls demand to be taken by force on their wedding night, but I could never imagine bespectacled, stuttering Hugh managing this. Perhaps he had been a hero of the Balkan campaign and a redoubtable warrior, but I never became close enough to him to learn the truth. This was because in the second half of the first year I withdrew from his tutorials. Because my history A level was in modern history, I had to pass the equivalent exam in ancient history at the end of my first year. But I found Hugh's tutorials too slow and too detailed for a mere A level. I didn't need to write long essays on individual books of their work to recognize that Thucydides was the father of history and Herodotus the father only of literary gossip.

When Hugh complained of my defection Freddie, who chaired the department, ruled that if I failed this exam on private study my undergraduate career would be over. So my situation was as in O-level maths, and I wasn't deterred. When my distinction in the exam bettered the results of all Hugh's more docile students, Hugh ignored me; but Freddie became my most important supporter. I was sorry to lose Hugh's favour because I admired his incredible memory (inherited, he told us, from his grandfather, a famous bishop). Hugh himself became famous many years later, anonymously, when Britain's most successful author modelled the most eccentric character in her children's novels upon him.

Robin was my Greek tutor; he was a married with a family, and he was tall, broad, and good-looking. He was also very bright, and he might have achieved more, had he not been so relaxed about life and so demanding about Greek verb-forms. He said my self-taught Greek was as good as that of other students with O levels, and he gave me confidence that it would be at A-level standard before the end of the academic year. At the close of my first term Robin began to suspect that his final-year students had forgotten some of the basics, and he set a giant Greek grammar exam for the students of all three years. My 92 per cent topped the table and from then on my position in the department was secure; as I confirmed this result in every subsequent exam it became unassailable.

I met Robin socially over twenty years later and he invited me to his home; his children had all scattered and he had lost his much-loved wife. His house was an Aladdin's cave of books that deadened the ghostly footfall of his loved ones. Robin was still a good drinking companion, but he was broken man. He spent his time rereading his favourite Greek authors again and again; as the novelist Coetzee pointed out, having something to offer on every rereading is what defines a classic. Robin's use of the classics reminded me of one of his favourite passages from Cicero:

Haec studia adulescentiam agunt, senectutem oblectant,
secundas res ornant, adversis perfugium ac solatium praebent.

('These studies inspire the young and comfort the old; they are
an ornament in prosperity, and a refuge and solace in adversity.')

This magic link between minds across 2,000 years is one of the things
that make me grateful for my choice of first-degree subject.

JK was the most unusual of our tutors, for Exeter at least; at Oxford
he would have been among a majority of his sexual proclivity. In Exeter
he became a legend for his wisdom, his charm, and his love of people,
particularly young men. The only other name JK was known by was
when he was a despatch rider in World War I, and the other soldiers
called him 'Gladys', because of his high squeaky voice. JK was a world
authority on Virgil: if you quoted him a line from the *Aeneid* (which
he translated for Penguin Books), he would continue reciting from
memory to the end of the book. He was our Latin tutor and, when he
discovered my facility in that language, he challenged me to translate
the English passages that he set us into the styles of two different
ancient authors. My favourite pairing was Caesar and Tacitus, when
I balanced the clipped Latin of an embedded journalist's war report
against the subtle, insinuating Latin of political dissent.

JK was an ardent spiritualist: he believed he was in touch with the
spirits of both Virgil and the dead mother he adored (and after whom
he named his home 'Caroline House'). JK was attracted to my mind
and Vic's body: thus Vic had to fend JK off, while I could enjoy a true
friendship with him. By my final year we had discussed everything
from love to religion, and when JK accepted a commission to write
a long piece about Ovid for a prestigious international journal, he
asked me to be his sexual adviser for a percentage of his fee. He wanted

guidance on the mass of *double entendre* in Ovid's poems about the titillation of women; since he had never had a woman, JK lacked a grasp of detail. Fortunately, by then my reputation as a pussy-lover was secure, and I was able to spend time in JK's home without setting off rumours in Mardon.

The tutor to whom I grew closest, however, was the blatantly heterosexual Freddie, who held the departmental chair and coached me on a one-to-one basis in verse composition. I had this privilege because the other students thought this special subject too difficult, but I knew that generations of English poets had done it before writing in English. Over two years, therefore, I translated almost half of Palgrave's Treasury into Latin elegiacs for Freddie, and we discussed every word in every line I wrote. He sometimes showed me his own version of the poem, which was always much better than mine. But by the time I sat finals I was able to polish off the obscure piece of Byron I was set in twenty minutes. And, most importantly, while other students had to wade through piles of books on their special subject, all I had to do was exercise a skill that I loved. It was like dancing with golden words on my feet.

Freddie's life story was a fascinating one, as I discovered many years later when I met him socially. By then I was a respectable businessman and could dare to call him Freddie, and I discovered that he was not only a great mind but also exceptionally entertaining company. Freddie had been at Cambridge with that university's famous ring of homosexual spies, but he himself had been condemned to a miserable war because he had married a German girl shortly before it. For this reason, and because heterosexuals were unloved by MI5, he was posted to India, where he spent the war years decoding Japanese aircraft signals. On his return he took his wife back to see her native Dresden, but it was he who suffered a nervous breakdown.

After successful treatment, his knowledge and brilliance assured him of a chair at a provincial university, but he felt he had fallen irretrievably behind his brightest contemporaries, and he hesitated to publish his own research. The academic establishment's loss was Exeter's gain, and Freddie was a great teacher. He also had a wonderful sense of humour and he was exactly the right person to translate Terence's bawdy comedies (Freddie's most successful book, published posthumously).

In the late 1990s the UK Data Protection Act opened all my employer's files, and my then boss read me the academic reference that helped get me my first job. In it Freddie described me as the ablest student he had ever taught, the biggest compliment of my life. By my own estimate I knew about five per cent of Freddie's Latin and less than one per cent of his Greek. Freddie died at the age of eighty, leaving a large and loving family and a cupboard full of unpublished masterpieces. The Japanese airmen whom he spent the war monitoring didn't know what a formidable brain they were up against until they hit the water.

I tried many new things at university: I ran for Mardon in a cross-country race and in the four-forty, without coming close to a medal. I cycled to the sea at Dawlish Warren, but only swam out to the nearest sandbank. I took an enthusiastic part in rag week, when we terrorised the local shopkeepers and collected a tidy sum for charity. I attended ballroom dancing classes for a year, but then joined a jazz club for nearly three. I took part in debates: I seconded a motion, 'that this house regrets the discovery of America', which got me a date with an irate exchange student from New England, and I proposed the motion 'that this house deplores the unfair sex', after which I walked two lesbians back to their bed.

I played very little chess at university, although a lucky draw with the club's unbeaten champion, who was about to return to his native Germany, won me captaincy of the chess club for three years. I soon forgot all the theory I had learned, and my results got worse and worse. By my final year I could still win an even endgame against anybody, but I couldn't reach one any more. At least my captaincy gave me a pass to the freshers' fair and hop each year and looked good on my CV. My captaincy of the college table tennis team was equally flattering, but we always got knocked out in the first round of the UAU championship. Vic and I usually won at bridge; on wet Sundays we used to play for small stakes against Mardon's warden, and we relied on winning the price of our cinema tickets. In our final year we won the college bridge championship for Mardon against a women's hall.

This life was enough for me, but I noted sadly that it wasn't enough for Vic, for several reasons. First, he had a much smaller grant, and he had to work as a furniture remover throughout all three vacations; secondly he had all that mass of Greek literature to cover; thirdly he read more slowly than I; fourthly, he hadn't done A-level English and took longer to write a good essay. I tried to persuade him to change his course to mine, and so get rid of the Greek literature burden, but his competitive spirit would not let him: he had never given up on anything before; and so he paid dearly for his courage in finals.

One of the things for which I am grateful to Exeter is that it helped cure me of god-bothering. In my first year I shared a room with the son of a clergyman, named Louis, who was reading English, and we discussed literature and religion endlessly. We visited each of the protestant churches of the city in turn on a Sunday; they have beautiful names like St Mary Steps and St Mary Arches, and the West front of the cathedral is a religion in itself. Inside these ancient walls Louis found comfort in his old habit of praying, while I learned only that I was talking to myself. At the end of the year Louis left to study theology at another university, while I began a career in atheism. I have now spent much of my life studying ancient and medieval fiction, and it is among humankind's most amazing achievements; but as a result I recognise that all religions are human inventions. If there is such a thing as god's truth, it lies elsewhere.

Mine is not a shallow atheism like the trendy faith of Richard

Dawkins. Thus I recognise the vital importance of religion to human evolution: it is the fittest tribes, not the fittest individuals, that survive. And a tribe's survival has always depended on the readiness of its young men to kill, and to die, both of which require comforting lies. In the twenty-first century a faith as feeble, militarily, as Islam can challenge the armed might of the USA by the strength of its lies. I am also aware that humans cannot live without hope, and that billions of people have no rational reason to hope. This accounts for the triumphs of Mother Teresa on the streets of Calcutta. So I appreciate the appeal of religion, of all religions, but I am afraid they are not for me.

Fortunately I had come to Exeter not to find god, but to get a degree, and I relied not on long hours of work, but on my reading speed and good planning. I prepared for my finals over three years, much as I had planned for the Dupree chess tournament. My starting point was the papers set over the previous five years, which could be purchased cheaply and which I studied carefully. In my first vacation I set myself a schedule rather like Jay Gatsby's. I wrote it down and it read roughly as follows. By finals I wanted to be able to:

1) Turn any register of English into Latin and Greek efficiently, and vice versa.
2) Close my eyes and envisage the details of the 100 most famous Greek statues and vases.
3) Versify in Latin as easily as I could write prose.
4) Quote copiously from my favourite authors Virgil and Tacitus.
5) Write a better essay, made up of concise, balanced paragraphs, and carefully weighed words.
6) Cite and quote enough from another twenty authors to ensure that I would find three one-hour essays in any exam paper.
7) Perfect my italic handwriting so that no examiner would miss one word I wrote.

A schedule like this didn't help Gatsby gain Daisy, nor did it make me a great scholar, but it brought me the first in Latin and the distinction in Greek that I wanted.

The hours I put in to achieving this were actually fewer than many other undergraduates worked. In term-time I never worked after 6 p.m. lest it interfere with my sleep. I attended all my tutorials (except Hugh's) and all the literature lectures, and I completed all my essays and translations in the intervals between them. I read all day until six during the Easter vacation, when I found it impossible to get work, and in the Christmas vacation, once my post-office job had finished. My summer job was a fair-weather one, and when I was laid off for bad weather I also read solidly until six.

My love life in Exeter divides into two distinct periods: in my first year I was looking for someone to love, and in my second and third I had already found her. My romance with Rhoda lasted only one term; I soon knew it was doomed because kissing never produced an erection and her wraith never appeared in my bed. Although we kissed and hugged, and she allowed me a few other bodily familiarities, neither of our hearts was in it. Like good pathologists, we were just going through the motions. Our relationship provided us with congenial dancing partners and the status of having a big steady, but it didn't excite, and eventually we agreed to end it.

In my second term I took several girls home after the last waltz and met them again in the cinema, but none of these contacts went further. We couldn't say and mean the words that would have given them a chance of doing so. By now I wanted only wraiths in my bed who had made it clear that they wanted to be there. And I found one right at the start of the summer term. Her name was Sandra, she was reading French, and she came from Plymouth. I met her at a dance, jiving with someone else, and so I saw her thighs before her face; in motion they were magnificent, and when her petticoats subsided I saw that she had regular features, and that she was rather like Keats's *Belle Dame sans Merci*: her shapely feet were light, her brown hair was loose, and her blue eyes were wild. She had a slim athletic figure, ideal for dancing, and I asked her to join me on the floor for the next fast number.

By then I had honed my jiving at hops and jazz club, and I spun and caught her, and kicked and flicked well enough to impress her. We danced every dance together for the rest of the evening and in the last waltz I held close all that I had seen. I walked her home to her hall, which had one of my favourite shrubberies, and we kissed and hugged one another until the front door was half closed. By then we had agreed our next date and I walked on air back to Mardon. So Sandra became my second big steady and the first girl to swear, after a relatively short courtship, that she would love me forever. Sandra had a sweet and loving nature, but she loved too easily, and her upbringing had led her to feel apprehensive. One day she would be even more affectionate than I was, and the next she would be uneasy from guilt and fear, so that loving her was like taming a nervous animal.

All that term we spent four evenings a week in one another's arms, one of them uninhibited by other people. We went to the Saturday college hop together, never missed a Wednesday meeting of the jazz club, and on two other days we would go to the cinema and enjoy a session in one of Mardon's small common rooms. These were the rooms in which freshers were locked before interrogation, but they soon became my favourite places. One contained a piano and the other a radiogram, and hall members could book them for up to two hours at a time for musical purposes. Several Mardonians played the piano, but the rooms were mostly used for entertaining big steadies in total privacy. Besides the source of music, they had a settee with many cushions, thick carpets, and a chair to wedge under the door handle for security

The first time that Sandra agreed to be my guest we took in some jazz records and put them on the radiogram before we got into a clinch on the settee, but later we carried in some vinyl only for show. Putting the cushions on the floor was actually more comfortable than the settee, and the last part of our time together was spent putting Sandra back together again (which I quite enjoyed), and tidying her unruly hair so she didn't look too bedraggled, in case we met someone on the way out. I was keen to book the room more often but Sandra was too concerned about her year-end exams.

Sandra's wild look and charming giggle belied the fact that she was a worrier: she worried about pregnancy (the fate of her best friend back in Plymouth, whose boyfriend had promptly deserted), and she worried about her work. French literature is as voluminous as that of Ancient Greece and Sandra was a slow reader for a languages student. As well as more sessions in the small common room I wanted to take her to Dawlish Warren at weekends, where students enjoyed love in the fresh air. By the evening of a fine Sunday there was a couple behind every sand dune. But Sandra needed to work, so I never saw her bikini; to judge by her day-wear it would have been minimal and functional, and have shown her slim body to great advantage. When in July Sandra scraped through her exams, her relief showed, but it was not in time for a beach outing.

On our last cinema date we went to see the sad film *Carousel,* and I held her so close that Sandra's tears wetted my cheeks, and I didn't know whether the tears were mine. At our last hop we clung so close in the last waltz that we didn't notice when the band went home. Our last embrace was our warmest and when I saw Sandra back to her hall that night I thought that no couple could be closer than we were. But I was wrong.

I returned to Southsea, to Sarah, and to my summer job, while Sandra went to Provence for the summer to act as an au pair for a rich family. She said she would spend her free time reading French literature, but she had no free time. She met a young Frenchman who took her everywhere on his motor-scooter and she had a very lively, busy time. By contrast the weather in Southsea was awful and I was often laid off, so my three pounds a week for Sarah were in serious danger. I made my situation worse by choosing those weeks to read Ovid's works of exile, *Tristia* and *Ex Ponto*, and I clutched at all the Latin words for misery as straws to save me from drowning in my own.

We had agreed to write often, but very soon our love letters turned to recrimination and mutual accusations of selfishness. I felt she was betraying me and she thought I was begrudging her a good time. Our disagreement was aggravated by Sandra's not being a good correspondent: she sometimes said unwise things and expressed them clumsily enough to hurt me. There were hints that she had become the Frenchman's mistress, and I took a stray comment of hers to refer to his sexual prowess. In the end our letters saying it was all over crossed. And it *was* all over. After Sandra I abandoned wraiths, because I wanted a real woman whose desire and pleasure would match my own; for that I needed a real person, with a real name. Sandra was much more than a laughable love, but she had a lovable laugh, and much else besides, and for a very short time I loved her.

I spoke with Sandra for the last time at the end of the second hop of term that autumn. We were both waiting in the foyer between the dance floor and the cloakrooms, Sandra for a group of friends, and I for the fresh-faced fresher with whom I had danced the last waltz. Sandra admired my neat new front teeth, and I complimented her on her new hairstyle, which was shorter and less unruly. She said she had enjoyed her summer with the French boyfriend, but that they had agreed they had no future together. I told her that I had a new love, who wasn't the girl for whom I stood waiting. We wished each other well, and we spoke softly and calmly, but I sensed Sandra was near to tears. And then her friends appeared and we went our separate ways.

That term I saw Sandra less and less often at the hops, and she gave up jazz club altogether. There were as many thighs and petticoats as ever at both, but soon none of them were hers. Next year one of her hall mates told me (on the beach at Dawlish Warren) that Sandra had failed her year-end exams and was now at a distant teachers' training college. And so Sandra melted from my memory, like the mistress in Salinas's *Muertes*, who faded from his memory by stages until even the letters of her name were assumed into an alphabet heaven.

11

ICE CREAM

Within a week of my breaking up with Sandra the sun came out in Southsea and I was busy on the seafront again. But during my exile with Ovid I had thought long and hard about my paid work, and I had made a plan to improve my earnings. At that stage I had never encountered the work of the German sociologist Robert Michels, but I had worked out from my own experience the essence of his Iron Law of Oligarchy.

I saw that all human groups inevitably form a hierarchy, a pyramid in which an elite at the top gains control of the group's assets. That elite usually represents fewer than 10 per cent of the total group, because that sort of proportion is necessary to control the assets efficiently, and the elite's members demand average incomes that are around ten times those of the remainder of the group. The elite then extracts wealth from the remainder via rents, taxes, profits, interest, and fees, and it ensures that its members' children get the best jobs in the next generation, either by reserving occupations or by educational advantage.

In 1956 this type of oligarchy operated in every country I knew of. Thus in the USSR, for example, the Communist Party occupied exactly the same position as the boyars it had destroyed, or as the British aristocracy of birth, or the American of wealth. The two last-named countries were better places to live for most people because they were *electoral oligarchies*. The elite split into two or three rival gangs who took turns in running the country, and once every four or five years the ruling gang had to risk being changed at the polls, which made it treat its social inferiors a little better. But I lost faith in democracy at an early age, when I saw that it didn't work: it always gives way rapidly to an oligarchy, because humans are hard-wired for hierarchy.

Britain's democratic deficit increased in the twenty-first century: in three general elections the winning political party has gained the support of just over 20 per cent of the electorate, while almost 40 per cent have refused to vote for any of the parties on offer. None of the rival gangs now feels a need to consider the interests of those at the bottom of the hierarchy, so the poor have no party for which to vote. The rich can also use their control of the media to mislead the middle classes as to their best interests.

So I am neither a socialist nor a democrat: I vote on principle for an opposition party, because it is vital that no one individual becomes a monarch like Hitler, Stalin, or Mao. I am a social moralist, however: I believe that the rich can sleep easy in their beds only if the poor have a decent standard of living, and don't suffer the humiliation of being regarded as 'trash'. But the only thing that has ever moderated the greed of the rich is fear, either of hell fire or revolution. Yet it is not revolution, which creates a new elite, that is beneficent; it is the fear of it. Thus communism may have been awful for many people in Eastern Europe and China, but it was a very good thing for the poor of Western Europe (as French intellectuals pointed out at the time).

In 1956 my meditation on oligarchy led me to see that my own route to a better income involved two distinct hierarchies, one among groups of holidaymakers, and the other among the seafront workers. The locale where the two groups came into contact was a stretch of beach running for half a mile each side of South Parade Pier, with its shops, amusement arcade, theatre, and dance hall. Over this golden mile were stacked thousands of deckchairs, and holidaymakers were free to take chairs and move them wherever they wished; once they were seated, ticket salesmen pounced on them for payment. Southsea beach was backed by a broad promenade, or prom, lined with upright canvas chairs for which the same tickets were valid. The tickets cost sixpence for four hours' use of any chair, which the holidaymaker could simply leave on the beach for the evening gang to re-stack and cover with tarpaulins. The other responsibilities of the beach inspector and his team of labourers were a long series of glass shelters along the prom and a bathing compound with about twenty huts and three freshwater showers.

The beach was divided into sales pitches, from five each side of the pier when the weather was fine, to one each side when it was less pleasant; when it was raining there were no ticket sales. The beach inspector's duties consisted of hiring ticket salesmen and allocating pitches, and deciding how many men were needed at six to stack the chairs. At that time he also checked all the salesmen's takings against ticket numbers and deposited the total in a bank's night safe. At the maximum, Tommo, the beach inspector, needed ten salesmen on the beach, one on the prom, one in charge of the bathing compound, and about eight dockers willing to join the salesmen stacking chairs in the evening.

At the minimum, Tommo needed one salesman to man the bathing compound (because the hardiest swimmers in Southsea, some of them in their seventies, ignored the weather) and a small team of salesmen to clean the many windows in the shelters (a task left for bad-weather days). When the weather forced him to lay off men, he always started with those whose pitches were furthest from the pier, and the last salesmen working were always the man in charge of the compound and the one on the prom, where business revived almost as soon as it stopped raining. The pitches thus formed a hierarchy, with the best being the bathing compound and the prom, followed by the two nearest the pier, and the worst were obviously the two furthest from the pier.

Tommo, who was expected to maximise turnover and minimise costs, therefore believed he operated a meritocracy, giving the best pitches to the most successful salesmen. But like most meritocracies this was a fallacy. A vicious circle existed, in that the pitches nearest the pier got most crowded and offered the highest sales, and the men who sold most tickets held those pitches. It was a vicious circle that was hard to break, but as a relative newcomer with a pitch on the beach far from the pier, I needed to break it. All but one of the salesmen were students on vacation, but some from richer homes worked only for a month or so before motoring to Athens with their chums or similar expensive things. Our other, occasional tasks, ranged from digging out water pipes under the shingle to patrolling the water's edge when there was a plague of poisonous jellyfish.

The exception to the rule that all the ticket salesmen were students was a man in his seventies named Ernie; he had worked all his life for the council and refused to retire. He was very short, with a mop of white hair under a white cap, and he held a pipe in his mouth as he worked. Ernie was the resort's talisman and the local paper carried an article on him every few years. His takings were good because, although he spent too much time chatting to his customers, they waited for him to appear, and some old ladies gave him presents at the end of their holidays. Ernie had a year-round job; he did not stack in the evenings, giving him forty-two hours and just over ten pounds in wages each week. He worked six days a week in the summer, and five in the winter guarding the chairs in their winter storage, and supervising the carpenters who repaired the broken ones. Ernie's short legs were too slow for the prom, so he worked the pitches immediately next to the pier, alternating each day so he could have a wider circle of holidaymaker friends. On wet days he manned the bathing compound and beach office, and when he wanted to get out and about he changed places with one of the window cleaners.

Ernie and I became fast friends over four summers: I worked on the seafront for ten weeks in 1955, for fourteen each in 1956 and 1957, and for a month before I was called up for national service in 1958. I knew by the beginning of the 1956 long vacation that if I wanted promotion in the salesmen's hierarchy, I needed to improve my sales skills first. Skill was required because of the salesmen's worst problem: when some holidaymakers saw a salesman approaching, they vacated their chairs so as to avoid payment, especially on days of mixed weather. I had noted the previous year that different-sized groups of holidaymakers behaved differently in this respect.

Groups of men and single men did not sit in deckchairs, but sat or sprawled on the beach, thus gaining a 360-degree view of all the sunbathing women. Single women did take chairs, but rarely melted away on a ticket salesman's approach: their towels were usually spread beside the chair for suntanning their backs, and their bags and clothes were usually attached to the chair. They also liked being chatted up, and the young ones enjoyed the caresses of a man's eyes on their bare limbs. Couples would only melt away if they thought the salesman hadn't noticed them. Usually, if they were not married the man would pay graciously, and if they were the wife would tell her husband to pay up, and then tease the salesman for being a nuisance.

The melting-away problem was mainly with groups, either of women or of mixed sex. In those days Southsea attracted lots of holidaymakers from South Wales, and these particularly liked to sit on the beach in groups. They were also particularly likely to melt away, saying 'Now we came,' and 'We're not staying,' in lovely musical voices that reminded me of Kitty's. Obviously, a ticket salesman could lose large slabs of business in this way, and I gradually developed a five-part strategy for solving the problem. The five parts were: speed, memory, rank, persistence, and shame.

Speed was important so that groups, sitting and talking, would not see me coming until too late. This involved several things: the first was being inconspicuous, so I made sure that I looked more like a tramp than a council official: I went hatless and wore only my oldest trousers, heaviest shoes, and a brown overall open to the waist. I also wore my money bag beneath my overall and produced my ticket roll from my pocket only at the last moment. My chest went deep brown and my hair went yellow at the front, so I looked a bit like a honey badger: this offered me camouflage against the pebbles and helped me gain the group's attention when I arrived. The second aid to speedy working was my long legs, and the third was my memory.

The easiest way to lose a group was to waste time asking to see the tickets of people who had already paid. This I avoided by scanning all the faces on the beach and remembering at least one of those in each group. So I moved from one group of newcomers to another with unexpected speed and used all the customers between them as cover. I trained my short-term memory to remember faces as I remembered cards at bridge. There were many more than fifty-two faces each day, but the human brain is hard-wired to remember faces. Since all groups are hierarchical, I usually remembered the alpha individual in each group. The alphas were easy to pick out: if female they sat centrally, talked most, and had the largest handbags; and if they were male the eyes of the women in the group lingered on their faces.

On arrival I would immediately confront the alpha: if a man I would stand too close to his chair for him to rise and lead an exodus; if a woman I would kneel before her. I would then speak politely but firmly, telling the alpha that the council charged for sitting in the chair, not staying in it, but that the tickets were valid for four hours wherever they moved: that was a penny-halfpenny (just over one half a modern decimalised penny) an hour. If this didn't do the trick, then I pointed out that this was a trivial sum to such prosperous folk, but it was the unfortunate duty of tramps like me to collect it. I wouldn't budge until one of the other members of the group said, 'I'll pay, just to get rid of him.' And, of course, the alpha couldn't possibly allow that, and paid up, usually flourishing a note, which I was grateful to change because it weighed so much less than coins.

The Welsh groups then used to tell me that the deckchairs on Barry Island were free, and other groups found other ways of teasing me. It was usually all smiles by the time I left, and my memory ensured that the group wasn't bothered again. But the women laughed at me as I passed by, and I winked and grinned broadly back. In all my four seasons my confrontations with alpha males never led to a fight, first because the British were not very violent until they became Americanised, and secondly because no man in his smart holiday-wear wanted his womenfolk to see him rumble with a tramp.

Once I was confident that I could extract more money from any pitch than my colleagues, I persuaded Tommo to give my far-from-the-pier pitch to someone else, and to let me work other men's pitches on their days off. I always collected significantly more cash (and most in notes, which Tommo liked) than the regular holder of the pitch. And when Tommo found that this was no flash in the pan, he promoted me, first to the plum pitch the other side of the pier from Ernie and then to the prom. After walking on pebbles, striding the prom was like champagne, and my memory allowed me to make more sweeps of the mile and take more tea breaks, and get to know more of the workers on the seafront. Most importantly it gave me work on bad-weather days and the twelve pounds a week that I wanted. Of course, I didn't become a celebrity like Ernie, but my regular customers and seafront friends (not to mention Tommo) used to notice when it was my day off. And each summer Tommo used to try out different men on the prom until I arrived, measuring their sales against mine.

I made many friends on the seafront, from the coach drivers who touted for business from kiosks near the pier, and the policemen who patrolled the seafront, to Pete the photographer and his beautiful wife, who charmed holidaymakers into posing for them. The beach labourers were also a friendly bunch, most of the students and dockers getting along remarkably well. My closest friend was named Clive; he was a fine athlete, who studied at a sports-teachers' training college and ran the mile for Great Britain's junior team. When we all went swimming after work Clive swam rings around us. My best buddies among the dockers were Taffy, a short man who smoked as he stacked, moving the cigarette from side to side of his mouth with both arms full of chairs, and Bill, an ex-marine who claimed to have ruptured a sampan girl in Singapore. When Taffy and Bill were stacking they tried to find a lone girl changing at the end of the day. When they found one half in and half out of her knickers, they would stop to chat her up, Taffy teasing and telling dirty jokes, and Bill asking for a date. Occasionally he got one.

But best of all were the army of girl students who worked in the cafeterias and ice-cream kiosks along the prom. I dated several in the weeks immediately after my break-up with Sandra and flirted constantly with them all. I found I was welcome at the cafés providing I flirted as much with the manageress as with her prettiest employee. Ernie taught me this tactic, and I still have a photo of Southsea café society, taken by Pete outside one of the largest establishments. Ernie and I are toasting Pete with cups of tea, and I have my other arm around Pete's wife, while Ernie has his around the manageress; and beside us are a group of smiling girls in white overalls. Before the season was very old I could get a free ice cream at most of the kiosks.

The exception was the sweetshop at the head of the pier, which was staffed by two students, a bespectacled blonde named Daphne, who had a nice smile and a lively line in conversation, and a beautiful brunette named Dawn, who talked less, but asked intelligent questions and made cute comments. (From now on I give my heroines their real names.) Dawn's smile lit up the whole seafront, brighter than the weekly firework display, and I knew that my friend Clive was equally dazzled by her, as was at least one policeman and two other ticket salesmen: a tall, ginger man named John and a smooth Cambridge undergraduate named Graham. And the number of admirers I didn't know about was doubtless legion, so I knew that I needed to move fast if I wanted to woo her.

I was aided by the fact that John was slow in everything, Clive was less confident with women than I was, and Graham, having attended boarding school and a men's college, was a sexual ditherer. We were all surprised that Dawn was still in the sixth form at Portsmouth's poshest girls' school, because she had a perfect figure and a quiet composure that her friend Daphne lacked; she also had a lovely voice and a dazzling smile. On principle, and because their boss counted the number of thin slices in every block of ice cream, neither girl was generous with free samples. But I could slurp elsewhere and was intent on higher things.

Both girls earned a mere three pounds a week and Dawn did masses of overtime to make up her wages. One day when it was wet and there was no stacking, I asked Dawn if I could see her home after work, and she said yes and told me the time she would finish. (Later I learned that both girls were expecting me to date Daphne.) I went home and changed into a suit and a shirt with a collar and tie, and I called at the shop for Dawn at the agreed time. She was clearly amazed at my appearance, because not only had she never seen me in a suit, she had never seen me in a shirt before. I took her hand firmly in mine and we walked first to her bus and then from its stop in Fratton to her front door. There we stayed talking for some time before I got my first kiss and another date. The cliché 'over the moon' felt like an understatement.

I felt deeply at ease in Dawn's company from the first; she was kind and took a charitable view of everybody, and she seemed interested in everything. She was beautiful inside as well as out. We found that we liked the same things: books, and films, and tennis, and dancing, and we began going out together several times a week. We visited each other's homes and met each other's families, and found that we liked staying in together as much as going out. We grew more and more familiar with one another's bodies, and I found that hers was even more gorgeous than it looked in an overall. Dawn found that I could be gentle as well as aggressive, and that I put pleasing her before everything. She even liked my neat new teeth because they gave me an extra centimetre of tongue.

On our days off, we either paid romantic visits to beauty spots like Petersfield Lake or Seaview on the Isle of Wight, or we spent energetic days in Southsea. There we could play tennis in the morning, roller-skate in the afternoon, and dance in the evening. We might even find time in our schedule to swim, so that I could feast my eyes on all her assets, and she could float weightlessly in my arms. I was soon desperately in love with Dawn, and when she had come to trust in my devotion she became mine. Our evenings then ended with two cushions on the carpet of her home's darkened front room. And, because we both liked to take our time, I often missed my last bus and had to walk joyfully home.

Thereafter we spent all our spare time together in every vacation, and during our long separations we wrote to one another several times a week. Dawn proved as good a correspondent as Sandra had been a bad one. She knew that I thought of her, and her only, in my bed at night, and she said that she did likewise. At Christmas she presented me with a pair of flimsy briefs embroidered with the words *I love you* to keep under my pillow. And I used the differences in our incomes to buy her presents, including her first evening dress, a low-cut blue creation in which she looked more ravishing than ever.

Dawn visited me in Exeter for a long weekend at each half term. The first time she stayed at a discreet hotel, where I could exit from her room early in the morning, but when I got my own room in Mardon she always stayed with me. I had to escort her to the bathroom and smuggle her out through the table-tennis room window first thing in the morning, but at that age we were always looking for adventure. I think we must have had rubber bones then, because we could change positions in a narrow single bed, and we could move into and out of hold as slickly as if we were on a spacious dance floor.

One of those visits was to a Mardon formal ball, where Dawn met Adrienne and they became lifelong friends. Their dresses looked wonderful and Vic and I were as smart as emperor penguins. We danced with one another's partners and Dawn and I envied their foxtrot, while they envied our jive. But some of our best times cost nothing. When I first arrived home on vacation, Dawn would still be at school, and because it was so close she could visit me at lunchtimes. After a ten-minute sandwich and fifty minutes of love, she would hurry back to school, and her friends would tease her that she looked as if she had been running; she told them, saucily, that she felt as if she had been caught. And this continued until Dawn left school and gained a place in a teaching college in London.

We agreed that our separation should not interfere with our love of dancing or Dawn's enjoyment of college life. This meant that we would both be dating other people and dancing in other partners' arms. We thought of this as a test: I would compare every girl I dated with Dawn, and she every man with me. We thought that we would find no other partner that we could love as much, and that lots of congenial company and even a little foreplay would confirm this. But I wanted Dawn to wear my ring to remind her who loved her best. I knew it would not fend off other men, because it often does the opposite: engaged girls know their way around a man, and miss an absent one. Nevertheless, I asked Dawn to marry me.

I bought the best diamond I could afford (it was closer in size to a B&B than to the Ritz) and I proposed to her in a beach hut after a lunchtime swim. We hammed it up a little: I dropped to one knee and begged her to make me an even happier man, and she enquired about my prospects. I told her that the main one would be a lifelong orgy, and that won her. When she said yes I was overcome with joy, because earth hath not any thing to show more fair than Dawn wearing only an engagement ring.

I have long been filled with wonder that Dawn should have chosen to share her life with me. I haven't deserved the love of a woman beautiful inside and out. I was never a handsome hunk; I have never been strong, or brave, or good. Her choice may be rationalised at a shallow, psychobabble level: she had recently lost her father in a tragic home accident, and she wanted another man who would love her forever. Her widowed mother had been distraught with grief and, robbed of her husband's income, she and her four children were slowly sliding into bankruptcy; so Dawn needed someone who would bring her financial security. Dawn loved children and she wanted a father for hers who would join her in spoiling them. Finally, Dawn had a lively mind and so she wanted a life partner who would challenge it.

But none of these rationalisations answer the key question, 'Why me?' It is the question every ant can ask that swarms from the cracks in the pavement to be crushed by my foot. The answer is luck, pure luck. As I became more affluent I met many men and women who were convinced that their prosperity was the result of personal merit. But I could see that they were deluding themselves: social (and other) luck is the biggest factor in human success and failure. And so the only answer to my question is that of the great preacher: 'The race is not to the swift, nor the battle to the strong ... but time and chance happeneth to them all.' The ancient Hebrews believed that they had been chosen, but they knew they had done nothing to deserve it; and one of them, at least, sensed that their good fortune stemmed from the randomness of the universe

In the two years of our engagement I longed always for the next time we would be one flesh as well as one in spirit. And that prospect, along with Dawn's delicious letters, made life worth living even in my dullest hours. Of course we both chatted, flirted, and danced with other partners, and we kissed other lips, if only to taste the difference.

But we passed the test: our favourite song was always 'Save the Last Dance for Me!'

In Exeter I met many other girls: I danced and jived with them, went to films with them, and took them to Dawlish Warren in the summer. If we liked one another enough we might go out together for a few weeks, but my big steady was elsewhere. I never hid this fact, and some of the girls I dated admitted to having steady boyfriends at home. But none of these girls ever proved a rival to my love for Dawn. I loved to look at pretty faces, I really liked women, and I enjoyed their company, but Dawn was the one with whom I wanted to share my life.

Modern science has shown that humans can gorge themselves on ice cream because the receptors in their brains fail to tell them that they have had enough. And Dawn is my ice-cream girl, my land flowing with milk and honey. And so I have tried to live the advice of Ecclesiastes 9:9:

Live joyfully with the wife whom thou lovest
all the days of thy vanity;
for that is thy portion in this life,
and in thy labour which thou takest under the sun.

12

ORDERS

Once my final exams had started I did no further revision; the weather was fine, so I spent as much time as possible in the open air, which is the best way to ensure a good night's sleep (far more important to exam success than the last-minute skimming of data). All my exam papers went as planned, and Freddie told me that he had never doubted my eventual degree class in either Latin or Greek. He urged me to study for a PhD, but admitted that, as the rules stood, I would still have to do national service. Neither of us guessed that the rules would mean nothing when conscription was abolished, without warning, the following year. So I resolved to get national service over as soon as possible, marry Dawn, and get a job that paid better than that of an assistant lecturer.

Dawn's term finished a week later than mine and I spent that week in a B&B in Streatham. The landlady's rules allowed a member of the opposite sex to visit my room until 10 p.m., and so Dawn and I made up for weeks of separation. I met her college friends, who were friendly and charming, and made them jealous by plucking roses from other people's front gardens and presenting them to Dawn as a love gift.

She was as successful in her exams as I had been, and we returned to Southsea in triumph, and in sadness. When I was declared medically A1, the War Office ordered me to report to the training depot of the Suffolk Regiment (later the 1st Anglians) on 8 August.

I became an infantryman because there is little use on the battlefield for a Classicist except to advance and retreat, and so my legs, and not my mind, would have to see me through. Fortunately, I was used to tramping twenty miles a day and dealing with hostilities. Dawn and I were both stoical about our separation because we were used to separations punctuated by honeymoons, and I left for Bury St Edmunds where I would be imprisoned for twelve weeks of basic training. This consisted of rising early for a fifteen-hour day of drill on the parade ground, PT in the gym, and weapon-firing on the shooting ranges. There were other distractions, such as cleaning and polishing kit and barrack rooms, standing guard, doing fatigues, and learning to crawl both physically and mentally. For their labours national-servicemen were paid three shillings and sixpence a day, just under the price of a packet of cigarettes, which is why I gave up smoking in favour of buying an extra meal each day in the NAAFI.

The aim of boot camp (as it is known in the USA) is first to exhaust and humiliate the recruits, and then to instil in them absolute obedience. The exhaustion never happens because the more the body is hammered the fitter it gets; the humiliation lasts only for as long as it takes the NCOs to turn their attention to someone else; but the obedience is vital. And after twelve weeks I was capable of killing a stranger on my platoon sergeant's word of command. And I could do it with rifle, Sterling automatic, light machine gun, or bayonet. We weren't taught to kill in unarmed combat because British troops at that time were killing mainly civilians. But we were taught how to dislocate the thumbs of 'terrorists' when we arrested them: this was our battalion's trademark in dealing with freedom-fighters in Cyprus.

All but three of my platoon passed successfully from basic training: the first was an overweight man who impaled himself on a high spiked railing when a corporal forgot a key, the second a sixteen-year-old volunteer who admitted lying about his age and was released, and the thrid was a Suffolk ploughboy who was transferred to the Pioneer Corps because he had two left feet. But I never reached Nicosia: along with several other 'educated cunts' (as the NCOs called the graduates among us), I passed a War Office selection board (WOSB) and, after hanging around the camp delivering coal and peeling potatoes for a month, I was posted to an Officer Cadets' Training Unit at a place called Mons Barracks in Aldershot. The camp dwarfed that at Bury St Edmunds and was to prove a very different sort of test over the next four months.

As officer cadets, we were distinguished from privates only by our white belts and cap flashes, but if we passed that test we would return to our units as *subalterns*. In US English this word means inferiors; in UK English it means people who deputise for captains (that is, lieutenants). Our commissioning would promote us by six ranks, but on the day we assembled that prospect seemed an immeasurable distance away. The duties of training the officer cadets at Mons were divided between four groups: the overall command and tuition of military knowledge was in the hands of ambitious infantry captains; weapons training was the preserve of experts from the Small Arms School Corps; fitness was ensured by a team of PT instructors; and parades, smartness, and general bullying were the responsibility of NCOs from the Brigade of Foot Guards.

'Shiny A Company', of which I was a member, consisted of thirty men from these Guards regiments and ninety ordinary infantrymen. The Guards cadets had attended the nation's most exclusive public schools, but lacked the talents for university or the world of finance, so they had signed on as regular soldiers. If they failed to gain a commission, their parents would buy them out and send them abroad to avoid national service, which clearly affected their attitude to military life and to their fellow cadets.

Throughout the sixteen weeks these thirty-odd Guardsmen considered themselves a different species from the infantrymen, whom they called *trogs* or *plebs*; we called them many things, the most polite of which was *toffs*. Most toffs were three years younger than the trogs, who were almost all graduates, and the younger men appeared very childish to us. Many liked to boast about the *tarts* (attractive younger boys) they had enjoyed at school, and the *fillies* they hoped to enjoy during the *season*. (Fillies was their name for the *debutantes* they were now chasing in search of a *meilleur trou*.)[1] This pursuit involved the toffs in jumping into their cars most evenings and driving to London, and therein lay the first cause of friction between the two groups of cadets.

To make these expeditions possible toffs offered trogs about three days' pay to clean their kit and two weeks' pay to do their guard duty. At first there were eager takers, but many of these barrack-room debts remain unpaid today. (It is an old English tradition that squires never pay their grocery bills.) The toffs at Mons soon found no takers for their promised money, and they were left to bull their own kit with bad grace, cursing what they called 'the servant problem'. It also became impossible to bribe a trog to do a guard duty: on the night of one important social event this led a toff to burst into tears and tear a five-pound note into small pieces before our astonished eyes.

I suffered from a toff's laziness only once, when we were on a week's digging-in exercise: I was assigned to share my firing and sleeping

[1] I have forgotten the source of the French saying, *Si vous connaissez un meilleur trou allez-vous y* ('If you know a better hole go to it'),'but it describes precisely the motivation of some of the young toffs.

trenches with a toff I hardly knew, but while I went to collect pick and shovel he volunteered to lay phone lines. By the time he returned I had dug both trenches and they were a foot deep in flood-water. He smelt of brandy and squatted in the firing trench like a toad that night, but I waited until the lights in the officers' tents went out and crawled under the nearest bush to sleep.

The temperature was close to zero on that exercise and I had flu at the time (an epidemic that had put half the toffs in the infirmary so that they missed the exercise). I was practically dead on my feet when I arrived back at the camp and had to spend a forty-eight-hour leave in bed recovering. My exhaustion showed on the nine-mile march back, and my platoon commander assumed I was unfit and gave me a disciplinary warning. He already disliked me because I used to read through the précis of his military knowledge lectures and then doze off (the classroom was forty degrees warmer than the parade ground). Sometimes I opened my eyes to look into his.

I tried to redeem myself by demonstrating my fast finish in the inter-platoon cross-country race, and by the speed at which I could carry a man of my own weight on a lap of the running track. But the warning was only finally rescinded at battle camp in the Brecon Beacons, where in our attacks and fighting withdrawals I volunteered to be No. 1 on the Bren gun. It was twice a rifle's weight, but when I started firing, its rat-tat-tat showed the invigilating officers which cadet had arrived first. I must admit that I was inspired in these live-firing exercises by imagining that all the plywood targets were my platoon commander. Even then he was incapable of saying, 'I was wrong about your fitness.' He just congratulated me on my improvement, and himself for producing it.

The final *coup de disgrâce* of the toffs was related in the autobiography of one who became a film star. Our toffs were the intellectual also-rans of the public-school system, and their busy social lives ensured that they would all fail the final military knowledge exam. So they bribed and cajoled a Guards sergeant-major to open the company safe the night before the exam and let them copy down the correct answers. The following day they all gained about 90 per cent in the exam, in some cases out of craftiness and in others because they mixed up the answers. No officer queried the results, perhaps from stupidity, perhaps because it could have cost him his career.

I did no revision for that exam, but relied on my memory and passed with ease (but with less than 90 per cent, which gave my platoon commander one last chance to sneer). Apart from spending a couple of hours in the guard-room cells for smiling on parade (at a hungover toff who couldn't tell his left from his right), my time in Mons passed without other incident, and I emerged, like a butterfly from a chrysalis, as a second lieutenant in the spring. But just as I was commissioned national service was abolished, and so my trip to Cyprus was cancelled again.

The War Office realised that it would no longer be able to conscript newly trained teachers as sergeants for its military education programme, and it decided to make its teachers officers, like its doctors and dentists. The army educates its troops in map-reading (to help them find the enemy), English (so that they can communicate the fact), and maths (so that they can find the right elevation with mortars and artillery). In 1959 the War Office decided to make good the loss of sergeants conscripted from teacher training colleges by recruiting graduates as education officers. And to get the scheme kick-started they redirected new subalterns from the infantry and artillery to the Royal Army Education Corps for teacher training.

As so often, the army went over the top on this conversion and tried to recruit what they thought were the best graduates. They realised that those from the ancient universities had better options, so they offered red-brick graduates who took short-service commissions years of seniority on the basis of their degree class. My first would thus bring me five years' seniority, and so for the rest of my national service I knew that I could sign on for three years and become a captain almost overnight. The biggest drawback would be that the British army has always preferred its younger officers to get horses before wives, and officers under twenty-five needed their CO's permission to get married.

The cancellation of my posting to Cyprus delighted me: while I wanted to see the Greek islands, I had no desire to shoot Greeks or to spend more than a year without seeing Dawn. I welcomed the RAEC transfer because it made it just possible that I would spend the rest of my service in the UK. I knew nothing of the RAEC, but I had its flashes sewn on my uniforms, and I spent my officer's kitting-out alliance on the navy-blue No.1 uniform of that corps. I was posted for ten weeks' training to the Army School of Education in Beaconsfield, where I would be no further from Dawn than at Mons.

The only thing I remember of my commissioning parade was that it went well until the major-general taking the salute came to mount the platform. He suddenly caught sight of the father of one of the toffs in the audience. At the sight of a famous soldier who was both an earl and a field-marshal, the poor general slid down three steps, as he tried to climb them and salute at the same time. The British love to grovel (which is why they have kept a monarchy past its sell-by date), but they pay a price for it, not least in the way that Hollywood presents them to the world as hopeless wimps.

The Army School of Education was built around a fine old mansion, which housed the officers' mess, and its classrooms were in charmless huts behind it. I was one of a class of about twenty new subalterns, and a captain, who was a better soldier than a teacher, instructed us. The lessons centred on the army's own education certificates, which NCOs seeking substantive-rank promotion had to gain, and the basic literacy and numeracy texts for new regular army recruits. All these exams were of a very low standard: even warrant officers needed only to pass the sergeant's exam and then pass O levels in maths and English. Volunteers to the regular army were tested on whether they could read, write, and count, and if they failed these tests the War Office ruled that they must pass them within twelve months or be released. The RAEC saved about 1,000 men a year for the army by teaching them what they had failed to learn in ten years of schooling.

Our training consisted of some rudimentary instruction on how to teach, some teaching practice, and the acquisition of a few special skills, such as those of a cinema projectionist. We also learned how to produce a field newspaper under primitive conditions (tent, radio, typewriter, and duplicator). Our remaining lectures, and they were many, were on army educational administration. The nearest thing to mental stimulation I received was when the War Office decided that all NCOs should be encouraged to take an O level in general science, and all education officers should be trained to teach it. For this we went through the syllabus preparing and giving lessons, which kept me on my toes because the only O-level science I had was biology. By hasty preparation the night before I just managed to keep one lesson ahead of the class. For this I received an entry in my pay-book stating that I was qualified to teach a subject of which I knew almost nothing.

I kept fit at Beaconsfield by becoming an enthusiastic cross-country runner; it was now late spring, and Buckinghamshire is a beautiful county. We ex-infantrymen always left the ex-gunners behind, and I usually managed to finish in the first group home. I also remember the RSM teaching us sword-drill; compared with the Guards-Brigade NCOs at Mons he was a gentleman: when he called us 'Sir' he sounded as if he meant it.

We also learned the ways of an officers' mess, the home of heavy drinking, ribald singing, and rough but rather silly games. Since national-service subalterns were paid only twenty guineas a month, we often walked the Buckinghamshire lanes to save money. It was pleasant walking without packs or rifles and in civilian clothes: as we went we discussed Freud, Marx, and the latest vogue in French philosophy. Since we had studied a variety of different subjects, our minds got the exercise they missed during the day.

The highlight of our time at the Army School of Education was a formal dance to which Dawn came, and my friends were greatly impressed by her beauty and her jiving. I booked her into an old country inn with a four-poster bed and stairs that creaked alarmingly beneath our feet. Once safely inside her room, Dawn said she liked my No. 1 dress, and all my messmates had passed compliments on her gown; but we couldn't wait to tear them off and dive into the four-poster. Since most weekends I now managed to get to Streatham to see her, we did eventually get some sleep.

The things that enable the lower ranks to endure the institutionalised bullying of military life are leave and the prospect of leave. Leave sustained me in the first ten months of national service: there was none during basic training, but thereafter my morale depended upon 48- and 72-hour passes. During college vacations I spent them in Southsea, where Sarah and Dawn were both amused to see me in uniform; they took photos of one another with a smiling soldier's arm around them. Term-time leaves I spent in London in order to see Dawn as often as possible.

As private or cadet on thirty-five shillings a week, I had to do this cheaply; on one leave I stayed with my school friend Ant, who was now studying geophysics at University College. After leaving Dawn in Streatham late in the evening, I walked back to Ant's hall in central London, arriving at two in the morning. The only way into the hall was through the window of Ant's girlfriend, whose room was on the ground floor.

On another leave I stayed with Vic's mother in Queens Park, miles to the north of the city. Vic's final exams had been a disappointment (he should have jettisoned all that Greek literature). He had become a management trainee with a London printing firm, and he and Adrienne were happy to be reunited. Many years later, after numerous promotions and international takeovers, Vic became the UK boss of that firm. He had always been good with people as well as data and it was gratifying to see him prospering. While I was at Beaconsfield Dawn and I enjoyed a double date in the West End with Vic and Adrienne, which cost me more than a week's pay.

The rest of that leave I spent in Streatham, lunching with Dawn, or in Queens Park, keeping Vic's mother company. Her name was Catherine, and she was pleased that Vic had not had to do national service, especially when I gave her a lurid description of its worst points. Seeing how lean I was, Vic's mother tried to feed me up and her cooking was delicious. Vic's father was not the stern man I had imagined: he was now in a relaxed I told-you-so mood because Vic was enjoying work (and seeing Adrienne every evening) better than he had university.

As a subaltern paid twenty guineas a month, I was able to stay in a Streatham B&B. In her second year Dawn and her three closest friends shared digs, and had a landlady who hen-pecked her husband mercilessly and spoilt their only son. But she was pleased to have the money I paid for an evening meal, and she allowed Dawn and her soldier fiancé exclusive use of the front room 'to say goodnight'. The four students were very different, but became close friends, and I was soon on excellent terms with them all.

When my time at Beaconsfield came to an end, I received the posting that would take me up to the end of my national service in fourteen months' time. I was to take command of a Garrison Education Centre in Chester, the home of Western Command. Since Chester was 160 miles from London, and 235 from Portsmouth, where Dawn planned to teach, I wasn't sure whether this was good news or bad. But Dawn, who for the last year had dreaded waving me off to Cyprus, recognised it as a great improvement. Nevertheless, the home-posting mileages were formidable for penniless young people.

The lovely city of Chester is on the River Dee, which was once navigable and made Chester the major port for Ireland. It has a medieval cathedral, and a racecourse, and mock-Tudor Rows with double-decker shops, and deep-red city walls to keep out the Welsh; the walls were built by the Romans and reinforced by the Plantagenets, and today they are used mainly by tourists in the daytime and lovers in the evenings. My education centre, however, was located at the Depot of the Royal Regiment of Signals, more than two miles outside the town. This large camp stood in open country, was surrounded by barbed wire, and consisted of numerous black wooden huts (called *spiders*). Two of these held the officers' mess, and the Royal Signals lorry that met me at the station deposited me outside them.

I was welcomed by the mess treasurer, a retired colonel who had spent his life in India and had nothing and nobody to come back to. But he had brought back trunks full of souvenirs and he was a very interesting raconteur. I was shown my room, and met the batman I was to share with two Signals subalterns; it took me about ten minutes to unpack my kit and place a photo of Dawn in a swimsuit on the bedside table. This luxury was one of the perks I had enjoyed since becoming an officer cadet, and that photo had made me the envy of trogs, toffs, and NCOs at Mons.

When I met my fellow officers I found that the younger ones were aloof and snobbish: the Signals subalterns were minor-public-school boys who were obsessed with chasing classy fillies in the County of Cheshire; and the medic, who had been made an RAMC captain in return for signing on for three years, pulled rank if you dared to argue with him. I also disliked the way he joked derisively about the medical conditions of the soldiers and WRAC girls whom he treated; Hippocrates would have been disgusted. Fortunately, this medic was transferred elsewhere before I had to have my appendix removed. The surgeon on that occasion was a retired RAMC general and he left a scar that looked as if it had been made by a sword.

I much preferred the company of the older officers, some of whom taught me to play snooker, and did me the favour of refusing to play for money. The retired colonel, too, was good company, but the age gap prevented us becoming real friends. I had a similar problem with another possible soul-mate, a long-serving, long-suffering RASC officer in his forties, who completed the *Times* crossword in twenty minutes every morning. The Catholic padre also had a good mind (and good Latin), but his temper was foul. Military service robbed him of choirboys, but enabled him to enjoy the pope's concession on meatless days for serving officers. When he was late to lunch one Friday, he almost crucified a mess steward for saving him fish instead of his favourite steak.

I took over the education centre from a short-service first lieutenant who was due for demob. It was situated in a self-contained spider with a large office, several classrooms, a library, and a small cinema. There were also many intriguing cupboards filled with equipment for both teaching and sports, which included a canoe. My roles were as headmaster and administrator, and my staff consisted of two sergeant instructors, the last of the conscripted teachers. Their names were Barry and Tony and, since they were nearer my own class, they soon became my friends. They had been in the RAEC longer than I had, and I consulted them on almost every issue before making sure that I took the final decision.

We three all suffered from the same problem: underemployment. The Signals depot supervised the movement, in and out, of thousands of men awaiting demobilisation or their next posting. They were therefore not interested in promotion exams, and they were kept busy by fatigues (as army chores are called) and interminable training marches (which also kept them fit). The education centre's only customers were the troops with jobs at Western Command HQ or the Signals depot. Though few, they came from every arm of the service: not just the Royal Signals, but also the WRAC (clerks and typists), the RASC (drivers), the ACC (cooks), the PC (maintenance workers), and the RAOC (the quartermaster's staff).

My work enabled me to pick and choose between classes; I taught English at each army certificate level, and map-reading to the WRAC women, one of whom propositioned me on Helsby Hill. The hilltop has splendid views over Cheshire and Lancashire and three stretches of water: the Mersey, the Irish Sea, and the Manchester Ship Canal. The weather was fine, the grass was dry, and the woman's khaki blouse was well filled (most men like women in uniform), but I declined the invitation politely in the interests of good order and discipline. In this way I was able to return all the army's property in the same condition that I had collected it.

The other groups I taught included basic learn-or-leave classes, because the subjects of literacy and numeracy fascinated me, and I liked to discuss them with Dawn, whose course was full of psychology and pedagogic theory. I achieved some success by adopting innovative methods. Remembering that my pupils were adults, I made the *Daily Mirror* the set book for reading lessons, and I devised a game called pay-parade for maths. For this I divided the class into two teams and members took turns in acting the roles of pay-sergeant and soldier. I would choose a number of days for which basic pay, ration allowance, and living-out allowance were due, and the pay-sergeant's objective was to cheat the soldier. The class soon realised that basic arithmetic was a survival tool in the army and my Thespian pay-sergeants became less and less successful.

Unlike most new teachers, I had no discipline problems: I wore my licence to bully on my epaulettes and I had watched some very effective bullies during my military training. The first and only man to try to disrupt one of my classes doubled around the square holding a blackboard over his head as I had held weapons in Bury. The RSM, whose realm the parade ground was, watched him but said nothing. Later, however, he looked into my office to introduce himself and welcome me to the depot; and before he left he congratulated me on getting a grip so quickly. But from then on, everyone knew that the new *schoolie* (as the RAEC were called) liked playing soldiers, and was used to tougher nuts than the line-layers and wireless-operators in Western Command. And whenever I was orderly officer the shine on my brasses and boots, as I inspected or turned out the guard, said the same thing.

Despite my trying to develop new ways of teaching, and discussing them carefully with my sergeants, we still had time on our hands. There were many long breaks between classes, and only enough administrative work to keep me busy for about one day a week. This was on things like exams and timetables, equipment indents, building maintenance, and performance reports.

The sergeants filled their times in different ways: Barry, who was close to demob, spent a lot of time away in job interviews; Tony spent his time trying to meet and then courting a WRAC girl who was neither a lesbian nor a nymphomaniac (two categories particularly drawn to service life). I therefore had to find my own solution to boredom, and at first it was reading my way through the library. But my transfer to sedentary work had an alarming effect on my sleep patterns: I became an insomniac.

I tackled this in three ways, the first of which was to confide in the adjutant and volunteer to take as many squads of migrant signalmen on training marches as he wanted. He soon found me plenty of this work, and I enjoyed being in the open air and exploring the lanes of Cheshire. My long legs and quicker pace enabled me to move from the front of the column to the rear, and back again, encouraging the blistered and the flabby. The second measure I took was to walk into Wales on three or four evenings a week; this took me through the centre of Chester and over the bridge. After six or seven such miles I would sleep as soundly as a recruit in basic training.

My third measure was the craftiest: I realised that it was very easy to spend my entire pay on mess bills, and so I volunteered to do extra orderly-officer duties. Remaining the only officer on duty in the evenings not only kept me busy and active, it also stopped me drinking alcohol. Since I preferred spirits to beer, keeping up with my seniors had begun to prove costly. I made up for this sobriety on mess nights, when free port and Madeira kept circulating even when the senior officers switched to brandy.

But with time still on my hands, I missed Dawn badly, and gradually a plan formed in my mind and became the subject of our letters. My pay-parade game and the size of my first mess bill combined to produce an idea. Although a national-service subaltern was paid only half as much as a regular officer, their allowances were the same. This meant that seven nights' living-out and ration allowance would double my monthly income; it would also save me most of my mess bill. On the other hand, it would cost Dawn no more from her teacher's salary to live with me in Chester than to stay with her mother in Portsmouth. The answer to our problems was therefore obvious: we needed to get married as soon as possible. (We also needed a five-year plan not to have a baby, but the London Rubber Company had never let us down yet.)

As an officer below the age of twenty-five, I now needed my CO's permission to marry and live out. I approached the Signals Colonel with some trepidation because this move meant so much to me. I knew that he vaguely approved of me: my volunteering for regimental duties, my marching, and my openness had not escaped his notice. He was also a happily married man, and he thought that two years was a long enough engagement. He asked to see Dawn's photo, and when he saw it he was impressed. He gave us his blessing and said that he looked forward to welcoming Dawn to his mess. The practical considerations also no doubt helped me: I was in my last posting, in a year's time I would be a civilian, and I had found a flat in Chester. The Colonel was a man of goodwill and I was lucky to be serving under him.

Dawn qualified as a teacher with flying colours, but she now had much to do: first she had to extricate herself from a job in Portsmouth and find a school on Merseyside; as a last-minute applicant she had no choice but to accept a school in the industrial town of Ellesmere Port, some miles from Chester. Then she had to work lots of overtime in the shop on the pier in order to save money. And, finally, as a twenty-year-old, she had to persuade her mother, who hated bureaucracy, to sign a consent form. All of which she accomplished, with a little help from Sarah, who was very helpful and supportive. We married in the Southsea registry office on a bright summer's day, in the presence of our families and closest friends (who gave us sensible wedding presents like bedclothes and saucepans). In our photos we are surrounded by smiling and affectionate faces. And in the afternoon we made the long journey by train to Chester and left our guests to enjoy the afternoon on *our* beach, and in *our* sea.

The furnished flat in Chester was close to the city walls; it was down-at-heel, although the rent was sixteen pounds a month (compared with Sarah's seven in Southsea), but we didn't care; we were now one another's environment. In the longer term our finances looked sound: my pay and allowances would be forty pounds a month for six months, and after that would rise sharply to sixty pounds a month (because national-servicemen were paid as regular soldiers in their last six months). Dawn's salary would be fifty pounds a month, and so on 1 October (our first joint payday) we would be rich. In the short term, however, we had almost nothing.

In those early weeks we honeymooned at home: we spent as much time in bed as possible, and we spent our weekends exploring the city and walking in the fields by the River Dee. We picked blackberries in trunks and bikini, swam in the muddy water, and lay in one another's arms on the bank, regaining strength for the night. On weekdays we were assured of one hot meal at school or camp, and otherwise we lived on baked beans (which were cheap in Woolworths) and blackberries, which Dawn turned into delicious pies with the aid of cheap ingredients like flour and margarine. It was one of the happiest times of our lives.

Once we were receiving our salaries, we felt affluent. Ninety, and then one hundred and ten pounds a month was more than twice what Sarah had ever earned, and we had money for luxuries: we became regulars at Quaintways, the elegant local dance hall, saw all the latest films, bought a radio, visited the other cities of the North West, and went on a short camping holiday in the Lake District. Nor were we short of company: Dawn's college friends stayed with us in turn, and those of my RAEC friends who were serving in the UK found opportunities to visit Western Command. But, most importantly, we made a new friend who remained equally close to us both for the rest of his short life. This was the replacement for my sergeant Barry, a younger man named Ernie (another one) whose family home was nearby in the Wirral.

Ernie was only nineteen and had entered national service straight from public school. His father was a senior officer in the merchant navy, and he sent Ernie off to boarding school when he came home on leave and found that Ernie had acquired a thick Scouse accent. The school cured this: Ernie now spoke perfect posh if he wanted to, but he never forgot his roots, and one of the first books he lent us was called *Learn Yourself Scouse*. Ernie was very good-looking and had immense charm; he had charmed his way into the Army School of Education (and three stripes) by saying that he was thinking of becoming a schoolteacher. Ernie also had a magnificent sense of humour and was the worst male giggler I had met: when the three of us were together we spent most of our time in stitches from laughing.

Ernie knew the Wirral like the back of his hand, and he had numerous girlfriends, all of whom he introduced to us. Dawn and I shared many double dates with Ernie and his latest. Our range of amusements was extended because Ernie had an ancient Morris 8 convertible and this provided a way of getting a canoe to the river. A good example of his mad escapades was the first driving lesson he gave me. I started by driving around the camp, and Ernie stood up beside me as I drove, waving his hands and shouting, 'Get out of the way!' Then he had me drive through the Mersey tunnel to see his latest girlfriend; and I learned how to find the point of a clutch by being told at the toll booth that the handbrake didn't work.

On another occasion he bet against my being able to break into my own education centre undetected: my plan was to climb over the roof to the spider's inner well and then through a window with a broken catch. Just as I was straddling the roof's summit the RAEC major at Western Command arrived, and Ernie told him that I was conducting a security test. The major complimented me on my thoroughness, and Ernie and I could hardly contain our laughter. So, even if my first year in the army was mind-numbing, my second was hilarious.

My last adventure in uniform occurred during one of my orderly-officer duties. In the middle of the night an arsonist set fire to the officers' mess, and had chosen to start it beneath the corner of the spider that held the retired colonel's room. As the first on the scene, I had to go through his window and get him out. Since he wouldn't be parted from his treasures, this meant bundling all his trunks through the window before I helped him through and jumped myself. Within seconds of my exit the floor caved in and flames leapt to the ceiling, so it was a narrow escape.

The fire was made worse by the fact that I, and all the orderly officers before me, had spent too much time inspecting the guard's kit and weapons, and too little checking the fire picket's hoses. Since these were badly affected by the rust of years, I received neither reprimand nor commendation. After the fire, the military police found that there was a convicted arsonist amongst the troops passing through the camp, and they interrogated every man sharing his barrack room. But everyone swore the man had turned in early and hadn't left his bed, and so he was never charged. This incident showed the army at its worst and at its best: a hierarchy obsessed with bull and drill, and troops who united against the world.

Dawn and I spent a very happy year in Chester and were sorry to leave. I wasn't tempted by the offer of three pips to sign on for a regular commission, even though a captain's pay was much higher than that of any job for which I was qualified. I knew that I was not entitled to an army married quarter until I was twenty-five, and that my next posting might be as distant as Singapore. Dawn and I had experienced enough separation already, and it was imperative that I find a job near a school where she could teach. And so I re-entered the civilian jobs market with ideas that were inordinately ambitious for an ex-greengrocer, milkman, and seafront labourer.

13

SOAP

At the age of twenty-three I had plenty of experience of manual labour but knew nothing about white-collar careers. Since Dawn and Sarah knew even less, I sought advice from older men. I did not approach my CO, because he thought I was a better soldier than I was, and he would have urged me to take a short-service commission, even without a married quarter. As noted above, a regular captain's pay was much higher than that of any other job open to me, but Dawn and I were not just interested in money. She had a career, and loved teaching, and there would have been no job for her on an overseas posting. My uncles who had been wartime civil servants urged me to try for the civil service's fastest track, so I filled in the forms and waited. But the RAEC major at Western Command said that he thought I was far too creative for the civil service, and he recommended I try something like advertising, where my skills could be better used.

I read a book named the *Hidden Persuaders* and bought several issues of *Advertising Age* to discover a little more about it. I learned that Britain's largest advertiser was an Anglo-Dutch conglomerate called Unilever and that it owned a large ad agency called Lintas. I also learned that it recruited graduates for fast-track management careers and so I applied. And when I discovered that there was another British company as large as Unilever, called ICI, with a similar scheme, I applied to it too. Finally I applied for a copy-trainee job with an ad agency named Mather & Crowther (it had been recommended by the RAEC major, who had a relative working there).

Civil Service (administrative-grade) entry involved a general exam, in which I wrote about subjects of which I knew nothing and managed to pass. Then came a weekend assessment centre, where I revelled in IQ tests and group discussions. Most of the other candidates were still at university in Oxford or Cambridge, and they seemed very young, although most of them were the same age as me. As a married man and a serving officer, I soon found them deferring to my judgement, and this must have done my chances no harm. In any event, I gained a final interview with the Civil Service Commission in London, and I faced an assembly such as I had never encountered, even at WOSB.

The commissioners discussed only two things with me: one was my exclusive preference for the Ministry of Education; and they failed to convince me that the Treasury could be as exciting. The other was my belief that, if all the public schools were closed on Friday, state schools would be better by the following Tuesday; and I failed to convince them. They were, of course, all male, rotund, and unctuous, and I felt uncomfortable in their presence. As I left I noticed that half of them were wearing the black ties with pale blue stripes that I had first seen on toffs at Mons. I realised that if they had asked me if my mother had ever scrubbed floors they would have reached their decision sooner. When I received an official-looking letter two days later I knew what it contained.

Mather and Crowther set me a copy-writing test by post; it involved a breakfast cereal and a toothpaste, and it won me an interview in their office on Waterloo Bridge. After an hour's discussion they offered me a job as a copy assistant, at a salary well below my army pay, and they gave me the impression that initially I would be what was known as a gopher (or go-for). Since *Advertising Age* had shown me how prone agencies were to takeover by larger US agencies, and how much blood was spilled on the carpet when they occurred, I resolved to hold the offer in reserve, as a last resort.

ICI wasted my time, and their shareholders' money (the cost of a hotel, dinner, and travel) with a pantomime of an interview. The interviewer was a man with a northern accent who had not read my application form properly. ICI were clearly looking for people with firsts, but only during the interview did he realise that mine wasn't in sciences. He then interrogated me aggressively on why I hadn't studied a difficult subject like his (chemistry), and I retaliated by challenging him to demonstrate the one-word proof of Pythagoras' theorem. I left him the solution on a sheet of paper, and I collected my money and left. So far, then, my only option was to become a copy assistant.

My first interview at Unilever was with a young Scotsman who spoke slowly but was very shrewd. He asked searching questions about why I was leaving the army when the loss of conscription left them short of officers, and he asked for examples of how I dealt with people. He then convinced me that I didn't want to become a *copywriter* (who had to bend to the will of someone called an *account executive*), nor even an account executive (who in turn had to obey someone called a *brand manager*). He persuaded me that what I wanted was to become a brand manager and, when I agreed, he booked me a place at Unilever's assessment centre.

Unilever called such things *selection boards* and their fast-track scheme the *Unilever Companies' Management Development Scheme* (such a mouthful that it was always known as UCMDS). I spent a day and a half at Unilever's Blackfriars HQ on this selection board, having the time of my life, since my experience at WOSB and the civil service made me the most relaxed candidate. I was even able to help and encourage the others, who again seemed very young, and by the time the senior managers making the employment decision gave me a final interview they were chatting with me as if I were one of them. It was just like the officers' mess when the port had done a few laps. A psychologist had been present to administer IQ and personality tests and her advice was useful. She said that, while my IQ results had impressed the selectors, the personality tests had revealed a fiercely competitive individual who cunningly concealed his aggression. She advised me to show it politely, instead, and I thanked her for her advice.

I accepted Unilever's offer and asked to start as soon as possible. My uncle Teddy, who had an office in Kilburn at the time, had the keys of a tiny furnished flat in a place called Crouch End, and Dawn got a job in a slum school in nearby Finsbury Park. Within a week of my demob we were Londoners. The flat was exactly six miles from Blackfriars, but the journey involved catching two buses and an underground train. It usually took just over an hour, but on one occasion when both tubes and buses were on strike I walked home in exactly sixty minutes. Dawn's journey to school was much shorter, so she arrived home an hour and a half before me; this enabled her, by trial and error, to become an excellent cook. And, once she had absorbed the wisdom of Elizabeth David and Fanny Craddock, her cuisine was *cordon bleu*.

We were as happy in Crouch End as in Chester and we could now see a great deal of Vic and Adrienne, who had recently married. And when Vic and I had both obtained driving licences, we borrowed an old banger and went on a camping holiday together in Wales. We had lots of hilarious adventures that included losing the car keys on a beach and almost reversing the car off a mountain. We passed through Chippy on the way and found that Sarah's cottage was now a lock-up garage. Dawn and Adrienne expressed amazement that anyone could live there. I found the holiday a wonderful break from Unilever, where the work was often more cerebral, but otherwise less challenging, than running an education centre.

Unilever was vast: it had a turnover of billions, operated in every country this side of the Iron Curtain, and employed a quarter of a million people. However, it faced three huge problems, the first of which was its own organisation. It was decentralised to the point of chaos, and owned hundreds of different companies in scores of different countries, each with its own chairman (almost always a national of the country concerned). These company chairmen always refused to discuss Unilever with outsiders: 'My company,' the Birds Eye chairman liked to say, 'is Birds Eye Foods; Unilever is just my shareholder.' To make things more complicated Unilever had twin boards of directors, and its companies around the world were divided not only by industry, but also evenly between Unilever Ltd (in London) and Unilever (NV) in Rotterdam.

Its organisation had been designed for the Long War between 1914 and 1945 (which between 1918 and 1939 was solely economic). There were Unilever head offices for both sides and, regardless of which power occupied a country, its Unilever companies had somewhere to remit profits. After the war the decentralisation continued because it served a political purpose. Aneurin Bevan had a list of twenty giant British companies that he planned to nationalise, and apart from ICI, none was a fraction of the size of Unilever. Unilever's name was not on the list, because it was politically invisible, and its name appeared on none of its companies' products. This also protected it from trade unions: it allowed profitable subsidiaries to pay higher salaries, and Unilever's main board were able to ignore the TUC at its most powerful, even though its companies negotiated with all the unions.

Unilever's second big problem was that it tried to sell everything; although most of its companies marketed consumer goods (such as edible fats, detergents, packaged foods, toiletries, and ice cream), many sold things for which Unilever's giant research and development resources, and its advertising expertise, could do nothing. Examples of products requiring quite different strengths included: grocery chains, board mills, and plastic manufacturers in the UK; fish restaurants in Germany; trucks in Africa: dairies in Asia: and three transport companies, including a shipping line. It was even rumoured that at one time Unilever owned two brothels in Tangier, which had been bought by mistake and were hastily sold to the Mafia.

Unilever's third and most urgent problem was the aftermath of the Long War. Western European countries had engaged in an orgy of mutual destruction, and their economies became captive to either the USA or the USSR. The first of these was almost as damaging as the second. While Europe's factories were flattened by bombs and its research facilities requisitioned for military purposes, US factories and laboratories steamed ahead and developed new and better products, from frozen food to synthetic detergents. And, as US companies used these advances to penetrate European markets, the rich of Europe poured their capital into the USA. The outflow of capital was greater than Marshall Aid, which was all that made a European recovery possible.

After the war, Unilever battled to keep up with American competitors like P&G, Colgate, and General Foods, and Swiss ones like Nestlé. Neutrality, even for a couple of years, is an enormous economic advantage. Unilever drew some comfort, however, from American prejudices: for example, P&G long held off entering Indian markets because the country was 'quasi-communist', and American companies' attitudes to Africa were rather like that of the Ku Klux Klan. Unilever was also able to trade behind the Iron Curtain through its Indian subsidiaries, and with Arab nations hostile to Israel through subsidiaries in more conciliatory countries.

After my UCMDS selection board I was sent for a placement interview with Unilever's newest, yet oldest, company, Lever Brothers and Associates. Unilever owned four UK companies selling soaps and detergents and three of these, Crosfields, Lever Brothers, and Hudson and Knight, had just been merged. For many years they had been keen competitors, and Unilever's board thought that a good thing until the American company P&G began marketing its wartime inventions in the UK. To counter this threat, the three Unilever companies selling *Persil, Lux* and *Lifebuoy* Toilet Soaps, and *Omo* and *Vim,* were merged.

The three marketing departments, containing mainly short-serving and high-flying managers, had no problems with this merger, but the three sales forces who had battled one another in the shops for years were plainly unhappy. This was also reflected at the top, where the three marketing managers each became a group marketing manager with a list of related brands (laundry, household, and personal products); but the three sales directors had to be dealt with less equitably: one became the merged company's sales director, another his deputy (termed *sales controller*), and the third was posted abroad.

My placement interview was with one of the new group marketing managers, and he checked my enthusiasm for marketing and confirmed that the new merged company (LB&A) would provide my training and early career development. He also made a promise (which he later duly kept) to arrange for me an attachment to a London ad agency. The UCMDS basic training programme consisted of two months in a factory, one in a sales routine office, six months on a sales territory, and nine working on a brand. Of these I did the sales-routine-office training first, because I was joining exactly one month earlier than my cohort, and I did it in Hudson and Knight's office in Leeds.

I was put up in a very grand hotel from Sunday to Thursday night, and spent time observing every job, before being allotted one of my own for the last week. I got on well with the office staff and quickly noticed something that turned out to be important to my subsequent career. It was called a Hollerith machine, and used punch cards that automatically produced an invoice for each order and a delivery note for a transport depot. I realised immediately that the day would come when every purchase in a store would automatically trigger the replacement of stock, the payment of invoices, the production of more goods, and the order of raw material for those goods. The whole distribution chain appeared before my eyes, and I saw that such a system would make sales forces (and sales interviews) redundant. I did not realise, however, that it would be another twenty-five years before computer technology made this dream a reality, and that many years of my life would be spent managing the interim situation.

I met the remainder of my UCMDS cohort on our eight-week factory attachment; there were seven of us, and we stayed in a company-owned hostel in Port Sunlight village. Nigel, Terry, Maurice, David and I were marketing trainees, Philip was a technical trainee, and Peter (a man with a famous name) was the last of a cadre of 'junior' trainees recruited from the top public schools. Four of us came straight from national service and two from university; Peter was more intelligent than the average toff at Mons, and he made more effort to blend with his social inferiors. In the first month we visited every department of the factory, studied its work, and asked questions of its boss; in the second we donned overalls and plodded and packed soap or served the vast tower that blew powders. In the first month I found the endless presentations of departmental aims and functions boring, and I think all seven of us learned how to sleep with our eyes open and yawn with our mouths closed.

During the eight weeks we discovered that Unilever was more hierarchical than the army: there are eighteen ranks in the British army, from private to field-marshal; but Unilever had fourteen grades of manager, from JC (Job Class) 20 to JC 33, and half a dozen clerical grades below them. Unilever JCs were not marked by pips and stripes, but by offices and dining rooms, of which there were seven in the factory (for directors, senior managers, upper-middle managers, lower-middle managers, and assistant managers, plus male and female blue-collar canteens). In the first month the seven trainees were allowed the privilege of lunching with the lower-middle managers, but by the second we had learned that the best place to eat was the Red Cow, just outside the (strictly temperance) village. All the women we worked with seemed to eat there, and we trainees always knew when one of them fancied one of us because she would come into work without curlers in her hair.

The office demarcation was still in evidence in 1990 when a manager arrived in Unilever House from Australia to take up a new JC 26 job. She was given an office formerly used by a JC 27 manager and she spent the first morning watching two men changing all her furniture and carpets to slightly inferior ones. Unilever's problem was not that it was hierarchical, because all human groups (as I have noted earlier in this volume) are hierarchical. It is easy to see what humans will do when they no longer have an economic use: at best, they will form hierarchies and spend their time negotiating and changing them; at worst, they will spend their time gazing at screens, and gambling, and cheating one another.

Unilever's problem was that it had too many formal levels and too many managers with overlapping responsibilities. It took decades to change this and, of course, even when layers had been stripped out, there was still the informal pecking order that characterises every human group. Nevertheless, in a leaner Unilever the barriers preventing someone low in the pecking order having an idea, or doing something creative, would have been lowered. And the amount of time that people at the higher levels would have had to interfere with this would have been greatly reduced. But in 1960 Unilever suffered badly from giving people titles and status without responsibility.

We seven trainees socialised together a lot and didn't split into private- and state-educated factions. We went to pubs and cinemas, and on one occasion visited a dance hall *en masse*. I was the only married man, and Peter, who had the usual open-topped roadster and full social diary, used to give me a lift to London and back every weekend. Peter attended balls and horse races with *debutantes*, but I'm sure that my reunions with Dawn were more ecstatic. It was winter, and both travellers in the convertible got stiff necks from the draughts that streamed through the cracks in the hood; but we both thought it was well worth it. Peter was heartbroken when rheumatic pain forced him to exchange his convertible for a saloon car.

I also spent some evenings with my army friend Ernie, whose home was close to Port Sunlight. There I met his mother Millie, who was a warm, bubbly woman with a fantastic sense of humour. She had a delicious Scouse accent, like all the best comedians, and she and Ernie kept me in stitches. Millie was also the most hospitable person I ever met and she, Dawn, and I were to become close friends. In 1960 Liverpool was still an exciting and friendly place. Its council could do nothing about the decline of British industry in subsequent years, but it crushed some of the heart out of the people when it flattened the city's central slums and rehoused their residents in tower blocks further out. Its twin city across the Mersey, Birkenhead, reflected Liverpool's character, but its middle classes preferred to say that they lived on the Wirral Peninsula, the silted-up delta of the River Dee. In fact one side of the Wirral was all factories and oil refineries and the other all golf courses.

After the factory experience came the sales force: a month working with an experienced salesman and five working a territory. The latter was possible because young salesmen with promise were given the opportunity of an attachment to head office in exchange. (Unilever's aim was a senior management only fifty percent ex-UCMDS.) The three sales forces had not yet been integrated and my mentor was a Hudson and Knight salesman named Fred. He was very welcoming, and he taught me to sell Omo, Vim, and Castile soap to shops of all descriptions (there were 140,000 outlets in the UK selling soap in those days). The key to in-store success was not to use the planned presentation that came out from head office each month ('Mr Trader, your customers will be clamouring for the bargains I can offer you today...') except when our area manager was accompanying us, at which times the customer would smile, and wink, and buy out of personal loyalty.

Fred let me practise my driving on his company car, but when I had earned my own territory I had to work it by public transport until I passed my test, which was a good thing because it meant that I was given a territory in North London close to my home. The Cockney voices reminded me of Sarah's family and in sales interviews I spoke it whenever my customer did. When my obligatory black Ford Popular was delivered Dawn and I became mobile; I had to pay for private mileage, but it wasn't much more expensive than bus-fares, and we made great use of it. It enabled us to see Vic and Adrienne more often and to visit our mothers in Portsmouth.

My last sales weeks were spent in the London regional office, where the managers were reeling under the impact of having to learn three companies' price lists and employ a new and complex method of calculating order requirements (the *Lever Stock-Turn System*). My regional manager soon realised that I understood this system better than he did, and he used me to explain it to his managers and salesmen. After that he relied on me to interpret statistics for him and help him prepare his meetings, so I wasn't ever either idle or bored. I made some good friends in that office, and I was doubly sad when the time came to hand in my company car and move on to the marketing department.

This department suffered particularly heavily from over-management: too many people competed for space in every decision area. Unilever prided itself on following its founder's example in offering jobs for life and treating people well. This meant that it didn't hire and fire on the whim of one man. Hiring and firing decisions were taken by an employee's boss's boss, and both incompetence and personal dislike are easier to tolerate at one level removed. In the 1980s I recruited the man who would change all this when he became UK chairman at the end of the century. He shed one-third of the organisation's managers overnight and his successor faced Unilever's first ever nationwide strike when its final-pay pension scheme was scrapped. But in the general brutalisation of capitalism in twenty-first-century Europe both events went unnoticed.

My marketing experience began with nine months as a trainee assistant on Lever's biggest and most profitable brand, *Persil*. The brand's size mattered because the company's top management became involved with decisions that on smaller brands were left to the brand manager. Thus, for example, eight people would represent the client when the agency unveiled a new ad campaign ('What is a mum?'):

Marketing Director	(JC 30)
Advertising Director	(JC 29)
Marketing Manager	(JC 28)
Advertising Content Manager	(JC 27)
Product-Group Manager	(JC 25)
Brand Manager	(JC 23)
Assistant Brand Manager	(JC 20)
Marketing Trainee	(No JC)

When the commercial had been screened a few times, the agency's Account Director would invite comments, which were given in JC order, senior first, with each level of the hierarchy taking care to agree with the ones above.

In my first such meeting I was asked to comment eighth (*noblesse oblige*) and I drew attention to an important error that my betters had missed. The product-group manager looked black and tried to kick me under the table, a task for which his short legs did not equip him. This created an awkward pause, which nobody filled, until the advertising director then continued as if I hadn't spoken. Fortunately, the ad agency people had been awake, and in the next version of the commercial, which was sent over to the brand office, the error had been quietly cut. From this I learned that even the humblest member of a client delegation may serve a purpose, providing he acts circumspectly, but circumspection was something I had to learn, like faces on a beach.

My superiors on the brand were men of good will, but it was difficult for them to delegate much responsibility to their trainee when he kept disappearing regularly and for weeks at a time. Courses and attachments came thick and fast. First there were training courses making up a Unilever Education Programme that taught business theory to people who had studied other things. This was one of Unilever's great attractions, and some graduates joined the organisation solely for the training, which came free. Today they would go deeply into debt to get that same education at business school, and their MBA diplomas would guarantee them a career in management. Although the Unilever Education Programme gave no diploma, until the 1990s it made a Unilever manager a favourite with head-hunters.

In my thirty-five years with Unilever I spent about fifty weeks in classroom courses, heavily weighted towards the early years. Courses, however, were only the tip of the training iceberg: there were attachments to market research and public relations companies, to perfumers, packaging suppliers, and distribution depots, and to laboratories and development departments. Trainees were also often assigned to project teams engaged in experiment and innovation. Thus the *Persil* brand manager saw me frequently, but not continuously enough to delegate anything substantial, and I enjoyed variety but not responsibility. In that it was the opposite of my time in the sales force.

The most enjoyable of my attachments was the month I spent with an ad agency in St Martin's Lane. To my kind and generous hosts I was a client, and therefore an excuse to lunch at a fancy restaurant, so executives of all levels regaled me with their knowledge over good claret for a couple of hours, and then answered all my questions. In between lunches I would attend meetings with clients from other industries ('This is Martin, our latest trainee.'), or read voluminous reports and write comments on them. I learned some interesting things: for example, Ford fired their ad agencies often, but one art director who had acquired the skill of making their models look a couple of feet longer always moved with the account (unknown to the top people at Ford).

I spent some time on film sets and in studios making commercials. One was for a chocolate bar, and the agency tried to save money by hiring a model, not an actress. She had to walk along a street with a pram and insert chocolate bars between her sensuous lips. She was a posh girl, too well brought up to obey the technician when he warned her to spit the mouthful of chocolate out after each take. After sixty takes I held her head while she vomited for ten minutes into the gutter. When her boyfriend arrived in his sports car to collect her at the end of the day she was still in tears. A *debutante* who wants a career does not have a life that's all champagne.

The producer who introduced me to the cold and uncomfortable world of making commercial films was a friendly man whose brother was the highest-paid British film star of his generation. In the week before Christmas I asked him what sort of Christmas present he gave a brother who had everything. He replied that they both knew one another's favourite brand of malt whisky, and that the agreement between them was a single bottle each way. By and large, I found that agency's people refreshingly free of status snobbery. This I had found not to be the case in the famous agency that held the *Persil* account. It had prestigious offices in Berkeley Square, employed only Oxbridge copywriters, and appointed contacts who matched their client socially at each level.

In Lever Brothers' marketing department there was still some social snobbery; not long ago it had recruited only men leaving public school or one of the ancient universities. By the 1960s, however, its UCMDS trainees were a mixture of state- and privately educated men, plus a few token women graduates. Statistics showed that almost all UCMDS women left Unilever within a few years to start a family, and so their expensive training wasn't a good long-term investment. This actually enhanced the value of those that did not leave: there were half a dozen women CEOs of Unilever subsidiary companies, and they were all exceptionally able. But they were all either single or divorced, which reflected British society in general, since the time when women expected (and gained) it all had not yet arrived.

The *Persil* brand office, like so many privileged corners of employment in Britain, was also an exception, in that it was an Oxbridge enclave. As a red-brickie, I felt I was underrated, and I had few chances to prove myself; those I did have were mostly in the area of analysis. I sometimes discovered, in the mass of figures that made up market and research reports, key correlations that my bosses had overlooked. Once my insights were recognised, however, senior managers saw them only as emanating from the brand office, and I gained no personal credit. Yet I did note that there were advantages to being underrated: one quiet brand manager named John often stole a march on his rivals in the competition for scarce resources just because his rivals underestimated him.

As my nine months' marketing training drew to a close my cohort was being assessed to determine which trainee would be promoted to assistant manager on which brand. This was something I was not prepared to leave to chance, and so I invited the product-group manager (who oversaw three brands, including *Persil*) for a drink one evening, and I made my pitch. I chose him because I felt that he was my severest critic, but thought it beneath him to show this openly. In the nearest bar I broached the subject of the overcrowding of the decision area in the marketing department, and he reluctantly accepted my analysis; then I told him that I would prefer my first management job to be in sales, where two things were happening that I found fascinating: the integration of three rival sales forces, and the company's reaction to the self-service revolution that was changing the face of British grocery retailing.

My erstwhile fiercest critic bought this line (which happened to be genuine) completely, and I was suddenly as popular as someone in an overcrowded lifeboat who has offered to swim. He immediately became my greatest advocate, and he used his influence to convince the sales director that I was the greatest thing since sliced bread (which had just been introduced in the UK). In later years I suspect that he took credit for kick-starting my career in sales, which brought me senior management (JC 27+) earlier than any of my cohort. If so, that attempted kick under the table was not a total miss.

Thus it was that eighteen months after joining Lever Brothers I found myself in one of the most creative roles in the entire company. I was only an assistant manager for the first six of those months, but during that time I had all the autonomy, complexity, and recognition I desired. In fact, I had to invent and reinvent my own job every day.

14

SPACE

The retail revolution arrived from the USA around 1960, when Brits began to accept that the UK was now no more than a satellite. Rather than resent the success of the US war aim to destroy the British Empire, the people of Britain threw themselves into the American dream and dreamed a new British dream: that they were honorary Americans. Today, Brits cannot live or work in the USA, much less vote in its elections, but they can be extradited to the USA on zero evidence and tortured, tried, and executed under its infamous injustice system. This the Brits term a *special relationship* and they enter into it with gusto, proudly dressing in vests, plimsolls, baseball caps, and faded blue denims. They even have US place names like *Yorktown* embroidered on their clothes to boast of their subjection. This enables British actors to monopolise parts as wimps in Hollywood films and British troops to act as cannon fodder in the Pentagon's wars.

The most important elements of the retail revolution have, just like American leisurewear, proved irresistible all over the world: for the consumer they were greater choice, self-service, and mass display; for the retailer they were vast stores, in large numbers, massive volume, and the power to coerce both suppliers and governments. There had been self-service stores in Britain in the fifties, and even before the war, but they were small and cramped, and offered no more choice than the largest counter stores. There had also been grocery chains, such as International Stores, Allied Suppliers, and the Co-op, but they were conservative and bureaucratic. The nearest things in Britain to a US supermarket were the stalls on which market traders piled their goods high and sold them cheap. But a stall could hold only a limited number of items, whereas even the first supermarkets sold in excess of 2,000 lines (a fraction of a hypermarket's range today). In the retail wars that broke out in the sixties Britain's market traders would wipe out the conservative chains, leaving small shops to immigrants with family businesses, which could open all hours.

Unilever's cleaning companies (including one not merged until the 1970s) employed 800 salesmen calling on the same 140,000 stores, most of which were doomed. The company's situation was fraught with peril, but rich in manpower, and Lever Brothers was blessed with two men of talent and optimism who saw opportunities everywhere in this crumbling British marketplace. The first was its new sales director, Maurice, a tiny Jewish intellectual with remarkable energy who had reached the pinnacle of the Indian Civil Service before joining Unilever in Bombay. His next post was as Unilever's chief economist, and then he occupied the chair in economics at a northern university until he retired. He and his equally diminutive journalist wife were stimulating company. Between them they set the conventional Lever sales force alight; she also liked to accompany salesmen into the shops (where there were news stories to be had), and the two were a powerful thinking unit.

Lever Brothers' second prophet of the revolution was a man in his mid-twenties named Keith, a public schoolboy with an aristocratic surname. He was exceptionally articulate, charming, and persuasive, and he had more intelligence and imagination than the entire Brigade Squad at Mons put together. The fact that he would probably have stolen the exam papers from the company safe if necessary made him even more formidable an operator.

Keith was the rubber-tipped hammer with which Maurice beat the Lever sales force into a shape that could survive for more than thirty years. Keith had studied marketing and merchandising in the USA, and he arrived back in the UK armed with a mass of data and a head full of ideas. His ambition was to teach the UK grocery trade how to merchandise: to maximise their sales and profits by exploiting customer psychology and by the efficient use of the space on supermarket shelves and floors. To do this he would first have to teach the Lever sales force how to merchandise, and then motivate them to use the retail revolution to their brands' advantage. We were struggling, sometimes successfully, to match P&G in product development and advertising, but the balance could be tipped in Lever's favour by out-competing them in the stores.

Keith naturally made enemies: the opponents of change and those managers of his own level and above who felt threatened by his dynamism. There was no doubt that he was arrogant; he was afraid of nobody but himself; that is, of falling, even for one minute, below his own exacting standards of creativity and intellectual rigour. But he loved ideas and respected other people's, and he was lavish in his praise when one of his team thought of something before he did. In the spring of 1962 I was appointed as one of his assistants, and Keith and I got on incredibly well. From the first he treated me as an equal, and he soon accepted that I could be useful in damping down the smoking embers left by the fires he lit: I healed rifts with managers overwhelmed by his ideas and energy, and I trimmed any of his ideas that wouldn't quite work until they did.

Keith also approved of Dawn when he met her socially, and he tried to introduce us to some of his county friends, women whose titles ranged from the Honourable upwards. But, typically of Keith, they were women with brains, and they seemed to adore him. He was unbelievably cavalier about expenses; he submitted his roughly once every three months, giving his secretary a briefcase full of receipts and asking her to sort them out. His petrol receipts were mixed with huge bills from all the finest hotels and most expensive restaurants in the land. The secretary had to check his diary and find out the names of the people he had entertained. If she didn't recognize a name, she assumed it was a senior executive of a grocery chain. The female names she discreetly reduced to an initial and, since Keith was no snob, there were no titles in his diary. I don't recall him even glancing at an expense claim of mine; he knew my background, and he encouraged me to live well as long as I worked hard.

Keith's first task was to have his other assistant conduct large-scale (and expensive) experiments proving that a store maximised its sales and profits from all detergents when the amount of space each brand was given on the shelves was in proportion to its market share. Lever's payback was that *Persil* got a third of the shelf space, more than double what it would achieve on an equal-shares-for-all-brands basis. This research was turned into a brochure and sold by the sales force to thousands of grocery managers. Having sold the idea, salesmen helped install this plan, and they became closer to store staff as a result. A *Grocer* survey showed that its readers rated Lever as having the UK's most efficient and helpful sales force, and it was amazing what most store managers allowed our salesmen to do. They controlled the stocks of all our products, making sure that there was no danger of the stockroom ever lying empty, and they gained far more than their share of the space left at gondola ends for special displays.

Behind all this activity there was a massive programme of retraining, and sales managers had to be converted to the new creed before their salesmen. One of my roles was to help Keith plan and organise a series of conferences and training courses for this purpose. But my main job was to ensure that our displays dominated the available floor space in stores all over the UK. I had a great deal of travelling to do in a grey

Hillman saloon that the salesmen envied, and which Sarah thought the most luxurious vehicle in which she had ever ridden. My job was to invent schemes, one for every fortnight of the year, to win Lever the coveted space: these schemes included *atmosphere merchandising* (often seasonal, like Santa's grotto, but all the year round), *related-item merchandising* (port and Stilton at one end of the gondola, washing-up liquid and toilet rolls at the other), and *unrelated-item* merchandising (deckchairs and household cleaners).

I had never dreamed of a job where you were paid for having ideas, but now I had one, and I revelled in it. The most useful part long-term was learning how to handle artists, designers, printers and delivery companies, and how to address large sales audiences. My work took me from design studios in central London, to conference hotels in Brighton, to struggling minimarkets in the back streets of Liverpool. The Lever sales department at this time was sited in grand wood-panelled offices in the Port Sunlight factory, where the rooms of senior managers had en-suite facilities (to get the smell of soap off their hands and to enable women clerks to dry their tears after being verbally humiliated).

Once again Dawn changed schools in a hurry, taking any slum school she could find, and when we learned that much of Chester was being demolished to make room for a through-way, we resolved to live nearer to both Port Sunlight and Ernie and Millie, who welcomed us back to Scouseland with open arms. Because we loved the sea we found an unfurnished flat 100 yards from the promenade in New Brighton; it boasted a secure parking space and an unshared bathroom, and we filled it with cheap furniture. The company had an agreement with the Inland Revenue that a transferred employee received a disturbance allowance (sufficient to replace all carpets and curtains), and we spent it on the basics for our three rooms. The most important item was a sofa that turned into a double bed and this meant we could have house guests. The first was Sarah who, of course, relegated us to the sofa, and she confessed that she had never been able to afford a flat even half as nice.

Although Keith's introductions produced no new friendships, we had a very busy social life in New Brighton at our own plebeian level. Old friends came to stay with us and we had innumerable double dates with Ernie and his latest girlfriend. When he found a new girlfriend he was quick to introduce her and seek our opinions. We visited pubs and clubs on Merseyside and spent days out on beaches in North Wales. Most Saturday evenings Dawn and I would dance at Quaintways. We were only a short walk from the New Brighton Pavilion, but the resident band there couldn't spell the word *beetle*, and all their music was rock and roll. We preferred the variety of music at the Chester ballroom, and enjoyed a cool drink on the Rows, or a stroll on the walls in the interval. When we confessed this to friends in later years, as we listened to the Fab Four's records, they wrote us off as hopeless romantics.

We also saw a lot of Ernie's mother Millie, who devoted considerable time to helping Dawn build up her culinary repertoire. Millie was an even better comedian than her son and when she took up the latest craze, called the Madison, she drew us into a different sort of dancing.

Dawn grew very fond of the children she taught from the slums of Birkenhead. One of her class was one of thirteen children, by ten different men, and when he was taken from his mother and placed in a council home we took him and his sister out at weekends. They were fabulous kids: we spoiled them and let them run wild, but they never cried, even after a bad fall. We used to feel embarrassed that when we collected them they were neat and tidy, and when we returned them they looked as if we had rolled them round the beach.

That summer we had, after three years of marriage, saved up enough money for a honeymoon, and we went to a quiet fishing village in Liguria for a fortnight. It had sand and rocks and mountains behind it, and was the ideal place for this purpose. I tried to practise my Italian, which sounded a bit too much like Latin, on the waiters. Each evening we would enquire in detail about what we were eating, and found that the meat was always *vitello*, even though it never tasted the same twice. That was where we began to appreciate the supreme value of sauces; and for lunch in the day we often climbed a hillside to a shady spot and picnicked on wine and peaches. We returned very brown, physically tired, and very happy.

Life seemed perfect, but then things got even better. Keith had put me forward for inclusion on a selection panel for a new job, ranked between area sales manager (JC 21) and regional manager (JC 24). Most regions appointed their most successful area manager to this job, but Maurice, with his ICS background, insisted one such post be kept for open competition between all the younger area managers. The region with no obvious area manager for promotion was Scotland (the largest geographically), and I competed with five area managers from other regions for the post in a day of relevant group tasks and discussions. I was expected to have an edge on knowledge of modern retailing, but I found that my experience leading a platoon up and down the Brecon Beacons also enabled me to fare well in discussions of motivation and leadership. Two days later I knew the job was mine and that I would start in the autumn.

Maurice's solution to Lever's overmanning problem was incredibly humane by twenty-first-century standards. Today, hundreds of people would have been fired (I detest the euphemism *let go*) overnight, and the remainder would have worked on in fear and resentment, leaving drugs, alcohol, and mental illness to accomplish the next downsizing. In the 1960s another British multinational, Beechams, head-hunted a new sales director (from P&G) to handle a similar merger, and he did so in the American way. Hundreds of salesmen were fired, and also half the people working in the sales-routine offices of the three subsidiaries involved. The result was that the management somehow lost all record of outstanding debts, and the merged company was reduced to writing to all its customers asking how much they owed.

This unprecedented move yielded a sum that was only a fraction of the sales recorded for the period. Millions of pounds were lost in this way and the new reduced and demoralised management's first task was to dig themselves out of a deep hole. Beecham's CEO began this recovery, admirably, by firing the ex-P&G sales director. Today, large audiences watch a TV programme where a celebrity bully fires photogenic young dreamers for failing to be entrepreneurs. The bully boasts that when he sees rubbish he fires someone. But the public would have been spared this theatre of humiliation if the bully had been fired when he produced a rubbish computer, or when he proved a rubbish football-club chairman. Unfortunately, a string of property deals after these two personal disasters, the man is a TV star and sits in Britain's unelected House of Lords. This shows that the benefits of not firing can be considerable.

In retrospect, I can see that Maurice understood something that twenty-first-century economists are only just beginning to realise. His study of economics, his knowledge of the differences between India and Europe, and the social conscience instilled by his religion combined to give him this insight. Maurice saw that the West's prosperity and the well-being of most of its people depended upon keeping men in employment and paying them well. Only this could produce long-term economic growth and allow women to raise their own children. This may sound sexist, but there is no reason why sexual partners should not exchange or share the roles of earner and carer once all their children are at school. And there is a great void in modern society where a caring industry should be meeting the needs of the sick, the handicapped, the old, and the orphaned. If mothers (of all sexes) owned and organised that industry and were well paid for it, the economy would benefit and one of society's biggest problems would be solved.

Maurice's way of handling overmanning also involved drastically reducing the number of territorial sales representatives (known as *reps* in the retail trade), and giving them the combined product list of the three companies to sell. But Maurice used time-and-motion-study experts so that each rep was given time to interfere with shelves and commandeer floor space for mass displays. This still left more than 100 of the three companies' reps without territories, but they were formed into regional merchandising teams, whose role was to install the Lever shelving plan in stores and thus give our brands the lion's share of detergent shelf space. The job of regional merchandising manager was to motivate all the reps so that they used that extra time productively, and to supervise the installation work of the merchandising team, or *merchandisers*.

The merchandising manager's task was a delicate one: he had to accompany area managers and help them persuade grocery head-office buyers to accept the shelving plan. He also had to motivate territorial reps to give priority to display-building and selling the Lever shelving plan in-store. And, finally, he had to ensure that his merchandisers always had a full day's work and did not feel like second-class citizens. This was a danger because they had to do lots of manual work, and their main task of installing new shelving plans was self-liquidating. Maurice planned to use early retirement so that the merchandisers replaced the older reps by the time Britain's shelves had been captured.

This sounds an elaborate and tortuous plan, but it worked, at least until British supermarket bosses themselves mastered the new art of store-wide merchandising. By the time I left Scotland almost all of its self-service stores had Lever shelving plans, and Lever's sales reps believed that good merchandising was essential to the future of their jobs. My ability to derive satisfaction from manual labour was undoubtedly an asset at this time, because if a manager could build a ten-foot-high display with a little store help, so could a rep. And Scots do not allow a Sassenach to outshine them at anything.

My new salary was almost £1,200 p.a., which was a very significant figure. At the end of my national service Dawn and I were earning just short of this sum between us, and we had agreed that when my salary exceeded our total we would start a family. We hoped then that it would take only four years, but in the event it took a little more than two. The job came with a very large car (a high-mileage Ford Consul, which I soon changed for a new Ford Zephyr), and another (far larger) disturbance allowance. Our first move was to abandon contraception and our second was to weigh the pros and cons of mortgages and rents. All my cohort were sufficiently middle class to want to own property, and they convinced us that a mortgage on a house would be cheaper than the rent of a flat.

I was nervous about going into debt, an evil I had spent my life avoiding, but we eventually saw it as the bank's owning our home and promising to gift it to us if we kept up with the rent for twenty-five years. Dawn, however, had a contract to teach in Birkenhead until Christmas, and so we would have to face being apart on weekdays that autumn. Ernie and Millie, who had become a second mother to Dawn, promised that she would not be short of company, and Keith told me that I would be so busy at first that leaving house-hunting until the New Year would be a sensible measure. With this vast saloon car to take me home to New Brighton each weekend, I felt confident that we would both survive the separation. And every weekend would be a honeymoon, as it had been so often in the past.

We proved to be good at making babies and very soon Dawn was pregnant, which made us happier than ever. Millie's advice and support became invaluable and Dawn bloomed, while I soon became used to a new routine. At 5 p.m. on Fridays I would begin my journey from Glasgow to New Brighton, and at five on Sundays start back again. There were no motorways yet, only a busy single carriageway, and it took me about four hours to get home on Friday and three to get back on Sunday. Dawn would go to bed at six on Fridays and set an alarm so as to be awake when I arrived. We crammed all our loving into forty-eight hours, as when I was in the army, and we felt that both the five days of waiting and the journey were worth it.

Although my weeks were spent travelling all over Scotland, Friday was a meeting day that always brought the region's management team to Glasgow, and so for three months we managed this schedule. But that was a diabolically cold winter (in 1962-63 hell almost certainly froze over) and the east side of Scotland was covered in snow for many months. Glasgow, in contrast, was cold but very wet, and somehow I was always able to get on the road home at five. But Merseyside was colder than Glasgow and Dawn soon found our water pipes frozen solid, so she could not take a bath and had to carry buckets of water every day from a standpipe. It proved a bad time to be pregnant and, to our great unhappiness, she lost the baby just as we began our move of home. Our furniture was going into storage and the company had booked us into a very comfortable hotel in Glasgow until we found a home.

Dawn was devastated by her loss, and I was in agony with her. Fortunately, Millie rallied round, and Dawn's gynaecologist urged her to try to conceive again as soon as possible. Ken, my boss in Scotland, gave me several days off after the move to make sure that Dawn was not alone, and our friends, and my colleagues at many levels, sent letters of sympathy and good wishes. Most importantly, Ken agreed with Maurice that no pressure would be put on us to move out until we had found a new permanent home. Thus it was that we lived in luxury in a posh hotel on the south side of Glasgow for the next five months. We were not trying to take advantage of the company's generosity, but the complications of the Scottish housing market were horrendous. Dawn, however, quickly recovered her health and high spirits under the influence of good Scottish food, and local goodwill.

Under Scottish law house ownership is exchanged with the aid, not of estate agents, but of attorneys, with all the delays and costs that lawyers can inflict. In my lifetime the USA became the first nation to boast a million lawyers, which led to the conundrum: 'What do you call a thousand lawyers at the bottom of the sea?' The answer was: 'A good start.' Scotland's lawyers ensured that a system of legally binding sealed bids deterred mortgage companies, frustrated both vendors and buyers, and made every sale a game of roulette.

In desperation we bought a new three-bedroomed house on a private estate in Bishopbriggs, just north of the city, and waited for the builder to finish building it. The house that Jock built was, as always, well behind schedule, and we waited until the beginning of June 1963 to move into our new home. In that time we enjoyed our hotel's good Scottish food and I learned to enjoy good Scotch whisky, of which there were many brands in all Scottish bars. These bars are more businesslike than English pubs: they put intoxication before ambience, but the goodwill flows as freely as the ale and spirits.

Most sales managers love to drink, tell crude jokes, and laugh at the world around them, and I rapidly became on good terms with all my colleagues. Ken, my boss, was a man in his fifties, who was wise, generous, and hospitable; and the three area managers were much older men who lost any resentment at my promotion when they discovered that I valued their experience and would heed their advice. I learned a great deal about Scotland and its retail trade from them, about individual salesmen and buyers, about our competitor's sales methods, and about life in general.

These men taught me how to value single malt above blended and how to drink Scotch with a little water ('for the hail'). They taught me how to avoid snow-blocked roads and keep a spade in the boot of my car to dig myself out, and a bottle of malt in case I couldn't. They taught me how to pronounce names like *Dalziel* and to recognise unique Scottish terms (I had no idea what *neeps* were and guessed that a *gigot* was a dance). But I was twenty-five years old, and the only members of the Scottish sales force who were within ten years of my age were my merchandising team, chosen for being the youngest and fittest of an old bunch. The two with whom I became closest were Alistair, who became our friend and neighbour, and Harry, whose game of tennis was just a bit too good for mine. His wife Lilian was as warm and welcoming as he was, and Alistair's wife Dorothy took over Millie's role of adviser to a first-time expectant mother. My friendship with both men lasted until Lilian and Dorothy became widows many years later.

Dawn soon recovered her health completely, and by Easter she wanted to resume her career. As usual the only schools with vacancies at short notice were in slum areas, and she got a job in a school in the delightfully named suburb of Springburn. She found teaching in Scotland both bad news and good: the bad news was that Scottish education is so superior to English that her qualifications weren't recognised; the good news was that an unqualified teacher in Scotland was paid as much as a qualified teacher in England. Dawn's only problem was that she couldn't understand what the children in her class were saying and they couldn't understand her. Since it took her only three weeks to master the local tongue, I guess that both parties were speaking sorts of English. (What we now call Scots was called Ynglis until the number of Gaelic speakers dwindled.)

Dawn immediately found evidence of Scottish educational superiority: at college she had been taught that children with IQs below 85 cannot be taught to read, but in her new school many bairns with IQs around 80 could read very well. She began to suspect that IQ tests have a hidden class bias, although I wondered if the strap she was given for discipline wasn't part of the reason for superior Scottish literacy. (I have also known many Irishmen who were excellent scholars, which they attributed to the regular beatings the Christian Brothers had given them at school.) Dawn believed that slum kids were more spontaneous and exuberant than posh ones, and she loved teaching them. She refused to use the strap she had been given for discipline, and her colleagues were surprised how well behaved her charges remained.

At weekends Dawn and I visited as many of Scotland's beauty spots as we could, and they are many; we both learned to love the country, from the lochs of the west to the snow-capped peaks of the east, from the warm sea in Ayrshire to the icy waters of Aberdeen, and from the gritty humour of Glasgow to the haughty heights of Edinburgh. We believed that Scotland was indeed 'God's ain country', and when we moved into our first house we even bought a tartan carpet for the stairs. In the room above them Dawn conceived again, probably on our first night in this new home, and in celebration we chose a Scottish name for our son. We enjoyed Scotland, like life itself, and thereafter I described myself as 'Londoner by birth, Provincial by education, and Scotch by consumption' (*whisky* is 'the water of life').

In 1963 we experienced a typical Scottish summer, which left our two most important guests with contrasting views of the country's climate. Compared with England, Scotland is quite large and very empty (its population is much smaller than London's), and it has so many beauty spots: mountains and moors, burns and lochs, rocks and beaches, and fine and proud historic cities. In July Sarah came to stay with us for a week in which the sun never stopped shining; she thought Scotland a paradise. In July Vic and Adrienne came up and we planned a fortnight's tour of the north west, the highlands and islands that I hadn't explored because they hold so few shops. Our friends, unfortunately, saw Scotland at its worst.

It began raining as we left Loch Lomond (our nearest beauty spot) and it didn't stop for one second in the next week. Visibility was close to zero and to give the windscreen wipers a rest we trudged up a few hillsides in Wellington boots, but we didn't linger. We stayed in B&Bs and stopped for large meals, which we ate slowly, because we were getting way ahead of schedule despite the difficulty of distinguishing roads from rivers. Our planned destination was Skye, but when we reached the Kyle of Lochalsh we couldn't see the end of the ferry pier, let alone an island. The radio weather forecast predicted more heavy rain for the following week in the north west and intermittent showers elsewhere in Scotland. By that time we were feeling overfed, under-exercised, and depressed. But, filling in time in our B&B, Vic found an ad for Butlins holiday camp way down in Ayrshire.

From the ruins of our aristocratic grand tour we saw a plebeian solution: we phoned Butlins, booked two chalets for a week, and sped south towards better weather. It was dry when we reached Ayr and that week it rained only occasionally, and we threw ourselves into making use of all the facilities: we spent our days on the tennis courts, table-tennis tables, and roller-skating rink, or in the heated swimming pool where Vic and Adrienne did rapid lengths while Dawn and I thrashed about or floated lazily. The two wives even went horse riding on the beach, which was very brave of my pregnant darling, and she looked wonderful on all this exercise. For the evenings there was a dance hall, where we danced and jived after watching a show to better digest our meal. The food was edible (we were always ready for it) and the beds were comfortable.

The only drawback was being woken early to a loud chorus of Zippadee-doo-dah. The chalet walls were thin and when we began to greet this with loud groans and screams the other campers thought we were having sex. There is much to be said for plebeian holidays, and I'm sure many grand tours have been miserable (especially if you were travelling with show-offs like Byron or Shelley). But we had a great time in great company, and when we all returned to work we felt that we had really had a holiday. The saddest part of it was telling Vic and Adrienne that we wouldn't be seeing them again for two years, because something exciting had happened on my twenty-sixth birthday.

Glasgow's centre is described up Buchie, down Saughie, and along Argyle, and the Lever regional sales office was on the first of those streets. On 30 July 1963 I was sitting in my office trying to compose a circular when I received an unexpected phone call from Reg, Maurice's deputy. 'Two things,' said Reg, 'Happy birthday, and would you like to spend the next two years in India?' His cheerful Cockney voice continued: 'Don't reply immediately, go home and discuss it with

Dawn. Phone me back at four p.m., and tell me what the two of you have decided.' This call was typical of Reg's cheek and of his warmth and talent for friendship; he was soon to retire, but those qualities had made him one of the best salesmen in the country.

I promised to phone Reg back and, since Dawn's school had just broken up for the summer, I went straight home for a council of war. Our first priority was the expected baby and we rang a colleague who had worked in Bombay to discover that there was an excellent maternity hospital next to Bombay's European swimming club. I checked with Sarah, who was very good at letting go, and she confirmed that she would be happy with whatever we wanted. Dawn said she had never felt healthier in her life and she was ready for new adventures. She felt that marrying a penniless soldier had been a bigger risk and she wasn't afraid of change. So I rang Reg back to say that we were very interested, but wanted to know a bit more about it before finally accepting. This seemed to be exactly what Reg was expecting and he closed the sale on that basis.

The deal had been brokered by Maurice with his old friend Prakash, who was chairman of Hindustan Lever. I would do a two-year exchange of jobs with an Indian brand manager named Narayanan, who came from Madras. He was a physicist with an excellent mind, and he was seen as a high-flyer (he eventually flew as high as Chairman of Ponds). I would maintain my job class and salary, but I would also receive a very large overseas allowance and a hefty final gratuity. My holiday entitlement would be seventeen days' local leave during the two years, and four months' leave when I returned to the UK. We would be found a flat in Bombay, for which I would pay only ten percent of my salary. The company would pay for our personal possessions to be shipped to Bombay and for our furniture to be stored in our absence. They would also take responsibility for selling our Scottish house. It was a generous package and we took it.

Our knowledge of India at that time came from the *Kama Sutra* and the *Ananga Ranga*, which had long been among our bedside reading, but we now read everything about the subcontinent that we could get our hands on. Maurice's wife had written a book called *India Changes*, which was an excellent introduction, and we managed to see Satyajit Ray's *Apu Trilogy* at an arty-crafty cinema in Edinburgh. We were soon bursting with enthusiasm and disappointed that it then took three months for my Indian work permit to come through. Unilever usually obtained work permits for more senior managers by arguing that they had skills not available in India, but Narayanan clearly had comparable skills to mine. Only when his UK appointment letter (plus some rupee notes) was waved under an Indian government nose did the word *exchange* sink in, and my permit arrived in October.

In the interval we had armfuls of jabs and a tropical kit allowance to spend. A manager who had recently returned from India advised us to wear nothing but cotton (which was sensible, given Bombay's heat and humidity). He also told us that outwardly the Hindus we met would be puritans, but that the *Kama Sutra* would lurk not far below, and he advised Dawn to take two years' supply of tampons because they were like gold dust in India. Because of her condition Dawn ignored this advice, and we thereby lost a great profit opportunity. Buying cotton clothes in an English autumn was very difficult in the days before cheap foreign holidays, but we found some at last in the West End, when we went down to Unilever House for our jabs. As we drove the 300 miles back to Glasgow our arms grew more and more painful, and we completed the journey only by my holding the steering wheel with my good arm while Dawn changed gears with hers. This is what the King James Bible meant by a 'helpmate' (or *help meet*).

Our last, and best, chance to learn more about India was when Maurice invited us to dinner in his Knightsbridge service flat. There were just six of us and, unfortunately, the other guests were a politician and her philosopher husband, and a BBC man and his wife. The politician talked non-stop for three hours about her recent trip to

Rhodesia and addressed everything she said to the media man. He tried vainly to change the subject and include the other guests in the conversation but she was unrelenting. The only other person to get a word in all evening was her husband, who corrected her logic on a couple of occasions. It was easy to see that the marriage wouldn't last, because he was all mind and she was all mouth. So we didn't get to learn more about India, but we did learn to keep well away from Rhodesia and avoid politicians like the plague.

In November we flew to Bombay via Athens and Cairo, and we took a week's holiday in Attica. Fresh from Scotland, we wore lightweight clothing while the Athenians were in overcoats; we kept one another warm. We admired the Acropolis, watched the sun set over Sounion, solved the mysteries of Eleusis, and searched for ruins on Aegina; we moved among the ghosts of gods and goddesses and were suitably ecstatic. We ate wonderful food in Piraeus and an old fisherman rowed us around what was then the *Tourkolimano*. He had a weathered face and a permanent smile, and I tried to engage him in conversation. He found my Ancient Greek hilarious and I found his Modern tongue almost impossible to follow because [*b*] had become [*v*], many phonemes had turned into [*iː*], and stress had appeared from somewhere. The old man said that Dawn looked Greek, and I told him that she was good and beautiful (καλή και 'αγαθή) like the sea.

The flight was smooth, we stopped in Cairo only for long enough to have a cold drink with ice in it, which gave us both diarrhoea, and we arrived in Bombay at just after half-past four in the morning.

15

HEAT

'Welcome to Bombay; local time is four-thirty-five a.m. and ground temperature is twenty-eight degrees centigrade,' said the disembodied voice. 'You may now unfasten your seatbelts; please collect your hand baggage and wait for the doors to be opened.' When we stepped onto the tarmac of Bombay's Santa Cruz airport the dark air almost knocked us over: it felt hot and slightly damp and was filled with strange perfumes. There were sweet and heady fragrances, of exotic flowers, of spices, and of pine-cones, and there was the smell of yesterday's warm sun, of sweat, and urine, and even a hint of faeces. As we became used to the smell, it faded slightly and, still half asleep, we trudged to the terminal, a dark silhouette shaped like an aircraft hangar, which indeed it had once been. It looked as if it hadn't been painted or repaired since the British left sixteen years ago.

Entering the building was another shock: the reception area contained an ocean of humanity beneath a sky of creaking fans. Hordes of short, brown men in brown uniforms were shouting, gesturing, and darting from one counter to another, and a mass of anxious faces competed for their attention. As we waited for our luggage I realised that one shining, smiling face was familiar: the broad features of my

Mysorean friend Surindra, who had been attached the previous year to Keith's department in Port Sunlight. He waved vigorously and we waved back, and the brown uniforms parted and allowed us to join him and pump his hand. Surindra said that he had come to get us through customs. It might take an hour, he said, but alone we might have taken five. He slipped notes surreptitiously into several hands as our cases were identified and opened by the customs men. After the briefest of questionings they were closed again and we were waved through the barriers.

Just beyond the barriers two men blocked our way, one with a notebook and the other a large camera. They said they were from *Bombay Life* and they did their job; it was five in the morning and we were dog-tired, but we tried to smile. We asked whether the airport was short of celebrities that night and Surindra said that Hindustan Lever (always called HLL) was a celebrity, the largest private company in India, and that *Bombay Life's* readers wouldn't know how unimportant a brand manager was. At the airport Dawn and I couldn't help noticing that most of the passengers were men, as were most of the employees. We began to wonder where all the women were.

We both found the long drive from the airport to the city a disturbing experience; the car wasn't air-conditioned, and two of its windows were partly open. The first few miles were through the gigantic slum that surrounds the airport; makeshift wooden, corrugated-iron, and canvas shelters rising from the sewage-filled swamps. The sounds, smells, and sights of the dirty, half-naked, and half-starved slum-dwellers battered our senses and left us feeling exhausted. There were lights everywhere, and the entire city seemed to be awake at an hour that could have been called ungodly if we hadn't seen so many lurid images of gods. We felt relief when the slums gave way to shabby streets and then more dignified buildings, some with high-walled gardens and guards on the gate (whom Surindra called *chowkidars*).

Surindra took us to the West End Hotel, near the centre of the city, and helped us book in. This was a run-down, second-rate establishment that had been built under the British Raj. Here we caught up on sleep, got used to the heat, and went for a walk in the evening when it wasn't so hot. But as we left the hotel the heat still bounced from the cracked and filthy pavements and I had to stop to get my breath. The scene was bewildering. Bombay life seemed to be lived on at least two different levels: at eye level and at pavement level, and the two levels of human being interacted only by cursing one another when their paths crossed. Among those squatting on the pavement dogs sniffed and excreted, and flocks of ugly crows scavenged and cawed. There were piles of filth everywhere.

But there were also women, and I marvelled at how such elegant women picked their way among the squatters and the filth. These women wore saris, or dresses, or the blouses and bloomers that are called *salwar kameez*. Many people wore white, but still more wore colours so bright that no European would dare to don them. I suddenly realised what was the strangest aspect of Bombay's streets: in Europe almost everyone wears the same type of dress; in India people wear every type, and sometimes none at all: the women ignored the naked *sadhus*, old men with pot bellies and limp penises, as readily as they did other strangers. Our senses overcome by the experience, we returned to the hotel and retired to bed.

At eight the next morning Surindra arrived to take me into my first day's work by taxi. We were driven to a new part of the city, not long reclaimed from the sea. Here there were government buildings and office blocks and it could have been any European city, except for the strange array of vehicles that formed the traffic jams around us. There were cars, usually old and battered, and those that were relatively new were of three makes, the only ones manufactured in India. The most battered vehicles were the yellow-roofed taxis, which I soon discovered were unbelievably cheap; I also noted that Bombay drivers used both sides of the road at random. It did not take me long to decide not to run a car of my own: it would be cheaper and less stressful to be driven.

Smoke rose from the queue of ancient lorries, which made life unpleasant for the bullocks and men pulling carts around them. There were two-wheeled vehicles of every sort and even the bicycles carried passengers, some of whom were women in saris with loads upon their heads. We arrived and I found that HLL House was a very modern office block, six storeys high, in a broad street mostly flanked by government offices. Inside, it was spacious and rather bare; but it was extremely clean and the lifts worked.

I was shown to the office I was to share, and introduced to my co-tenant. Vinoo was a quiet middle-aged man with a friendly smile, and he was responsible for departmental administration. We were to work alongside one another cheerfully for a year without ever really understanding what the other did. I received another shock when I was introduced to my secretarial help. One of an HLL director's perks was a female secretary, but it was male *stenos* who served managers as gofers and provided their shorthand and typing services. This was because in India most graduates can't get better jobs and most parents don't trust their daughters with strange men. Vinoo and I shared the services of a small Goan named Alfie and he was safe with both of us. Alfie wore the vestigial beard affected by Portuguese grandees; he was polite and efficient and played a good game of table tennis.

HLL was a gigantic business: in the UK Unilever owned dozens of separate operating companies, but in India one integrated organisation marketed all the group's products. It did this through three divisions, each with its own marketing controller: Food Division's main business was cooking fat, and its *Dalda* brand served ordinary Indian families as a cheaper substitute for *ghee*, the clarified butter that gave the rich heart disease (*Dalda* was also less perishable because it was sold in tins). The division's less important products included frozen vegetables and cattle feed, and it was eyeing India's largest ice- cream company, which seemed ripe for takeover.

HLL's Soaps Division had the lion's share of both the clothes and personal washing market: *Sunlight* and *Lifebuoy* bar soaps each sold tens of thousands of tons, *Lux* was the favourite beauty bar of the middle classes, and the powder *Surf* was growing fast in India's cities. Fortunately for this division, P&G did not yet operate in India because it heeded the Pentagon's warning that Nehru's India was a *quasi-communist* state. HLL's main competition was therefore cheap sodium-silicate-filled bars, made locally, and imitation products. (Local crooks put the crudest bar soap in look-alike packaging with names like *Fux*, and filled packets with names like *Skurf* with powdered chalk.) The Indian consumer had good cause to be wary, and HLL's brands were a haven of reliability, just as Billy Lever's had been in nineteenth-century England.

Colgate and Ponds did operate in India, and very successfully, which made it tougher for HLL's Toilet Preps Division. Their most profitable brand was *Himalaya Bouquet*, a talc that poorer people rubbed into their faces to lighten their skin, some creams that were used for the same purpose, and *Pepsodent*, a toothpaste that suffered from being based on chalk, while *Colgate* dentifrice was based on dicalcium phosphate, which tastes better.

I was placed in Toilet Preps Division and my job was to get two new brands on the market: *Sunsilk* shampoo, which was a major brand in the UK, and *Erasmic* razor blades, which were very successful in France. Since both were still on the drawing board in India, my responsibilities were boosted by *Pears* transparent soap and *Pears* talcum powder, both of which were widely believed to lighten the skin. Skin colour was enormously important in India, where the population results from the intermarriage of light-skinned Aryan and Mongol invaders with dark-skinned Dravidian serfs. My skin soon became darker than that of any of my colleagues because I sought the sun and they shunned it. And Dawn had such a magnificent suntan that our friends teased her, saying that she was beginning to look like a *Dalit* (untouchable), and advising her to cover up. Since I loved her skin best when it was the colour of well-cooked shrimp I urged her against this.

Dawn spent many hours at Bombay's European swimming club, which had a wonderful open-air pool next to the sea (in contrast, the nearby Hindu swimming club boasted an excellent indoor one). All but two of my close friends in Bombay were Indian, and I tried to persuade each of them in turn to become my guest at the European club. But years of exclusion by the Brits of the Raj made this beneath an Indian's dignity, and my friend from Ghana and his wife were so harassed on the streets of Bombay that they accepted only invitations to people's homes. Since black GIs had been my wartime heroes, I was delighted that crowds of protesters against its *kala bar* eventually forced the European club to open its doors to all races. (*Kala* is Hindi for black.)

My boss *Krishna* was the Marketing Controller of Toilet Preps Division; he was a South Indian who had finished his education in the USA with a doctorate in development economics. Krishna was a Dalit who had achieved everything by scholarships, and he was very bright, enthusiastic, and ambitious to the point of marrying an American wife. Once in India, like most Americans, she was horrified by the shortage of air-conditioning and the primitive plumbing, and she left Krishna with two small children. The script had run just like the story of David and Bathsheba: Krishna had been general sales manager at the time, and his British boss sent him off to distant markets while he bedded the American wife. After the two lovers left for the UK Krishna had been promoted to a post where he could see more of his children, and he was now as wrapped up in his job as ever. In fact he was a workaholic and he volunteered to take on additional governmental responsibilities. The first was for the national birth-control advertising campaign, from which we nicknamed him *Krishna Pessarywala*.

Krishna's boss was now an Englishman named Doug, a man in his forties of great sensitivity and shrewd judgement. His wife Margaret was an angel, and they had four children, of whom the only boy was at boarding school in England (at Unilever's expense). Eventually Doug persuaded Unilever to find him a British posting and the family was reunited. Margaret took Dawn under her wing and introduced her to life in Bombay, and for a woman expecting a baby Margaret was an invaluable source of advice on everything. One of the many good things about my retirement party, more than thirty years later, was that Doug attended; he leaned on a walking stick, but he was the same cheerful, observant, witty man who had guided my career in India. I was proud to number him among my lifelong friends

Doug's boss, the chairman, was Prakash, a Punjabi who was an author as well as a businessman, and who had a Swedish wife. Prakash managed to combine success as a businessman with being a loyal supporter of his government. Inevitably, he graduated from HLL to work on government and educational projects. As the boss in the boardroom Prakash was rather formidable, but as a guest in my home he was gracious and amusing. I addressed him as chairman in both places, out of respect, but he asked Dawn to call him Prakash.

He kept in touch with Indian reality by touring extensively and taking as much interest in bazaars as in new factories, and by holding a 'Prayer Meeting' every Tuesday morning to which his entire management team was invited. Managers who had been out of Bombay on business were asked to relate the most interesting things they had discovered. Prakash was brilliant at steering a discussion that was not of his own choosing and he promoted a learning culture. He was well aware of his government's foreign exchange problems and he coped well with the harsh rules against importing plant and raw materials. I could not have guessed that by the twenty-first century Unilever's international business would be under Indo-Dutch (instead of Anglo-Dutch) management, but I saw in Prakash the qualities that led to that outcome.

After a few days at the West End Hotel, Dawn and I moved into a spacious flat in a very expensive area of Bombay; it occupied the first floor of a mansion named Alhambra, and Doug and his family occupied the floor below us. This flat had two double bedrooms, two bathrooms, and a long room that divided into a dining room and lounge. When Margaret, who showed us around this flat, raised the question of servants, Dawn said she hoped she wouldn't need them. Then Margaret led us to the tiny airless kitchen, which had no mod cons, and Dawn thought again. The kitchen boasted servants' quarters, a small room with two bunks in it, a luxury that all our friends envied because their servants had to sleep on the landing or the stairway outside their flats.

Dawn agreed to hiring the minimum of servants, whom Margaret found for us; they were both Tamils: Shanku, a cook-bearer, and Taniskoti, a *hamal* or cleaner and dishwasher. Their wages totalled 180 rupees (£14 a month), and Margaret explained that foreigners always had to pay a premium for servants who could prepare Western as well as Indian food. I found it difficult to believe that a man could live on so little, until I learned that both servants sent money home to their families. The building also had a sweeper who cleaned all the bathrooms, a task below caste for our two. As our friends predicted, our cook, like many Indians, was a carrier of amoebic dysentery. Dawn proved to be as immune to its symptoms as Shanku, but I missed a trip to Rajasthan because of mine, and I was very glad to bid my amoebae farewell.

On my first day in HLL House I was taken to lunch by Soonoo, a chubby smiling man with a keen sense of humour, who managed *Pepsodent*. Prakash was a great admirer of Gandhi and Nehru, and so he would have none of the dining hierarchy found in Unilever's UK companies. Directors, managers, and all staff ate together in a large self-service restaurant. The cuisine was multi-regional Indian: there were meat dishes from the North and vegetarian ones from the South, a variety of curries but also plenty of blander dishes for overseas visitors. The drinks available included tea and the Indian drink known as *nimbu pani* (lemon water).

The disadvantage of this democracy was that Prakash might choose to sit at your table, but he was considerate enough to talk business only with managers. If he joined a non-management group, he would make small talk unless one of them raised a business issue. I don't know if he was really interested in everyone's opinion, but he listened to us all. The advantage of this democratic eating was far more obvious: it left space for a large games room, where older workers played *karom* (a cross between snooker and *Subbuteo*), and younger ones could play table tennis. After our meal Soonoo explained the rules of *karom* to me and we watched our steno Alfie thrash several opponents on the table-tennis table; when Alfie invited me to play I managed to beat him 2:1, and thus began a pleasing ritual that I followed whenever I was in head office: a twenty-minute lunch helped down by forty minutes of exercise.

When I handed over my bat on that first day, Soonoo observed that joining a sports club was obviously my second priority, but that getting a liquor permit must be the first. I agreed to let him help me do both at five that evening when the air conditioning was shut off and everyone went home. Diligent senior staff who wanted to extend their working day could arrive at six in the morning, but our evenings were our own. To my chagrin our Saturday mornings weren't: the air conditioning was on from six until midday, and attendance was compulsory.

During the Raj the Brits had made the club one of the bastions of civilised life, and India's ruling elite embraced this custom, so HLL paid the subscription to a club for each of its managers. Directors' choices were the Willingdon, which had a golf course, and the Yacht Club, which had a marina, while most younger managers joined the Bombay Gymkhana, which, as its name suggests, was a gym with *khana* (Hindi for food, and very like the Latin *cena*). The Gym, as the club was known, had numerous tennis, squash, and badminton courts with a team of professional coaches called *markers*.

It was widely believed that regular exercise promoted health in India's testing climate, and I was delighted by the opportunity to play sport on at least a couple of evenings every week. In my first weeks I sought opponents for tennis but found that those of my colleagues who played regularly were far too strong: expert coaching and a perfect climate for nine months of the year had created a gap in standards that I couldn't hope to close in two years. Most of my Indian contemporaries, however, played squash or badminton to keep fit, and so I migrated to both those games; in Bombay I benefited greatly from some expert tuition in badminton and made visible progress.

In addition to clubs, India's elite believed that there was a second necessity for survival: alcohol. The Congress Party, on the other hand, were more concerned with the well-being of the masses: the only way they can live with low status and poverty is by praying or getting drunk. Since drunkenness leads to domestic and civil violence, India's new rulers preferred to lead them to religion, and they introduced laws against alcohol in a rather uneven fashion. Thus it was illegal to drink in Delhi only on Tuesdays, whereas in Bombay, where the chief minister was so religious that he drank his own urine, there was total prohibition. The result, as in the USA a generation earlier, was bootlegging and police corruption on a massive scale.

So dependent were the badly paid Bombay police on bribes from bootleggers that in the driest season they beat up people who tried to draw water from standpipes. This protected one of liquor's raw materials, but caused great misery and popular resentment. There was also no redress for the ordinary folk because the chief minister's son was one of the principal bootleggers. Nobody with a father who insisted that urine was healthy and delicious could be blamed for following such a career. As in all societies, however, measures were taken to ensure that an elite could escape the law. Those measures were liquor permits for registered alcoholics, and government-owned liquor shops that charged ridiculously high prices.

There were two ways you could become a registered alcoholic: the first was to have two doctors certify that you were incurably addicted; the second was to prove that you had been raised in an alcoholic country. I therefore only had to show our passports to a government official and Dawn and I became registered alcoholics. As such we were allowed twelve bottles of spirits or 144 bottles of beer a month. We never actually got through our allowance, because all our friends had reliable bootleggers, but the opportunity to become a real alcoholic was there. Fortunately, however, smuggled spirits cost the earth and the local whisky tasted like a cross between Scotch and methylated spirits. Nevertheless, I gradually acquired a taste for this mixture, which was as inebriating as the best single malt.

The drinking at the Bombay parties we attended was indeed frenetic, but this was because in the early days of prohibition a judge had ruled that empty bottles at a party did not constitute evidence against any one individual. Once a party had begun, therefore, it went on until there was no evidence left. At that point (usually around midnight) the hostess would serve the food and, after they had eaten, everyone would go home. We attended about three such parties a week and learned to balance eating and drinking in this way. And once every two or three weeks it would be our turn to be hosts. The spaciousness of our flat was a boon.

In Bombay Dawn and I found it easy to make Indian friends, and I got to know scarcely half a dozen of the city's 3,000 Brits. Dawn was on good terms with many she met at the European swimming club, but our best friends were almost all young managers in multinational companies or their spouses. We were surprised by how close we became to members of their social class: for example, Brahm's and Dayanand's fathers were industrialists, Soonoo's a judge, Jaspal's a general, Anil's a senior naval officer, and Arup's a top civil servant. What their CVs had in common was that most had attended the Doon School (India's Eton) and most had studied (usually overseas) to gain additional degrees. Foreign companies in India clearly had selection methods that favoured those who were very bright, very confident, and who spoke perfect English. I was thus a pleb among toffs, and our acceptance was a sort of intellectual compliment.

The group prided itself on its cosmopolitan outlook, but at our parties the men drank alcohol and smoked, while the women teased and flirted, but everyone joined in the conversation which ranged from local gossip to international politics, sex, art and religion. The men wore shirtsleeves and the women were arrayed in dazzling saris or crisp *salwar kameez*. Her friends taught Dawn to wear a sari: she went from swimsuit by day to sari in the evening, and she was very popular with both men and women. The men enjoyed my competition and the women my compliments, but at the end of the evening (and the booze), after we had eaten delicious curries, all the couples would re-form and go home to their own beds.

Some of my Indian friends' marriages were discreetly arranged by parents who kept introducing them to members of the right caste and opposite sex until they found one they really fancied. But others had rebelled and married partners that shocked: a Sikh manager had married a Muslim girl whose brother was a famous actor, a second Sikh had married a German girl during his stay abroad, a Muslim manager had married a South Indian Christian, a Southern Christian manager had married a Bengali Hindu girl, and a Hindu manager had a Parsi girlfriend who was preparing to shock her parents with an engagement announcement. All this was very different from the norm in Bombay, where the local newspapers were full of marriage ads: 'Female graduate seeks fair graduate of medium height; must be Shivite Brahmin.'

Although many of my friends' marriages must have involved them, dowries were largely the subject of jokes at our parties. Our conversation often touched upon whether arranged marriages were preferable to love marriages, and the speakers all had their personal viewpoint. I admitted that arranged marriages rarely ended in divorce (which was an unthinkable disgrace for women in India because the husband always won custody of the children), but pointed out that love marriages rarely ended with the mother-in-law pouring cooking fat over a childless bride and setting fire to her in her own kitchen. The debate usually ended in a draw, but many of my friends' marriages eventually broke up, regardless of whether they had an arranged element or not. They had chosen cosmopolitan lives and paid cosmopolitan penalties.

My chief regret about my stay in India was that it was scheduled for only two years and that I was immersed in English (which even taxi drivers spoke in Bombay). HLL paid for me to take Hindi lessons in my first year and Telugu lessons in my second. My Hindi *munshi* was an old and solemn Sindhi who lectured in philology; he earned more from HLL than from his teaching post at Bombay University. But on discovering my interest in his subject he taught me the basic grammars of Sanskrit, Hindi, and Urdu, plus a vocabulary that allowed me to appreciate the poems of Ghalib. The Urdu Shakespeare saw and sang the collapse of his culture, and in his lines beginning *'Ishq ne Ghalib nikamma kar diiya* he caught one of my favourite moods:

> Love has robbed me of all my force and pith,
> Else I had been a man to be reckoned with.

Translations of Ghalib were among my first published poems, and he caught another of my moods in his lines beginning *Ghalib, chhutti sharab*:

> I have promised to keep away
> From the cups of my delight,
> But I take the odd draught on a cloudy day,
> And a sip on a moonlit night.

My dilettantism prevented me from achieving conversational fluency in any Indian language, but I learned three different scripts (the *devanagri* of Hindu India, the *nashtaliq* derived from Arabic, and the spidery script of the Andhras), and I developed a fascination with comparative linguistics that has lasted to this day.

In my first months with HLL I was underemployed, so I visited factories, labs, sales offices, and advertising agencies, always trying to ask the right questions and to suspend judgement. I also toured bazaars extensively in four Northern and three Southern states (India at that time comprised sixteen linguistic states, most of them larger than the UK). I was amazed and humbled by the size of the country, the variety of its cultures, and the energy of its people. My tours also enabled me to visit Agra's Taj Mahal, Delhi's Red Fort, many temples and mosques, and the ruins of cities that were ruins when London was first built. The longest distances I travelled by air, but I much preferred travelling by train. India's railway system is vast, and it carries all human (and much animal) life; it is the proudest achievement of the British Raj, and in 1963 its most elegant monument was Bombay's Victoria Station.

Indian stations are always packed with people before and after a train arrives; and when trains disgorge their sardine-packed passengers they are still more crowded, and their mass heaves more. Since every departure and arrival involves a whole family, threading through the crowd and finding your seat is an adventure in itself, one impeded as much as helped by the army of red-turbaned porters trying to keep track of the owners of the bags on their heads. Magnificent steam engines drew the packed carriages in 1963 and insanitary, but delicious, food was hawked aggressively on every station. Once aboard, the varied scenery of a vast continent provided entertainment, and fascinating strangers provided company. The book, but not the racist film, *Bhowani Junction*, always brings back to me the thrill of rail travel in India.

One of the most interesting companions of my travels was Anil, who, as a Bengali, saw Calcutta through different eyes; to me it resembled a bigger, dirtier Birkenhead with cows. Another was Soonoo, who showed me the depths to which the Buddha's sacred state of Bihar has sunk, and who explained the columns of half-moons beside the railway tracks each morning (nursery training in India is about when, not where, to excrete). A third companion was Jagdish, Krishna's deputy, who introduced me to the steaming South, with its jungles, beaches, waterways, and temples. In Southern cities brightly coloured figures fill the streets, and turn to stone as they climb the towering *gopurams* (ornamental gateways) of temples. At the time, their message seemed to be that nothing changes, but Southern Indian cities now challenge Silicon Valley for the title cyber-capital of the world.

In later months I was kept busy by my brands, when my new product launches moved off the drawing board into reality, and by the latest initiative from Unilever House in London. The latter involved the writing of *strategy documents*: marketing strategies, brand strategies, advertising strategies, and distribution strategies. I was the person who knew least about the markets of India, but the one who wrote the clearest and most concise English, and so I produced a series of these, not only for my own brands, but also for those of other managers.

Of my own brands, *Pears* caused me least work, because its advertising budget was small and its campaign well established. My chief tasks on *Pears* consisted of replying to consumer queries, and liaising between the sales force and the factory so that production levels matched projected sales. The brand's consumers were divided between those who complained that *Pears* soap didn't lighten their skin and those who confirmed that it did. The former I advised to try the combined use of *Pears Soap* and *Pears Talcum Powder*; the latter usually sent in a hundred wrappers to claim an encyclopaedia that was out of print (it was an offer that had long expired); I sent these loyal consumers a free sample of both soap and face powder, recommending that they keep out of the sun.

My factory visits were always tussles with the Calcutta factory's manager, a diminutive and uncharitable Christian who was a devotee of Mother Teresa. On one occasion he certainly had good cause to be bad-tempered. *Pears* soap's transparency is the result of saponifying it in an alcohol medium and allowing the alcohol to evaporate slowly. For this process, denatured ethyl alcohol was used, which was simply sugar spirit rendered foul-tasting by unpleasant chemicals. On this occasion, we in the marketing department were convinced that if the factory changed the medium to benzine it would save many rupees per tonne. So we carried out an experiment on a test batch, and the following morning five men from the factory's night shift were found dead by the incoming workers. The victims had become connoisseurs of denatured alcohol and had taken their usual tipple from the test vat. Negotiations with the HLL union led to the return to denatured alcohol and the sacrifice of the potential savings.

In early 1964 I readied my two new products for test market, and *Sunsilk* shampoo was the more exciting of these. Indian women like to wash their hair every day, so the Indian shampoo market should have been the biggest in the world. But it was actually tiny, and it consisted mainly of poor, cheap products made from coconut oil, which was traditionally believed to strengthen the hair. Most Indians used either ordinary soap, the alkalinity of which damaged hair, or a natural product called soap-nut, which lathered poorly. HLL aimed to alter this with the aid of India's biggest ad agency and the latest shampoo formulation that Western laboratories could produce. It sounded easy, but there were a thousand complications, such as obtaining decent bottles and finding a local chemical company that could produce the active ingredient and the perfume. When the search for a local perfume proved unproductive, HLL had to get a temporary import licence from the government, which was a slow, frustrating, and expensive business.

In the summer of 1964 local *Sunsilk* bottles at last reached quality-control standards, the vacuum-packing machines were now working to capacity, and the imported perfume was proving stable. But unfortunately the perfume import licences that the government granted HLL could not supply the entire Indian market, so to minimise transport costs HLL decided to launch *Sunsilk* only in the quarter of the country nearest Calcutta. We planned to wait for a local perfume supplier to be developed, so that the brand could be extended nationally, but our market calculations were upset by Indian entrepreneurship. So popular was the brand in test market that wholesalers from other parts of the country swooped on Calcutta and bought up all the stock of *Sunsilk* they could. I left my successor to calculate how much the brand would sell if supplies were ever sufficient for national distribution.

HLL was also embarrassed by the success of its razor blades. A razor blade in the West shaved smoothly for as many as twenty shaves, whereas an Indian razor blade gave scarcely one good shave. This was because Western manufacturers gave their blades an electrolytic coating: Gillette coated carbon steel with Teflon, and Wilkinson, to outflank Gillette's patent, coated stainless steel similarly. Then one of Unilever's French companies outflanked them both by coating carbon steel blades with soap, which was much cheaper. Neither Gillette nor Wilkinson could manufacture in India because the government would not allow them to import Teflon (in its wisdom, the Indian government allowed unlimited imports only of books and contraceptives). The way seemed open for HLL to launch Unilever's French product, but carbon steel also required a licence, granted only to small-scale Indian industry for political reasons.

HLL circumvented this problem by going into partnership with a small Indian razor-blade manufacturer near Delhi, and we hoped that when his sales rocketed the government would reward him with far bigger import quotas. In 1964 market leadership by value in razor blades belonged to the absent *Gillette*: millions of their blades could be packed into a small boat, and smugglers sold them at a premium of 1,000 per cent over Indian blades. Since the Indian government lost tax on this vast sale of smuggled goods, it was very much in the economy's interests to develop the market as HLL wanted. But there were two sets of people bribing the government officials concerned: all other Indian blade manufacturers and the smugglers. HLL had only a 'Delhi Director' who visited Bombay for board meetings and whose activities were strictly secret.

My job was to launch HLL blades into two test towns in North India with local press and poster advertising. The campaign chosen described *Erasmic* as 'the silk edge blade' and the ads featured Europeans using the product; it was a deliberately unsubtle campaign and the ads tested well. We also had to find the best way of dealing with the manufacturer's quality-control problems, because his electrolytic coating process was inconsistent: some blades were perfectly coated, others unevenly so. The latter could not be reprocessed and the French company simply destroyed them, but this was India and import licences were like gold dust. So we launched a cheaper brand called *Taj* ('Crown') to sell the rejects, and it was given minimal advertising (theme: 'from the makers of *Erasmic* blades') to make sure its sales were profitable.

When we launched, both blades were runaway successes and production could not keep up with sales. This was because entrepreneurs from all over India sent lorries to the two test towns to pick up blades and sell them in other parts of the country at a premium. So our test market proved useless for the purpose of calculating how much we could sell if we launched nationally, but we still had a case for the government to give us licences for much greater quantities of carbon steel, and for new machine tools. To our dismay the government made this expansion conditional upon our selling our share of the blades business to our local partner, so that it would be a 100 per cent Indian enterprise. The two sets of people bribing the relevant officials had probably grown to three. But that was India, and HLL bowed out gracefully, like the league of gentlemen we were.

I became even more cynical about the farce that Indians called a mixed economy when Nehru, India's Augustus, died, and he was succeeded by the urine-drinking Morarji Desai from Bombay. The best minds in India weren't running the country, because they hadn't served terms in a British jail; they were either busy selling soap, cooking fat, and toothpaste, or they were building vast criminal gangs and running a separate 'black' economy that made huge profits and ripped off consumers. Marxism had never appealed to me, as it had to Nehru, and I saw its deep faults as clearly as I did those of unbridled capitalism.

It was easy for me to bear HLL's disappointments because of a wonderful event at home: I became a father. Unto us a child was born, making 7 April a second Christmas for the rest of our lives. Dawn looked beautiful and stayed fit throughout her pregnancy, and when she became overdue she engaged in strenuous exercise, which was meant to help, until her contractions began. She was given a light and clean room in Breach Candy hospital with a window overlooking the sea, and she pushed a nine-pound baby boy into the world. We called him Mark, because it can't be shortened, and Andrew in gratitude to Scotland, and I and my friends surrounded his triumphant mother with flowers. The scent of tuberoses always reminds me of hospitals, and Dawn, tired but radiant, and the sun, and the sea.

The hospital was very solicitous of mothers but rather cruel to fathers. The latter were not allowed to be present at the birth, because an American had been watching when his wife had complications, and he had tried to interfere (a national failing). Mothers were ensured a peaceful sleep by having their babies taken from them and kept together in a room with oxygen on hand. Dawn watched anxiously to make sure that Mark was correctly labelled and I was allowed to see him only through a glass wall. I was sure that the nurse held up a different baby each time I visited, but I comforted myself that at least they were all perfectly formed.

To compensate for this separation, all hours were visiting hours, and HLL gave me time off to spend with Dawn. Many of our friends arrived, too, with bouquets, kisses, and congratulations, but she was delighted to bring the baby home to Alhambra, where even more friends came to admire him. I think the nurses handed over the best of the perfectly formed babies I had been shown, so my patience was rewarded.

Women are programmed to love babies, and men programmed to love women (or so the scientists who measure brain activity say). Both find common cause only in cherishing the soft bundle of genes that are intertwined as tightly as a man's and a woman's bodies at the moment of conception. Dawn and I would never be one another's all again, but we now had a shared stake in the species. Animalcules that had met in the confluence of our juices would walk the earth as humans and feel the overwhelming desire to repeat the same pattern. Bombay, which religious fascists have now given a new Hindu name, will live in our memories not as a place of heat and filth, but as our *Inn of the Sixth Happiness* (the happiness you wish yourself).

16

DUST

In Bombay the monsoon arrives in June: it rains heavily, often for days on end; the downpour floods roads, fills reservoirs, and brings relief to parched land. At the end of August the inhabitants of the city take garlands, and coconuts, and statues of their gods, and they throw them into the sea. The monsoon then ceases, and the city steams for a while before recovering its perfect climate. During the monsoon, buildings turn dark green, books and the contents of drawers get mildewed, and swimming pools become covered in green fungus. The last restricted Dawn's activities, but she found new ways of passing the time: she took up badminton, attended painting classes, gave Margaret's children piano lessons, and became quite proficient at chess. Dawn soon regained her energy and her figure, enhanced by breastfeeding, which she greatly enjoyed. She insisted on doing everything for Mark but wash clothes, for which we found an *ayah*, who also served as babysitter. So we were both busy and happy.

Dawn played chess with our new English neighbour Linda, whose husband Alan had arrived to take over HLL's cattle feed business. Alan was a few years older than I and more senior in the company, and he skilfully managed to socialise with both my age group of

Indian managers and Doug's yacht-club friends. Alan had read history at Cambridge before joining one of Unilever's animal foodstuffs companies. He and Linda, who came from a farming family, thus had country interests in common when they wed only shortly before coming out to Bombay. Alan was a keen cricketer and Linda became an expert at making cricket teas, so they knew many more Bombay Brits than we did. The only sport I shared with Alan was squash, at which he was by far the better player. But he found a good match in my friend Jaspal, and we all became firm friends.

Soon after the monsoon closed Doug summoned me to his office and announced that I was now ready to take over a sales area, and that it would be one in the larger and more profitable Soaps Division. He asked me to choose whether my area would be in the North or South, since he had two young area managers whom he wanted to give head office experience, one in each half of the country. I would simply change jobs for about a year with the manager of the area I chose, and the other would soon be found another opportunity.

I had learned on my travels that Northern India has winters with bitterly cold nights, while only hill stations in Southern India know what coolness is. At this stage Dawn and I had grown so accustomed to basking in Bombay's climate that we both opted for the latter. I had fond memories of the South, of Kerala, Karnataka, and Tamilnad: Jagdish had shown me jungles, waterways, beaches, and temples, and Rajni, HLL's market research controller, had taken me to a conference in Madras. She was a decade older than I, but also held a London degree (a doctorate in psychology); she and her husband, a nuclear chemist long resident in the USA, numbered among our friends. The Madras conference had somehow included a trip to the beach on the Bay of Bengal. I recalled the wind and the waves and research girls in bright saris, who spoke perfect English, and who giggled at my Hindi as we waded ankle-deep in the water.

Nothing could have been more different than the posting I received.

The linguistic state of Andhra Pradesh consisted of the lands formerly ruled by the Nizam of Hyderabad, once India's richest prince, and the districts he ceded to the Madras Presidency in order to gain Britain's goodwill. Andhra was 105,000 square miles in area (considerably larger than the UK) and by 1964 most of its population of forty million already lived in its towns and cities. The state capital was the largest of these: the twin cities of (old) Hyderabad and (new) Secunderabad boasted about two million people. The official language of Andhra was the Dravidian Telugu, but the Nizams had made sure that all posts of importance in their regime were held by Urdu-speaking Muslims, and these still constituted a large proportion of the population in the capital and the more westerly cities of the state.

Andhra boasted many types of terrain: thick jungles, steep hills, stony deserts, broad river deltas, and mile upon mile of agricultural land. The paddy fields in the deltas of the two great rivers, Krishna and Godavari, bear three crops a year; and drier lands bear tobacco, ground nuts, and coarse cereals, unless the monsoon fails. Many of Andhra's cities had more than 100,000 inhabitants, and some were also ports. Few of Andhra's roads were metalled, but the main ones were busy with seven-ton lorries, and all carried a procession of ox-drawn carts (*bandis*), goats, and cattle, so driving on them was far from easy. Two main railway lines crossed the state: one ran from India's west coast to its east, passing through Hyderabad, and the other ran along the edge of the Bay of Bengal from Calcutta to Madras. The two lines crossed in Vijayawada, Andhra's second city, which was usually known by its shorter Anglicized name of Bezwada.

For a year Andhra was mine as far as HLL Soaps were concerned, and I was responsible for several million pounds' worth of turnover and the motivation of twenty salesmen. I spent half of each *sales cycle* (of twenty-eight days) accompanying salesmen in distant bazaars and seeing what was happening in other cities for myself. The remaining half I spent in Hyderabad and Secunderabad, either working the twin cities' many bazaars (which occupied three salesmen), or sitting in the office below our home. From my desk I monitored daily sales, and wrote letters, circulars, and reports. And from time to time I received delegations of wholesalers, or dealt with taxmen and other government officials.

To aid me in my work I had a Tamilian deputy nicknamed Balu (Hindi for *bear*), an ancient Willis Jeep, complete with driver, and office help in the form of an English speaking clerk/steno who preferred to be called Mr Tilak. I operated from a house on the edge of Secunderabad that was both office and home: the ground floor held our dining room and kitchen, as well as the office, while the first floor was divided between a large lounge, two bedrooms, and a Western-style shower room/WC. Above was a secluded flat roof where we spent a great deal of time in summer, and on two sides the lounge was bordered by a cool verandah.

The house had a walled garden with parking spaces outside it; on our left stood the bungalow of a Mysorean Brahmin family, and opposite that was a house rented by a Brit working on a government project, whom we never met. (This reminded me of the joke about the two Brits shipwrecked on an island who never spoke because they hadn't been introduced.) Opposite our home was nothing but a giant banyan tree: under it was a wheel where a man drove an ox all day, crushing limestone, and behind it rocks of increasing heights stretched to the horizon. Nothing could have been more different from our home in Bombay, and it reminded me of my years in the farm buildings at Great Rollright. But our new home had electricity, running water, main drainage and a telephone, and we were very pleased with it.

HLL paid three servants to look after this home: a *hamal* named Rajamma, a part-time gardener, Rajamma's husband, who was known simply by his job description *Mali*, and the inevitable sweeper who cleaned the bathrooms that Raju would not touch. We had to find for ourselves an *ayah* to wash clothes and babysit, and a cook who was an essential because, although the kitchen held a large fridge, it had no sink, only squat-down taps and a floor-drain. Cooks also normally went to the bazaar to buy fresh food each day, but Dawn gradually became an expert bazaar shopper.

Servants became our biggest problem in our new home because, while Rajamma was a treasure, Mali was always off sick (drunk), and cooks who would touch meat and attempt European dishes were in very short supply since Hyderabad had never been ruled by the British. We managed with cooks and ayahs who spoke little more English than Rajamma: we retained an ayah by always keeping a supply of fresh green chillies in the fridge, which she stole and ate like sweets. But we hired and fired a series of lazy, drunken, and pilfering cooks.

From this account it is clear that Dawn almost became a traditional *memsahib*, one of the resourceful women who maintained the Raj by preventing its rulers from marrying local women, as previous invaders had done. Therein lay the Raj's doom: a population of many more million Anglo-Indians might have helped the Raj last as long as the Mughal Empire; as it was, it ended after only a hundred years of indirect rule and ninety of direct. Dawn differed from the traditional *memsahib* in that she had no delusions of racial superiority, and while the 'fishing fleet' sailed to India because they couldn't find husbands in England, Dawn could have found a husband anywhere. And her only reward for overcoming the traditional *memsahib*'s trials and tribulations was that every month she enjoyed a fortnight's honeymoon.

Although I missed Dawn when I was on tour, we made up for it passionately on each of my returns. Both our lives were busy and full of people, mine filled by dozens, Dawn's filled first by her baby son, and then by a small group that were also dependent upon her. Although we joined the Secunderabad club at HLL's expense we rarely visited it: most of its members looked down on *baaxwalas* ('trade' in English snob circles); and when I was not on tour we found ourselves busy and we enjoyed one another's company best. We did, however, make two close friends in Secunderabad, a Gujarati paediatrician named Jyant and his English wife Pat, whom he had met when he worked at a teaching hospital in London and she was playing the cello in an orchestra.

Jyant and Pat had a daughter the same age as our son, and Dawn and Pat spent such leisure time as they had together, comparing development, exchanging advice, and giving one another mutual support. Jyant shared a home and a practice with his brother, who was a GP, and Pat had bravely moved in with his family. When Jyant died of leukaemia at a tragically young age, Pat settled into an Indian life with Jyant's brother as head of the family; by then she had a son and so was an honoured member. We saw Pat regularly but infrequently for many years, because her son was educated at an English boarding school; we lost touch only when Pat no longer came to visit him.

HLL salesmen called on their customers at twenty-eight-day intervals, which they called the selling cycle. This cycle observed no weekends, because distances were vast and the men travelled by public transport, however irregular. For twenty-three days the salesman worked his territory and the remaining five he spent on leave with his family. During the twenty-three days he chose three as administration days when he would complete his paperwork and rest in his hotel or lodgings. My cycle was divided between touring and home. To the few towns that lay to the west and north of my home I could drive out in the cool of the morning and return in the evening, but I visited the many towns to the south and east by making huge sweeps, with overnight stays in the most important or convenient. During my year in Andhra I put thirty-five thousand miles on the clock of the ancient Jeep. Where possible, I met up with Balu, who toured by public transport, and between us we ensured that every salesman had at least one day's contact per cycle. Only in this way could its management keep control of HLL's business in a land where corruption is rife; and for me there was no better formula for getting to know and love a place.

Andhra is very beautiful and very varied: all the trees and the bushes bloom and the flowers are bright and fragrant, the fields glow luminous (or leguminous) green, and men with ox-ploughs and rows of brightly clad women tend them. The jungles are dark and menacing; the beaches are white and gleaming and washed by an azure sea; and the deserts are rocky and punctured by oases that shrink in the dry season and flood in the monsoon. The bazaars are full of bright flowers and heaps of coloured powder, and fragrant with garlands and spices, competing with the farmyard odours of cows, goats, chickens, and dogs, which wander everywhere. The roads are made of dust, which rises in red clouds as columns of bullock carts plod by, and becomes a veritable storm as seven-ton lorries hurtle past them. The lorry drivers are entrepreneurs: their loads are topped with paying passengers who make them rich; and these Deccan Don Juans have several wives along the route whose families make them poor again.

HLL regarded every town as a separate market and the area manager chose how to compete in it: one way was to appoint a registered stockist (RS) who would carry large stocks of our brands and sell them on to the retail trade. An RS would be given 2½ per cent commission on all our sales but would have to give extensive credit and let HLL decide how much stock he should carry. Because of the vast turnover wholesalers fought to become our RS, and they were even prepared to give HLL blank chequebooks so that payment could be taken on the day of delivery. An RS was also required to provide a handcart and man for instant delivery to retailers whenever our salesman visited the town, and to give away some of his margin when we ran a special promotion.

If the area manager decided to make a town a *closed market* he had to choose one RS or divide the town between two. The alternative was to create an *open market*, and trade direct with a number of large outlets that were both wholesale and retail. It was therefore important to know the financial state of the town's traders, and for this the area manager had to rely upon his salesmen. The salesman's aim was to ensure that every retailer in the town carried stock of all our products and to boost sales by special promotions that varied from cycle to cycle. The HLL sales team were thus walking a tightrope between missing consumer sales and bankrupting their customers. The power of the area manager was reflected in the company rule that he must accept no gifts from any wholesaler other than one basket of fruit per year. My favourites were melons, Dawn's were mangoes.

The RS's percentage sounds meagre, but the competitiveness of Indian markets is ferocious and almost all RSs were rich men. An anecdote that illustrates the competition is the story of the man who pays 144 rupees for a gross of bars of soap and sells them for exactly one rupee a bar. He then sells the empty wooden box for another rupee, and after buying another full box, returns to the bazaar. Whether his family lives or starves depends on how many times a day he does this. Trade margins in Andhra were so small that grocers bought schoolchildren's exercise books at the end of term and used the pages to wrap small quantities of dry goods like rice and lentils. In Andhra I always felt incredibly rich and lucky but, like my customers, I doled out alms to the horde of beggars only at the end of each day lest I be under constant siege. My customers had their gods' blessing, while I had only a random universe to thank for my good fortune. In India the wish for a better world is tempered by the hopelessness of the desire.

On tour I stayed in *Daak* (post) bungalows when in small towns, and in hotels when in large towns and cities. The first were government bungalows and civil servants had priority for them, but after the Raj few civil servants bothered to travel. Daak bungalows provided a bare wooden bed and, if you were lucky, a mosquito net; for this reason I always carried in the boot of the Jeep a bedroll: a mattress, sheets, and a pillow, with a waterproof cover and handle. I also carried an ice box that was refilled with fresh ice at each stop. In it I kept bottles of boiled water from home and soda water sealed in Hyderabad by the only plant in Andhra that knew what sand-filtration was. My other liquid intake was in the form of hot sterile tea and water from coconuts split open before me. On one of my tours I drove into a village where all its twenty-eight children had drunk water from the school's polluted well and had died of cholera.

Some of Andhra's hotels housed brothels, but the only one of these I stayed in regularly was in a town called Rajahmundry, where all the hotels were infested by vermin. As I passed from the restaurant to my room, girls standing in doorways would solicit me in a mixture of high-pitched Telugu and lewd sign language. Most were plain and all were grubby, but not half as grubby as the men from the street whom they entertained. In the gloom of their rooms lurked TB and leprosy, as well as syphilis, and some girls would have been kidnapped from their villages and beaten into submission. They moved me only to pity. Nothing can stop humans from selling their sexual services (some marriages are based on it), and such a transaction is often a woman's last insurance policy against starvation. But a decent society needs to take better care of its young women, because they hold its future.

The better Andhran hotels had mosquito nets, but Balu and my salesmen preferred to sleep under a whirring fan to destabilise insect flight. These hotels were known as *laadges* (no Indian language has the vowel of *lodge*), because a *Hindu hotel* was the name for a restaurant with a Brahmin cook. The laadges had bedclothes and the ones I stayed in had a Hindu hotel attached. Away from the coast all my meals were the same (forget breakfast, lunch, and dinner): they consisted of plates, or banana leaves, of *anamu kura* (the first word is one of the many Telugu names for rice, the second is analogous with our word curry). Good Andhran cooks vary the vegetables and spices in this dish, but in laadges I took pot luck. Since I developed favourites among hotels, I could soon tell the difference between *Kurnool kura*, *Warangal kura*, and *Nizamabad kura*. On the coast, however, which had been dominated by Tamils under the Raj, I could relieve this diet with good

Tamil food: delicious *dhosas* (rice pancakes filled with spicy veg) and convenient *iddlies* (conical rice cakes).

I lived as a vegetarian for half the month because in the South only the poorest people eat meat, which is often lethal because it has died from some disease. At first I tried smuggling cans of meat into my room and eating them before the evening meal, but my salesmen said that all the other guests could detect this from the smell of my perspiration. So, when I dined with Brahmins, on food cooked by Brahmins, I ate as a Brahmin. This diet did not agree with me: at my fittest army weight I was a lean twelve stone, but in Andhra I could scarcely maintain eleven. A vegetarian diet, however, is good for absent husbands: my libido on tour was negligible but rose sharply when I got home. Or perhaps that was just Dawn. In the twin cities we had access to mutton in the Muslim shops, and live chickens for the latest cook to slaughter and pluck. Although chillies and pulses contain protein, there was a limit to how much of them I could stomach, so I got most of my protein intake in one half of the month.

HLL paid me a travelling expense allowance that covered my hotel bill plus forty-five rupees a day for meals and incidentals. Outside the twin cities it was difficult in Andhra to spend even the odd five rupees on meals, so I spent much of it on books, often ones protected by US or UK copyrights. I read mostly non-fiction and tried to compensate for not having read English, philosophy or sociology at university. The Indian government allowed the import without licences only of books (influenced by Nehru) and birth-control devices (probably influenced by his daughter). And, since English is the medium of Indian university education, I had masses of choice.

I could have spent my spare time in deserts and jungles studying Telugu, but I realised that one year of study would not make me fluent. Fortunately, the traders in the bazaar either conducted our sales interviews in Hindi (which I could just about follow) or showed off their excellent English. The little missionary whom HLL employed to teach me Telugu settled in the end for helping me write a Telugu grammar for English speakers, of which he took a copy. This left us time to discuss my latest reading (the *Quran, Dhammapada, Analects, Paradise Lost*, Russell's *History of Western Philosophy*). I was sorry for this humble and sad man because, like all Christian missionaries, he found it impossible to convert either caste Hindus or Muslims, and had to be content with untouchables and tribal people.

When Dawn gave up breastfeeding we also re-entered the other unlicensed market: Jyant warned us that Andhran hospitals were death traps, so we postponed adding to our family until we were back in the UK. There is much to be said for condoms, although today's young people don't say it, despite the advent of fruit flavours. But these products help the man to last longer and tell him when he is halfway there (by external saturation). They also give the woman peace of mind and allow her to concentrate on her pleasure. In Andhra they were distributed free to the poor, many of whom, amazingly, preferred vasectomy and the bribe of a free radio.

Apart from reading, I used my free time on tour to visit the cinema: I saw a few English films, many Hindi ones, and even more made in South India. I went to these with my younger salesmen when we were equally far from home; the older ones preferred a discussion of comparative religion, which of course leads nowhere, but is often more entertaining. All Telugu films at that time had only two plots. The first was one where an Andhran boy leaves his wife at home and lives for a while in the USA; and then he returns to despise his wife as a *jungli* peasant; his dissolute nature is shown by the fact that he keeps a fridge full of Coca-Cola and entertains bimbos with low-cut cholis. But when the boy's father falls ill and dies in his arms, he weeps floods of tears and returns to his wife and *nimbu pani*. In the second film plot obese actors with small moustaches fight out the battles of Hindu mythology, wearing robes so voluminous that a modern Punjabi in a tracksuit could beat either of the combatants to a pulp in five minutes. Both types of film run for nine reels and about twenty songs.

The twin cities have a very pleasant monsoon because they are on a 2,000-foot-high plateau. Every day the clouds build up slowly in the morning and release their load about 3 p.m. This serves as an air-conditioning system and makes it possible to plan picnics even in the wet season. In the deserts of Andhra some years it doesn't rain at all: the tanks of the oases dry up and the price of a pitcher of water rises and rises. Anywhere near the coast there is a full-scale monsoon and roads get flooded and washed away. At such times I abandoned the Jeep and travelled by train, which somehow always got through. To balance their good monsoon the twin cities had a short winter, where it was necessary to wear a sweater in the Jeep until the sun got warm at about 9 a.m.

At home Dawn decided that she would never be able to enjoy Telugu radio, so we hired a piano, which arrived upright upon the heads of six porters. I loved her playing classical music to me in the evenings, as Mark did in the daytime, and Mr Tilak became one of her fans. Most of our Bombay friends managed a visit, and although we took them to the Secunderabad club, they preferred drinking with us and enjoying Dawn's ingenious international cuisine. Her ingenuity gave her succession of cooks a hard time. Dawn's favourite visitor was Arup, who could play wonderful piano jazz and ragtime. All our visitors brought presents and news of the Bombay social scene, and for those who wanted to stay we moved Mark's cot into our bedroom.

I was entitled to seventeen days of local leave in Andhra, as was our former neighbour Alan in Bombay, and he and Linda joined us for a grand Jeep safari in the South. We traversed Andhra, and toured Tamilnad, Karnataka, and Kerala; we visited temples and mosques, game reserves and hill stations, and we saw both oceans. We stayed in major cities like Bangalore, Mysore, Madras, and Cochin, in all of which we found hotels far superior to Andhran laadges. We also had some unusual adventures.

In the game reserve we saw all sorts of animals, but none more menacing than the giant spider Dawn found in the WC of our cabin. On our way to the hills in Ooty we were caught up in a language riot. The Indian government proposed making Hindi the nation's sole official language, which offended Tamils, whose language is at least a thousand years older. We escaped the mob who surrounded our Jeep by learning the Tamil for 'Down with Hindi!' and joining them when they danced up and down chanting it. They accepted a small donation to their cause and scrawled a message on the side of our Jeep in large characters (if the Telugu alphabet looks like spiders, the Tamil one looks like crabs). Then we sped on our way to loud cheers. I have never met another linguist who has been in a language riot: it should be added as a practical element to all courses.

I spent a great deal of time with my salesmen, some of whom I accompanied in towns distant from their families. One such I shall call J, because to English ears South Indian names (of polysyllabic gods) are so similar. J had recently married a young wife who lived with his family in Madras, and she was unable to conceive because the HLL sales cycle did not mesh with hers. Allowing him to accumulate admin days and use them to go home when his wife was ovulating solved this problem, and Mrs J was soon pregnant. There was no clearer example of management effectiveness in my career.

The problem of R's daughter was more difficult to solve: R was a Shivite Brahmin whose son eloped with a Vaishnavite Brahmin girl. This disgrace made it impossible for R to find his daughter a husband of her own caste, and so she remained at home, a sixteen-year-old spinster with no prospects. But Leila excelled in English at school and I was invited to give her a chance to practise her skills. The three of us went to Telugu movies whenever I was in their home town and we discussed them in English afterwards. Leila was both pretty and intelligent, and she would have found no difficulty in finding a husband anywhere else in the world. I urged her to read English at university and recommended many books; and R conceded that she would need to go to one of India's big cities to seek a career. Compared to that task, finding a husband there would be a doddle. Leila's unhappiness and resentment soon turned to ambition, and I was convinced that India's future belonged to its women.

In the course of my work I saw a lot of Balu and Mr Tilak: they were as unalike as peas and pork. Mr Tilak was an Andhran of high caste who spent his holidays as a pilgrim visiting shrines. He had a family but we never met them. He was fairly efficient and very polite, and Dawn was glad that he was on hand when trouble with cooks was on the menu. But Mr Tilak's mind never left the world of his ancestors. Balu was a Tamil with a degree in economics from Madras, and on tour he wore Western clothes, smoked, and drank. He was excellent company and taught me a lot about Southern India. In his home, however, he wore a dhoti and Mrs Balu (as she preferred us to call her) would allow neither alcohol nor tobacco. The walls of their home were decorated only with pictures of gods and the females ate separately from the males. This was a way of life that had endured for thousands of years.

In ancient times the Dravidian peoples could weave but not sew (hence the Islamic word *darzi* for a tailor). Both sexes wore only a single piece of cloth wound around them, anchored by a string about the waist: the men wore the shorter *dhoti*, the women the longer *sari*. In 1960s Andhra *Sudra* (manual-working) women still dressed this way, as did men of all castes when visiting the temple. It was very convenient in a land with no public toilets: men squatted shyly to urinate while women relieved their bladders standing up, with their legs spread. In small towns both sexes used the open gutters in this way.

The Brits of the Raj had been crazy to wear European clothes in Southern India: petticoats, and later knickers, were as masochistic as waistcoats and trousers. I wore a bright-coloured loincloth at home in summer, because it was much more comfortable than Western clothes, and Dawn used to tease me about this. We had always slept in the raw, but now we needed the protection of a mosquito net: malaria was temporarily banished but mosquito bites still hurt and elephantiasis was common in the villages. If a mosquito managed to hide in the netting and spend the night with us it always bit me for preference, but when I returned from touring Dawn would show me her bites as additional evidence of how much she missed me. A mosquito net in the dining room also served to protect Mark's food from flies.

Dawn came to rely more and more on the cleaner, Rajamma, whose smile was constant, but unique, because she had no front teeth. Chewing betel had weakened them and made them easy for her skinny little husband to knock out. He never bullied her in our presence but I punished him anyway, by bringing home three-foot-tall cacti from all my tours and making him plant them in large earthenware pots. When he was absent, drunk, Rajamma used to do his work for him, once she had completed her own in her smiling and exemplary fashion. Rajamma had two equally smiling, mantis-like daughters, whom Dawn and I would spoil if they came to work with her. Mali probably beat her because she hadn't produced a son, and so Rajamma adored our son Mark. We broke caste by allowing her to hold him and play with him, much to the ayah's displeasure. We have a delightful photo of Rajamma and Mark exchanging toothless smiles on a rug in the garden.

My constant companion was Narasimulu, a six-foot-six giant among five-foot-tall Andhrans. I soon discovered that, behind his thick lenses, his eyes were in a very bad state. He saw poorly by day and at night he had to stop the Jeep at every headlight until his sight returned. I solved this problem by changing roles: I drove, and he became my mechanic/interpreter; and to save both our faces we changed places just before we drove into the bazaar. I spoke almost no Telugu, he almost no English, and we developed our own language: its grammar and most of its vocabulary were Hindi/Urdu but an increasing number of English and Telugu words were added to it over the months. My Cockney accent and Narasimulu's Telengana one added to its uniqueness. When visitors from Bombay heard us talking they were reduced to hysterics and claimed not to be able to understand a word.

His doctors said that Narasimulu's bad eyesight was linked to his age: many years before he had told HLL that he was twenty-one in order to get the job (like most Andhrans, he had no birth certificate): now he was officially fifty-five but physically well over seventy. Before I left I collected all the medical certificates for him that I could and got him early retirement on grounds of ill health, and a full-term pension. We were firm friends and had many adventures together: they ranged from sinking the Jeep past its axles in a dried-up riverbed to running over a suicidal goat and having to deal with its irate owner. At least we weren't charged by a water buffalo, which was the fate of one of the sales vans HLL used to reach remote villages.

In the summer of 1965, despite all my precautions with drinking water, I contracted paratyphoid B. I fell ill in the Andhran town farthest from Hyderabad, and by the time I reached home two days later I was badly dehydrated. My GP tried to dose me with chlorostrep, but when he found that I could not keep down even a spoonful of boiled water he despaired and left. Dawn called Jyant, who fixed tubes and bottles to our mosquito-net frame and fed me intravenously with saline and chloramphenicol. He thus saved my life, but a few years later was unable to save his own. Only in a random universe could such an injustice happen, or such a good man be wrenched from his good work and his lovely family. One chance, as the preacher said, taketh them all.

Dawn soon nursed me back to health and I returned to work for two further cycles in Andhra. The chief excitement in that time was a product emergency. A supplier had delivered a contaminated drum of cresylic acid to HLL's factory and it had been used to make a batch of *Lifebuoy* soap before the problem was discovered. The whole batch had been delivered to my RS in Guntur, a city near the coast, famous for its tobacco. My boss sent me the code numbers of the boxes concerned, but unfortunately it was the beginning of my salesmen's leave period.

The contaminated soap was likely to cause bad skin problems and I needed to uplift every bar; so there was nothing for it but to summon Narasimulu and drive to the coast.

When I arrived the RS revealed that he had already sold all the contaminated boxes to retailers. I had watched all my salesmen work bazaars, but now I had to try it for myself. The RS lent me his handcart man and gave me a pad of receipts, and Narasimulu went with me to explain the problem in good Telugu. It took us until nightfall to cover all the RS's customers and collect all the contaminated soap; and we were glad when the sun set, because the daytime temperature was 127° and we were drenched in perspiration. When I sank into bed in my usual laadge I slept the sleep of the just. There was no outbreak of dermatitis in Guntur that summer, and replacement supplies of *Lifebuoy* were in the shops within days. I was always keen to head sales league tables but, unfortunately, that month's sales of the brand were credited to me only once.

My boss, Rajesh, invited Dawn and Mark to accompany me on my next trip to Madras and he gave us important news. Sampath, the manager with whom I had exchanged jobs a year earlier, had asked to return to his area (he and his wife were Tamils, and much preferred Andhra to Bombay). This fitted well with Doug's concern for the health of my family, which since my illness had no longer seemed unassailable. (South India is full of the graves of British children). So I was to return to Bombay to spend my last few months as a brand manager, and Dawn was to regain her beloved home in Alhambra.

We were regaled with four farewell parties; one hosted by my colleagues in the Madras branch office, one by my sales team, and one each by my two richest RSs (those in Hyderabad and Secunderabad). Dawn wore her saris and ate among a host of men in the finest Hindu hotels. Many heartfelt *Namastes* were said and I had to make emotional speeches to enthusiastic audiences. We received presents that have adorned our homes for the rest of our lives, and packed them carefully with our personal effects for transit to Bombay. And suddenly it was time to leave. There were more emotional farewells to Balu, Rajamma, and Narasimulu at the station, and we left Hyderabad in a puff of steam.

Jyant and Pat bade us farewell by joining us for a short holiday in Aurangabad, which was on the line to Bombay. There we visited the famous caves at Ajanta and Ellora, hollowed from the rock a thousand years ago by Buddhist monks. The walls of the Ajanta caves are covered in beautiful paintings depicting the world the monks renounced: all human life is there; and the Ellora caves are covered in wonderfully carved figures from a legendary world. Our last stop in Aurangabad was the mock-Taj Mahal that Aurangzeb built to house the tomb of his wife Bibi. She was a simple country girl whose dying wish had been that she be buried where the wind would blow around her tomb and the rain would fall on it. Aurangzeb had vents cut beneath the dome of his cut-price monument so as to grant her wish, and the whole building has a melancholy air. In our photos I look newly recovered, and Jyant shows no sign of the illness he is carrying, but our wives and children look lovely.

Back in Bombay we resumed our former home and were welcomed by our old servants, and I took up my new job as brand manager for *Surf* and *Lifebuoy*. My work on those two big brands was very much the same as that of a brand manager in the UK. Our circle of friends remained: some engaged couples were now married, and some wives were now pregnant, but the partying resumed as if it had never been interrupted. When my new boss Bau invited us to a farewell dinner a fortnight before we were due to leave, I had to tell him that we had a party booked for every evening. So we settled for a lunch, and Bau gave us some books of South Indian poems translated into English.

On my last day in HLL I was called to the boardroom to find it crowded with smiling friends and colleagues. They presented me with many beautiful gifts and demanded a speech. By then I was well practised in farewell speeches, and I took as my theme the words of a

Hindi folk song: *Hamne dilko de diya* ('I have given my heart away.') There were wet eyes in the audience, including mine, and even Prakash was moved to offer me a job in India. He offered me a bigger sales area but a smaller salary, reminding me that my Indian colleagues were on less generous pay scales. But he was probably only joking and I politely declined; I knew my opposite number Narayanan was due back soon, and I had other jobs and lives awaiting me in the UK.

In particular, we were keen to see our mothers after a two-year absence and show them their new grandchild. We looked forward to Christmas back home, but I now had four months' paid leave; so we decided to return slowly by ship and delay the shock of an English winter. We travelled on a liner with wonderful Australian food, which took us through the Suez Canal slowly enough for us to visit Cairo and Alexandria. The Sphinx, the Pyramids, and the Cairo museum all impressed, but we found Egyptian attempts at Western food inedible. Nevertheless, Egypt seemed very prosperous compared with India: all cars and no bullock carts, no bare flesh in sight, and fewer beggars.

After disembarking in Naples, we flew to Rome and then Paris for sightseeing. We stored Roman ruins, medieval cathedrals, art galleries, and triumphal arches in our memories, alongside temples, caves, mosques, and Moghul tombs; and we marvelled at the boundless energy and rich history of our species. The hotels of Europe were much more comfortable than the laadges of Andhra, but they were unexciting by comparison. Our palates began to forget chillies, and we could soon taste the wine, but the streets were very grey compared with the brightly coloured bazaars, and bitterly cold. Mark, who had never worn anything but a nappy before, hated clothes, but we forced him, protesting, into them, as we all gradually became acclimatised to the European winter.

17

ASCENT

We arrived in the UK in December and rented a bungalow on Hayling Island for three months, and we gradually got used to grey skies and thick overcoats. With a tour-end gratuity from Unilever our savings were sufficient to buy a brand-new car, a Hillman Minx, which we used that winter to shuttle between Hayling and Pompey. My Aunt Edith hosted our Christmas lunch and Mark was smothered in the love of *grambies* as he called his grandmothers, as if they were marquises. On Christmas day he ate his lunch sitting in the pedal car that was our major Christmas present to him. Thus began the process of spoiling our children that Dawn and I maintained until all three were driving real cars. From 1966 Sarah had a little boy again to love, and I think she enjoyed her grandson more than her son because responsibility for his future didn't weigh heavily upon her.

While we were in India Sarah had been diagnosed with breast cancer. She decided to keep this awful news from us (there was no hint in her letters) because she was trying to deny it to herself, and she knew that we could do nothing to help her. She trusted in her doctors and radiotherapy and was rewarded by a full remission that lasted eleven years. Her sudden illness had had a big impact on her life: it hit her when she was still working as hard as ever, at the age of sixty-eight. She looked ten years younger and her boss could find no one half as productive to replace her. She enjoyed both her work and being indispensable, and she had built a strong friendship to replace me when I left home.

Her friend was named Marjorie, and she was twenty years younger than Sarah. Marjorie, in effect, became the daughter Sarah had always lacked. They shared the same tastes in music and films, and Sarah became the younger woman's confidante and mentor. Marjorie had recently lost her mother and was now a working girl who lived alone and wanted a man. But she was plain and shy, and Sarah tried her best to guide her to success, despite having had no good experience of men herself. Marjorie had no luck with the men she went out with, and Sarah was a warm shoulder to cry on. Sarah probably saw more of Marjorie than she had seen of me since I was four years old.

Sarah would have described herself as happy until her illness struck. She took an intense interest in life and wished she were young enough to wear the latest fashions, and to dare to do the new things women were doing. The latest films, the latest popular songs, the latest crazes, all fascinated her. And with no son to support, she had the money to enjoy them. Women of her class had never been as well off as they were in the 1960s, and she rejoiced in it. She enjoyed her work and status in the sweatshop, which was a bustling friendly place where people laughed a lot. She still knitted and read at the same time, and the world was full of new books and patterns. And television became a fourth element in her multi-tasking.

Sarah's GP guided her sensitively through her illness and helped her make the right decisions: she retired, which didn't surprise her workmates, because they thought she must be getting close to sixty, and her GP's efforts gained her a council flat on Hayling Island, where she could be near her sister. It was sheltered accommodation and the rent was so low that her old-age pension would keep her comfortably.

There was a warden, whose power Sarah resented, and other residents of her own age, one of whom named Hetty soon took Marjorie's place as her special friend. For eleven years Sarah lived what she called 'the life of a lady'; her flat was the warmest place she had ever lived, courtesy of the underfloor heating paid for by the council.

Although the flat was near Hayling's best shops, Sarah spent little, because food had never interested her much and knitting, plus her work in tailoring, had ensured she always had new clothes. As my income grew, I sent her a monthly cheque (but I had to insist). It was enough for little luxuries, but as often as not she spent it on presents for her grandchildren, whose photos adorned her flat. Her sister Edith lived less than a mile away, and when Ann and Harry retired to Hayling Sarah was even happier because she was brought back into close contact with more members of her family.

For eleven years Sarah had all that she had lacked for most of her life: a warm home, financial security, and hours of leisure. She knew how to fill them. When our children were small, Dawn and I rented a holiday bungalow each summer on Hayling, so that Sarah could devote a fortnight to being gramby. As they grew up, this became a fortnight as a guest in our home; Sarah enjoyed the game of finding new things for children to do in their school holidays. At Christmas both grambies came to stay with us and share the excitement of the midwinter festival. By then we were living in houses so large that Sarah thought we were very rich; we weren't, because I was paying a stiff rate of income tax, but that is the time when people need large homes: when three generations have to be brought together to enjoy one another.

Back in 1966, in the warmth of our bed in freezing Hayling, Dawn conceived again, and we waited in awe and anticipation. It made us keener to get established in a more permanent home and I found four months of idleness frustrating. My good friend Horace, the personnel director of Lever Brothers, had sold our house in Scotland for us in our absence because he knew that my next job would be in London. When

I went to see him, Horace told me that there was a brand vacancy coming up that should suit me. And so, at the winter's end, I took over the very old brand, *Lux Flakes*, and three other fabric-cleaning brands that were still in development. There was very little for a brand manager to do on *Lux Flakes* except to keep up the advertising campaign that had been running for almost a century, and to find cost savings. But it enabled me to get to know the people on the London agency scene and the menus of the best restaurants. The development brands, however, were much more challenging.

For most of the twentieth century new brands showed Unilever at its best and also at its worst. The best was that a marketing team in any of a hundred countries could invent a new brand and put it on the market (thus a Swedish shampoo called *Timotei* temporarily became a big international profit earner); and the fact that a subsidiary company could adapt a brand's formulation or advertising to local conditions often worked in its favour. The worst was that successful brands often spread from country to country very slowly, so slowly that competitors could anticipate them and cash in.

The reason for this tardiness was the decentralised nature of the Unilever business: individual company chairmen had the power to move at their own speed and develop their own versions of Unilever brands. The international board's power lay in being able to change the subsidiary chairman, but that was a slow business compared with issuing an edict saying, 'Do it now.' P&G, who issued edicts from Cincinnati (and also fired executives faster), had an advantage in this way; but it could also be a disadvantage: In the 1950s the US fabric-washing market leader *Tide* had been a flop in the UK because British washing machines differed from American ones and were damaged by the US formula.

In the 1960s Unilever tried to overcome its weakness by appointing one main board director to take charge of each industry as its *World Coordinator* (a title borrowed from the adventures of a comic character called *Dan Dare*). So the brands I managed existed at the coordinator's behest, and the chain of approval went upwards beyond my chairman. Another factor in my operation was that Tony, my chairman, had been Lever's marketing director in Germany and that the new coordinator, Mr S (whom I never met), had been his chairman there. One of my brands, *Skip*, was a brand leader in Germany, and the wives of these two mega-bosses owned German washing machines. The first *Skip* off the UK production line thus had two VIP customers, and their impatience for *Skip*'s launch affected my department's marketing strategy.

Deutsche Lever's major fabrics brand was called *Skip* because Unilever did not own the brand name *Persil* in mainland Europe. The physical differences between the two brands began with *Persil* being soap-based, while *Skip* was a synthetic detergent; but the more obvious one was that *Persil* foamed, while *Skip* produced a very low lather. *Persil* had been formulated to suit British top-loading washing machines, and *Skip* to protect continental front-loading machines, which were suds-intolerant. Front-loading machines, with their revolving drums, washed more efficiently, went wrong less often, were simpler to manufacture, and easier to repair. In the 1960s a whole generation of top-loaders was gradually being replaced by front-loaders, but in 1966 barely 3 per cent of British homes had front-loading machines.

Two of them were in the homes of Tony and Mr S, and therein lay my greatest problem. When, several years later, Lever wrote up the history of this market as a case study for business schools, it contained no mention of the two ladies whose influence was so powerful. Case histories in marketing are the worst sort of history: they are the post-rationalisations of lucky survivors. For this reason it is difficult to make *business studies* an intellectually rigorous subject, and its popularity today partly results from this: at least 60,000 British youngsters enrol each year to study it because it is undemanding, and they think it will lead to a career. But executive vacancies in the UK are a fraction of this number and falling; so business graduates are little better off than *media studies* graduates, who find that the hundred jobs in TV all go to Arts graduates from Oxbridge. My advice to bright young people applying to redbrick universities is, 'Study science.'

The problem for *Skip* in 1966 was that the homes with front-loading machines were unevenly spread, and at 3 per cent barely merited placing the brand on British supermarket shelves. I put *Skip* into test market in Yorkshire and persuaded the Lever sales force to get it wide distribution, but the result was that store managers found it sold very slowly indeed. When their head offices picked this up they wanted to delist it immediately, because future growth and long-term profitability were not the priorities in their cut-throat markets. I spent many hours writing documents that proved it would be at least five years before *Skip* was viable in the UK. I argued that the UK brand should carry the *Persil* name and share its facings on the shelves. No retailer would delist the *Persil* of the future, and it would slowly but surely grow into the nation's biggest brand, as home after home replaced its washing machine.

The last people to be convinced were Tony and Mr S; the first was my colleague and friend David, who was *Persil* brand manager, and the next was our immediate boss, another David, who was both pugnacious and persuasive. He fought the issue through and commissioned the studies that proved a low-suds automatic variant would not confuse ordinary *Persil* users. When the two VIPs recently returned from Germany signed an armistice, *Persil Automatic* was launched, and its success exceeded all our expectations. I handed over all my data on low-suds detergents to the *Persil* brand office with relief: I cared nothing for the credit, I simply wanted to stop flogging a dead horse.

My reputation as the axeman of doomed brands grew further as one called *Luvil* gradually metamorphosed into one called *Radiant*. In the early 1960s detergent companies suddenly realised that enzymes could be dry-mixed with detergent powders and digest stains. The laundry industry had been using enzymes for decades, but they are dangerous beasties, and it is one thing to take risks with your employees and another to take risks with your family. In 1966 there was one big problem with putting enzymes in washing powders: the oxygen bleach in the detergent destroyed the enzymes in storage. Unilever's Dutch company, however, had just made a success of a brand with the unpromising name of *Luvil* by selling it as a pre-soaker. It contained no bleach, and Dutch housewives (who clean their saucepans so that you could eat off the outside of them) accepted the chore of soaking biologically stained garments in *Luvil* before washing them in a brand with oxygen bleach.

Unilever's decentralisation stopped it from launching *Luvil* immediately across Europe, which might have worked. But Unilever's slow reflexes allowed another firm to launch an enzymatic pre-soaker called *Biotex* in the UK, and *Biotex* sold well and became a very profitable brand. My job as *Luvil* brand manager was to try to get a second profitable pre-soaker onto the market quickly, even though British housewives resisted pre-soaking all but the worst-stained garments. I put *Luvil* into test market in the far North East and watched it struggle, almost as badly as *Skip*. To British retailers *Biotex* was a specialist brand and there was neither demand nor space for a *me-too* brand alongside it. (This was exactly what was happening in Holland, too, but to *Luvil*'s advantage.)

From the first I suspected that the future of enzymes lay in making them compatible with oxygen bleach, but the Unilever research lab in Holland that worked on the product said it was quite impossible, and its scientists concentrated on the much easier tasks of making *Luvil*'s formula cheaper and more effective. Senior executives in P&G, however, with their 'can-do' philosophy and 'do-it-now' style, did not accept this from their labs. In the course of time their scientists discovered that giving the enzymes an electrolytic coating (termed *encapsulation*) protected them in storage and solved the problem. I found this frustrating, because I had seen how electrolysis protected the edges of razor blades; but no company allows a Classicist to solve scientific problems.

It took several years for P&G to launch *Ariel*, the first heavy-duty enzymatic detergent, but it was an immediate success, threatening *Persil*'s market leadership for the first time in 1970. Once the secret of encapsulation was known, Lever launched a me-too brand called *Radiant*, which never caught *Ariel*, but severely restricted P&G's profit: consumers switched to *Radiant* whenever *Ariel* was three pence a packet more expensive. I felt that having an enzymatic variant of *Persil Automatic* was the answer to *Ariel*, but by that time enzymes were someone else's baby. The baby proved troublesome with Lever's unions, because the dry-mixed enzyme dust did terrible things to some workers' skin, and for a while Lever moved out of enzymes. When the company discovered that dressing the operatives exposed to the dry dust as spacemen cured this problem, they began using enzymes again. But the withdrawal killed *Radiant*, and Lever were eventually forced to launch a *Persil Automatic* biological variant.

P&G, in contrast, kept with enzymes throughout: they allowed no unions and bought off disfigured employees with large sums in compensation. This was a small local difficulty for P&G, who had launched a tampon called *Rely* that actually killed women with something known as *toxic shock* (a good name, I always think for a girl band). The business philosophy in the USA is to shoot first and pay compensation afterwards. Causing disasters and then spending your way out of them was never the Unilever way. The advantage of the US way was that, with luck, a company might escape paying compensation altogether, like Union Carbide-DuPont, who walked away scot-free from the second worst industrial disaster after Chernobyl (the grim details of which are given in Indra Sinha's prize-winning novel *Animal's People*).

When my arguments were finally recognised, my bosses were left feeling pleased that everything had worked out for the best, but uncomfortable with my modus operandi. I was a no-man in a steep hierarchy that wanted yes-men, and so, like almost 80 per cent of UCMDS trainees, I began to look outside. The vast sums Unilever spent on training meant that head-hunters would always welcome a Unilever brand manager and in next to no time I had a job offer as marketing manager at a much higher salary. The offer was from the multinational Beechams, who wanted to launch enzyme products and thought they could buy in expertise.

Beechams was run by the future medical miracle of British business, a man named Saunders, who got Alzheimer's disease when jailed for the Guinness fraud, and who recovered immediately he was released. Britain's ruling class are always protective of their own when it comes to imprisonment, because there are so many of them who think, 'There, but for the grace of God...' I saw Beechams under this man as a company managed by fear, and a very uncomfortable place to work. Once they had drained my knowledge of enzymes they would undoubtedly have fired me. One of the reasons that head-hunters are so friendly is that they know a good prospect means repeat business.

As so often happens, I remained with Unilever because in Lever Brothers' house there are many mansions and a very desirable residence was coming my way. When I wasn't being entertained by an ad agency, I lunched in Lever house with my colleagues, and we soon got to know one another very well. One colleague, whose name was Gerald, was very keen to learn about Unilever overseas (he ended his career in the perfume industry, with the whole world as his territory). Gerald was surprised and impressed that in India I had operated my own price list in every town and had hired and fired wholesalers as if they were cooks.

Gerald's job gave him the ear of Len, Lever's sales director, who was desperately looking for a future sales chief of my generation, because his senior management (none of whom were graduates) had an average age of over fifty. Since he felt no younger manager in his department had the necessary vision, he had even tried advertising outside. Len knew that most of the bright young managers in the marketing department would never leave the glamour of the London advertising scene, but when Gerald told him of my Indian experience Len realised that I could be the answer to his long-term personnel problem. And Len was good at the long term: although an accountant and not a graduate, he had invested in a business education in the USA, and he was eventually to become Lever Brothers' most successful chairman. Len had a West Country accent and an obsession with profit (his first book was about it), but he did not fit the image of Unilever top people. Under his leadership Unilever Ltd would surely have been internationally more successful than it was under the Anglo-Irish aristocrats who ran it in the 1970s.

It was easier for me to bear the frustrations of the marketing department in 1966-67 with equanimity because things were going so well at home. As we threw coins into Trevi fountain on our way back from India, Dawn and I had both wished for a daughter, and Roxane was born in the autumn of 1966. This time I was present at the delivery and marvelled at how brave Dawn was. I always counted the pink limbs of my newborn children and stared into their bright eyes, and thought how wonderful it was to have a perfect human being to love. One of my colleagues had two children who were paralysed from birth and I knew that the random universe had no favourites. I was lucky; I was almost always lucky; even Dawn's miscarriage had made Mark possible.

We were now living in a detached house in Bromley, just over half an hour's journey from my office. We liked our neighbours, both the quiet couple on the left and the Antipodeans on the right, whose children ran barefoot in the quiet suburban street. The family opposite, however, became our closest friends. Barbara, like Dawn, was a schoolteacher, and she eventually became a headmistress; and Reg, who was quite a few years older than we were, created a very successful business. They remained our close friends for the rest of their lives and over the next forty-five years we were guests at one another's homes in Surrey, Nottingham, Devon, and Andalucía. We watched one another's children grow, and one another's grandchildren arrive, and the loss of Reg and his beautiful wife still weighs heavily upon us.

Reg talked to everyone he met, and he teased and charmed them all. But he was very competitive and for many years we competed to see who could be the most extravagant host. Reg had hero-worshipped Chelsea football team as a child in Croydon, just as I had Wolves in Chippy, and we kept the rivalry between blue and old gold going as our favourite joke. When I lived in the Midlands, Len, a keen football fan himself, had introduced me to the Wolves manager Ronnie Allen. This led me to visit Molyneux stadium on many winter Saturdays, and when I returned to London Reg and I never missed a match between our two clubs at Stamford Bridge. Since home teams are at an advantage Chelsea usually won, and Reg lived to see his team become champions of Europe. By then the four of us had travelled thousands of kilometres together on holiday, and shared many gallons of good wine and tons of good food. Our wives were as competitive as cooks as Reg and I were as hosts.

By the time I returned to the sales department I had achieved all my ambitions in life, which were very modest, as befitted my lowly origins: living in a house, running a car, and earning more than twenty pounds a week. Sarah never dreamt of such a life, but I had now spent years among men who wanted far more. And since hell to a Unilever high-flyer was saying to the devil, 'enough,' and being cast to perdition, I was trapped on an escalator. So I decided to enjoy it.

Once he had made his choice, Len's ambitions for me were greater than my own. The advert he had used to lure a high-flyer into Lever sales management had promised responsibility for the whole field-sales operation, and Len had probably already decided on the hurdles the successful applicant would need to clear before that happened. The first was managing one of Lever's largest sales regions, and the second was setting up a special unit for negotiating with the country's major grocery chains. Thus it was that I became Midlands Regional Manager (JC 25) in 1968, and the head of a new National Accounts Department (at JC 27) in 1969, before my coronation as General Sales Manager (also JC 27) in 1970.

Lever's Midlands region accounted for about 15 per cent of the company's sales, a figure in millions, which could be compared with the 6 per cent of HLL's soap sales that had been my responsibility in Andhra. I had a team of three area managers and thirty divisional sales reps (merchandising had been built into their workload as numbers fell). My deputy was in charge of all the region's major customers, and we worked from an office with five staff in the centre of Birmingham. One of my first tasks was to move that office to the (less expensive) suburbs. Like all bosses in this situation I found an office close to my home, in a location that also had the advantage of being on the A45 to Coventry and London and very close to the airport.

In my year in the Midlands I also had to carry out a reorganisation of territories, because the number of shops in the UK was shrinking rapidly but unevenly, and new supermarkets were springing up everywhere. I recognised that this redistribution of work would have to occur on an almost annual basis for the foreseeable future, and I worked with our sales-routine office to develop a smooth and rapid process for reorganising territories. I also learned how competitive both sales reps and sales teams are by nature: Lever had a sales incentive system with cash prizes for sales reps and group holidays for areas and regions, and this played a big part in getting men out of bed in the morning, and in getting them to build bigger displays and gain bigger orders. It also focused the whole management team on results.

My region's results that year were more than adequate, and the best performers in my team received due recognition, while the worst were encouraged firmly and clearly. Most of the Lever sales force had more than twenty years' service, and their sense of self-worth was intimately tied to their belief that they were good at their work. A sales manager's job is to ensure that every sales rep feels that his achievements are appreciated, and that his shortcomings are known only to someone who is on his side and will help him succeed in the future.

I was aided by the fact that my reps sensed that there was no class barrier between us. I had had the luck to have an education at the age when they had had to fight a war. I might have the greater responsibility at work, but their lives had probably been more valuable to society. They accepted that my mind might move more quickly on occasion, and that my reward for taking the blame for bad outcomes was that I must have the last word, but they knew that I respected their experience, knowledge, and common sense. I gave myself no airs and enjoyed nothing so much as a good laugh in their company. For this they even forgave me for being a mouthy Cockney, and I made some lifelong friends among both managers and reps.

One of the things that bound us was football, the culture of the plebs, of which I am one: I not only went to Molyneux whenever I could, I invited any rep who was a fan of the opposing side. The Midlands has many famous clubs and I discovered some of their grounds when my reps invited me for the return fixture. On social occasions we enjoyed a drink together and, while I drank whisky to most people's beer, I was never slow to suggest a chaser. My liking for an occasional cigar was also forgiven when they realised that their cigarette habits actually cost them more and that I was generous with the cigar box when I was entertaining on the company's behalf. (Those were the days when the government taxed away most of your earnings and business expenses were a manager's only luxury.)

When we arrived in the Midlands Dawn was again pregnant, and we found a much larger home to accommodate our growing family. It was in a posh avenue, near a golf course, in the satellite of Birmingham called Solihull. We had a garden 100 yards long and by turfing over a large area previously given to vegetables I converted it into a mini-park, with swings and sandpits for the children and a large putting green for the adults. Pregnant women can be very good at putting, and many of our visitors played golf and wanted to beat us on our own course. Along with my new job came an enormous Vauxhall Cresta, which often broke down but had plenty of room for a wife and three children. Dawn now ran the Hillman Minx that had been our first pride and joy, and two children, a little morning sickness, and a new home kept her busy and very happy. My work took me to different towns for three days each week, but I always managed to reach home in time for a good evening together.

In March Dawn was delivered, at home, of another baby girl (we had both wished for the same thing at the Trevi fountain). We gave her another historical name: *Roxane* had been the wife of Alexander, and *Ximena* the wife of El Cid, so you can see that we were ambitious for sons-in-law. Mark, who was now at infant school, had a long argument with his teacher, who said that his new sister's name must be *Jemima*. Ximena's life began ominously: she turned yellow in the hours after she was born and I rushed her to hospital, leaving Dawn in the care of a professional who gave her the pampering she deserved. But it was a time of anxiety for us both, and we were greatly relieved when the baby's condition rectified itself: apparently a minute duct in her tiny body had at first failed to open.

This temporary setback gave us food for thought: each of our babies had been smaller than the previous one, with a smaller placenta. We realised how lucky we were to have three healthy children, and Dawn soon found three children under five a taxing task. Although my weekends were now devoted to doing things as a family, we were outnumbered. While each parent was levering a child into Wellington boots the third child would disappear somewhere around the house. By the time we had rounded up all three we usually discovered that one child had the wrong foot in the wrong boot. It did not take many weeks of this before we agreed that three children were enough.

In Solihull we were able to entertain grambies and friends, and took them to see the local sights. They played and lazed in our garden-cum-golf-course and thought that the industrial Midlands was a nice place after all. Mark was acquiring a broad Brummie accent and Roxane learned to walk on the carpet of my new office as soon as it was laid. I made the mistake of getting the children the cat they wanted, thinking that with such a large estate we needed livestock. We named the cat Orange, because it was bright orange. Unfortunately it was psychotic. Like all such conditions, the origins were in its childhood: it had been born in the wild, the mother bringing her kittens back into the owner's home only when they were weaned.

Orange sometimes thought he was a dog: he used to jump up to greet me when I arrived home and came to my whistle. This frightened the children and made them wary of him; when he was feeling lonely he used to rugby tackle them at the ankles, which alarmed them even more, and it was a good thing that I had laid lawn over the whole garden. At other times Orange thought he was a parrot: he used to settle on one of my shoulders but never managed to say, 'Pieces of eight.' He also displayed a lack of delicacy and intelligence in the way he caught birds: in spring he brought home fledglings by the mouthful, and for the rest of the year sat on the bird table and wondered why none came. When he went completely wild in our next home, we had to have him put down; I missed him, but our garden was soon full of birds.

Once again Dawn rapidly recovered her figure, and she looked so young that our neighbours thought she was the children's au pair. Since she was breastfeeding, as always, she made a very striking one. Most of our neighbours were the owners of small engineering firms or other businesses and they were surprised that these new residents of Links Drive were so young. One neighbour was curious enough to ask Dawn what I did for a living, and when she replied that I sold soap (millions of pounds' worth of it) the neighbour said she wasn't surprised, because I came home looking so clean in the evenings. But when I was laying that lawn I got as dirty as a navvy, and I was glad of my neighbour's help: he fed me with wheelbarrows full of turf like a conveyor belt. I repaid him and his young sons in visits to Molineux.

I was lucky in my bosses in Birmingham. My immediate boss, the GSM, preferred the name G to his Christian name and once he was sure I was competent, and that I was loyal to him and looked to him for advice, he became a sort of father-figure. He was a fount of good sense and sincere feeling and his insight into people was remarkable. G had spent the war as an artillery officer in the Far East where he had had the privilege of being shelled by the US artillery and bombed by the US air force. He assured me that friendly fire was no different from any other bombardment. G survived both Japanese and American shells and emerged from Burma minus only one thumb; he clearly felt lucky to have emerged at all.

In 1968 G had recently lost his wife and was grieving still; one of his consolations was Scotch whisky; at that stage he had considerable capacity but knew when to stop. Although G had two children of his own, he was greatly taken with Dawn and became a welcome guest in our home both before and after he retired. On retirement G took a world cruise with another elderly widower and they had an agreement that, if the worst happened, the survivor would push the other through a porthole. When G returned he found a flat on the Solent, but he had too few hobbies; when we visited him there we discovered that his alcohol intake had grown, and a little later we were glad to hear that he had met a woman of almost his own age who set him back on the straight and narrow.

During my time in the Midlands Len had moved on to become marketing director, and Tony accepted the appointment of a new sales director. I say accepted, because Mike, who was more than ten years younger, was Tony's strongest rival. Mike came from Unilever's toilet preps business and was tipped as the next world coordinator of that industry. Tony was the favourite to succeed Mr S as detergents coordinator, and resented Mike's faster-moving career. (There was plenty of rivalry in what was known as fast-moving consumer goods or FMCG). Mike was short and stocky, and was urbane, eloquent, and persuasive, on top of which he was very bright and a good mathematician. Mike reached the main Unilever board slightly ahead of Tony but, while Tony eventually retired as detergents coordinator, Mike went on to become our international chairman.

Mike delivered a very polished and funny speech at the Midlands Christmas party, and the next time I met him was, at his request, in a posh hotel near his home in the Chilterns. As we ate, we discussed at length the future of grocery distribution in the UK and Lever's reaction to the changes on the horizon. Mike finished by offering me a job that would take me back to Lever's head office in London. So our cosy and comfortable life in Solihull would have to come to an end, and I would become a small fish in a big pool again. I would also have to become that most wretched of beasts, a London commuter, but the consolation for this was that the job brought a much more expensive car that didn't break down. It was a Triumph 2000; and so I returned to the Smoke in triumph.

18

UPLANDS

The job that Mike offered me was a new one at the very interface between two countervailing powers (as J. K. Galbraith termed them): manufacturers and distributors. Manufacturers had long been used to making the decisions in this area (particularly on the retail price of their goods), but now strong retailers were growing to challenge their power. Among the managers of Lever Brothers were some who believed that the strength of our brands would enable us to maintain the *status quo* in this power struggle indefinitely. Len and Mike were not among them, but both were determined to hang onto the notion of a manufacturer's recommended price for as long as possible. And it was vital to do so until retail head offices solved the problem of *buncing* in stores: store managers could cover their losses through pilferage by selling at full price stock that the chain had bought, and intended to sell, at a bargain price. Only the development of computers would bring retail head offices the desired level of control.

In the meantime the board of Lever Brothers was determined that the millions they spent on promotions would get through to the consumer. They also could not afford for our brands to have lower market shares in the growing sector of the market (retail chains) than in the declining sector (independent and Co-op outlets). By the end of the 1960s supermarket chains were growing fast at the expense of our other customers. Lever's best interests, therefore, lay in having higher shares in the chains, and the corollary of this was that special attention had to be given to such customers.

Mike asked me to set up a new sales unit in head office that could steer Lever Brothers through to the future of British retailing. The unit would consist of three negotiators (at JC 23-25), an admin manager, and a team of secretaries, and I would be responsible for the profitability of our business through the largest and most powerful supermarket chains. This job would be graded JC 27, a sizeable promotion with a sizeable raise in salary, and it would make me the first member of my UCMDS cohort to become what Unilever termed a *senior manager*.

Mike, who had spent most of his career in close contact with the advertising world, wanted to model the titles of the department's managers on ad agency practice. By calling the negotiators National Accounts Executives and their boss National Accounts Director he hoped to increase their status in the eyes of their customers. The latter title would also protect Mike, because many of the big chains were beginning to appeal over the heads of their normal contacts for what they wanted. In future, when the buying director of any chain wanted to see a Lever director, Mike intended him to get the National Accounts Director.

Only in a firm as complex as Unilever could this finesse of nomenclature find objections. The main board of Unilever intervened to ban the title National Accounts Director on the grounds that in its smaller subsidiaries there were board members of JC 27; since I would not sit on Lever's board, my proposed title would be unfair to them. It was a Unilever weakness that its board tended to interfere on minor issues and allow the chairmen of its subsidiaries to decide major ones. So, although Tony argued strongly for the disputed title, he did not succeed. Later, in one important case, Mike and Lever Brothers would pay a price for this. My title was amended to National Accounts Controller and, because my style was never to make my executives look small in front of their customers, many took me for the chief accountant and wondered why I had so much influence in negotiations.

The first perk of my new job was a fortnight's study-visit to Lever Brothers New York. Unilever senior sales managers from a dozen countries (in a party led by Mike) were given the opportunity to observe the future of grocery retailing, and to see how our US subsidiary managed it. This was actually very badly, because LBNY's top management were all P&G rejects bent on enriching themselves. They underspent on advertising, research, and development in order to make the short-term profit on which their bonuses relied. These men held off the Unilever main board by exaggerating the severity of US legislation restricting foreign companies from managing (as distinct from owning) US businesses. Only in the 1980s did Unilever grasp this nettle, and it made me realise how corrupting any bonus system is if the beneficiaries are allowed to make the rules. But, unfortunately, the fat cats of British industry today seem to be no better than their US counterparts in the 1960s.

The Unilever study-visitors spent a week in New York, and each then visited a sales region for a further week: I was one of three foreign managers allocated to Cincinnati for this second week, so could observe P&G on their home ground. The LBNY sales force resented their ex-P&G bosses, and the Cincinnati team took special pride in holding the best market shares in the USA. As well as visiting some mighty big stores, we three breakfasted in the Playboy club and appeared on a local daytime TV programme sponsored by *Dove Beauty Bar*. That US audiences watched daytime TV horrified me, but our compère was a good comedian, known as the 'Mayor of Kneesville' because his all-female audience were seated in tiers above the set. We three foreign sales managers were interrogated and gave as good as we got, and for the rest of the day we were accosted in supermarkets by women who said, 'I know you from television!'

I preferred Cincinnati to New York, which was just another big, dirty, noisy city; rather like London but with giant concrete slabs looming above us. The weather was hot, and I explored the streets and Central Park in shirtsleeves late every afternoon, looking too poor to be worth mugging. Every evening the sales director of LBNY regaled us with parties, theatre visits, or trips into the New England countryside, so we had a great time socially. The board of LBNY were thorough and imaginative in the way they kept Unilever at bay.

The drinking was fast and furious at these parties and the laughter catching. I asked one of my hostesses why New York drivers weren't content with leaning on their horns but kept a window open so they could shout insults at other drivers. She replied that everyone in New York was trying to fuck everyone else up the ass. Another lady explained to me that in the USA every wife would leave her husband for a richer guy, and every husband leave his wife for a younger woman. My informant was attractive and flirted promiscuously, but financially she was out of the foreign managers' league. Manhattan cynicism is taller than its buildings.

When I returned to London I found my new post both challenging and frustrating. Lever Brothers' marketing department had been quietly restricting the allocation of promotional resources to my customers in the fond belief that they could prevent the advent of powerful buyers. It took me some time to gain my unit a bigger say in resource allocation. The other internal issue that I had to sort out was that our weakest negotiator had the most difficult and demanding account. A change was needed to ensure that sales to that account grew and that the weaker negotiator began to get a good night's sleep. As the youngest member of the department I had to proceed with caution and, occasionally, cunning. But the biggest benefit of my year in national accounts was that I got to know our biggest buyers.

From Tesco I learned that the customer who complains loudest gets the most attention: a very charismatic lady named Daisy was their buying boss, and she liked to rave and rant a bit before serving us tea in expensive china. Sometimes she bought the line that she was our most valued customer and we were already offering her the best price; at other times we found a little extra. What was important was that Daisy knew when you would give no more. The account exec and I were with her and her boss Jack one day, when we noticed a bust of the Tesco founder in the corner of his office. He asked us what we thought of 'old ugly mug', and we said it should be at the front of the building. The next day it was, with the addition of a 'Sir' on the plinth; he was a fierce negotiator but an exceptionally charming man, and should have been made Lord Cohen, at least.

On another day the buying director of Sainsbury's phoned me out of the blue and announced, 'We have decided to sell soap.' Until then the JS chain was renowned for selling fresh food of the highest quality and little else; and only in the South of England. JS now wanted Lever and P&G to deliver a case of each of their brands to the Sainsbury head office, and to make a pitch for the space in their stores. We persuaded JS to stock all our brands and base their space allocation on market shares. JS soon became a national grocery chain and their stores stocked thousands of non-food lines. The only things that distinguished them was that their owner, 'Mr John' called his buying director by his surname, like a butler, and also refused to allow suppliers to entertain his minions.

In 1969 F. W. Woolworth was our biggest customer, just, and it was a slow- moving and conservative business under the iron rule of a Mr C. His buying director, Albert, had risen largely by sycophancy and was an anxious little man afraid for his job. This generally worked in our favour, but on one occasion something called the Trades Descriptions Act frightened him. The act was badly worded (as often) and Albert feared, wrongly, that the packs we sold in his stores marked 'Xp off recommended price' were about to become illegal. He refused to have our lawyers resolve this with his and cancelled an order for half a million pounds' worth of Lever products that were already on railway wagons en route for his stores.

My only recourse was to appeal over Albert's head and I requested an appointment with Mr C. Albert, of course, was livid, and Mr C refused to see Lever's National Accounts Controller: he suggested that I talk to his Chief Accountant. So, reluctantly, Mike asked for an appointment with Lever's Sales Director and got one. Mr C turned out not to be the ogre that Albert painted him. Mike was very skilful and persuasive in getting Mr C to hear my case, and he accepted the mass of supporting evidence I had from Unilever Legal Department. He overruled Albert, and the whole of Lever Brothers heaved a sigh of relief. My account exec commiserated with Albert that those upstairs had taken the matter out of their hands, but Albert was relieved that the burden of risk had been lifted from his shoulders.

Dawn and I sold our house in Solihull, for the asking price, to the first person who came to see it. It had been built by a builder for his own occupation, and the structural survey raved about its quality of build: such things as its 90-degree corners, and an underfloor space for inspecting floors and foundations. It made us realise what a shoddy job most builders do most of the time. It was more difficult to find a new home near London, even though de-industrialisation had not yet produced today's enormous price gap. For six months we lived in a rented flat in Blackheath, in what had been the house of Spencer Percival, the only British prime minister to have been shot on the steps of the House of Commons. (Unlike US presidents, most of our PMs get away with it.) The village of Blackheath, where golf was invented, is inhabited mostly by snobs and eccentrics, and we got to know some of the eccentrics. In the end we coped with the difference in prices by buying a house in Bickley (near Bromley), which wasn't detached, but at least had five bedrooms and two bathrooms.

In 1970, soon after moving to Bickley, I received another promotion and handed over national accounts to my friend David, the brand manager who had absorbed *Skip* into the *Persil* brand. By then Mike had moved to the Unilever main board and I had a new sales director. Tom was a public schoolboy who had fought in the RAF, and he was nearly twenty years older than I was. He had had a long Unilever career, which culminated in his becoming Lever's marketing director in Nigeria. He relinquished this post early for family reasons, and Unilever, *pour encourager les autres*, made him restart his career in the UK as a brand manager. It says much for his character and resilience that he fought his way back to the board of Lever Brothers. Tom's example showed me that an international career is always a balancing of the business and the personal, and men's lives, at least under the old patriarchal dispensation, were always divided between their families and the labour that they took under the sun.

In the summer of 1970 Tom announced my promotion to General Manager of a sales force that did not yet exist, even though almost 500 of my troops were already fighting the good fight in the shops. Lever had a smaller sister company called Domestos Ltd, which had its own sales force, and my first task was to combine the Lever and Domestos sales forces into a single unit. The Lever Brothers board had taken responsibility for Domestos marketing several years before, but they left two separate sales departments for good reasons. *Domestos* bleach (the UK market leader) and *Stergene* liquid (a light-duty fabric brand) were sold in returnable glass bottles and the Domestos sales force was originally a team of van drivers who delivered crates of product to the point of sale. They also sold *Sqezy*, the first washing-up liquid in plastic bottles, and briefly market leader.

The supermarket chains did not like returnable bottles, although they made the product significantly cheaper, because they took up valuable floor space and store managers found them a nuisance. When all the retail chains ganged up and threatened to de-list both *Domestos* and *Stergene*, the board of Lever Brothers decided to sell them in non-returnable plastic bottles and raise their prices. Since Unilever's labs had recently found a way of making hypochlorite both more effective and less likely to burn its way through plastic, a *Domestos* price increase was sustainable: in fact sales rose for many years once the brand had become a thick and clingy bleach in robust plastic bottles.

Thus only the environment and Domestos van sales paid for the retreat from glass. There was now no good reason for two separate Unilever detergent sales forces and the two were to be merged. For a while sales management was about the sale of vans, the redundancy of drivers, and the competition for jobs in the new organisation. As retail chains had grown, the Domestos sales director had promoted about 100 drivers to become sales reps calling on head offices and larger outlets, with van drivers simply delivering their orders. The 100 reps had to be combined with the 300 Lever reps and the two management teams had to be welded together. This made the job of general sales manager (times two) a complex and challenging one. The new combined sales force was divided into nine regions (seven under ex-Lever regional managers and two under ex-Domestos), and I spent a great deal of time travelling to places as distant as Glasgow and Bristol.

When all was ready, I chaired meetings in every region in which I conducted a ceremony of marriage between the two sales forces. The ceremony was a pastiche, beginning, 'Dearly Beloved, we are gathered here today to celebrate ...' and ending, 'Whom the Board hath joined let no man put asunder.' My audiences realised that belonging to a bigger team might be great fun and my regional managers continued the meeting in the same light vein ('I'm not sure whether I'm the father of the bride or of the groom, but from now on we're one family.') It was an opportunity for nine very different managers to sell themselves to the troops, and they used it well. I was very fortunate in the management teams I inherited: they were men of many talents.

One of my priorities was to ensure fairness in the treatment of personnel from the two backgrounds: one group had begun their careers as van drivers while the other had always worn collars and ties (and, when I first joined Unilever, hats). And my regional managers soon learned that fairness was demanded of them, too. All nine were older than I was and had more years of sales management experience, and they all to some extent began by resenting the fact that a young upstart from the marketing department had taken the job that would have represented the peak of their careers. Steadily, however, they came to realise that I shared their most important values, had a clearer vision of the future, and was quicker in prioritising the demands of the present.

At sales conferences Tom always reserved a room with a bar for the regional managers to discuss things in privacy. It helped weld the managers from two different backgrounds together and it enabled new regional managers to find their bearings. Tom usually looked in for a drink or two to cement his relationship with his senior team, and Len occasionally appeared to say hello and thank us for our efforts. On these occasions the RSMs sat long and late, drinking and chewing the fat. In these sessions nine very articulate men who were cocks in their own barnyards tried to cap one another's stories, pull one another's legs, and find common cause. I always stayed with the conversation all the way, but took a deliberately quiet role, and in this way I was able to observe the nine.

I soon came to know their strengths and weaknesses, and their talents and foibles. And I trust they came to see me as one of them, someone who would fight for their interests. My monthly meetings of RSMs, held at airport hotels, followed a similar pattern and the nine gradually realised that they would never reach consensus without me. I listened hard to what everyone had to say, and when I had summarised and decided what was the best course of action the debate was over. Only the youngest of the original nine managers was too impatient to wait for our business relationship to develop. He was a fiery energetic man named Brian who had taken over the Midlands region after me.

Brian decided to sell his experience and Unilever training (which had the status of an MBA when MBAs were unknown in Britain). He accepted a job as general sales manager for a firm in the Midlands with a comparable salary to mine and a bigger car. Two weeks later he was in the office of Horace, the Lever personnel director, pleading to be reinstated. The owner of the firm he had joined was clearly a crook and was speeding towards bankruptcy. Tom who, like Horace, had a heart of gold, offered Brian a job in sales head office that had fortunately just become vacant, so he was saved. Once he had settled into his new job, Brian and I established a good working relationship and became drinking pals. His brandies matched my whiskies and we had many good laughs together.

Establishing my ascendency over the RSMs was not my toughest initial task in my job as GSM: that came from Unilever's usual problem of an overpopulated decision area. G was promoted from Lever GSM to become Tom's deputy (with the typical title of *Sales Controller*), and Charles the sales director of Domestos was left in transition. He kept his title until he had disposed of that company's depots and vans and had finalised the redundancies of its drivers. But he was named as sales controller for when G retired in a year's time. So I had two sales controllers to manage, and twenty regional managers would have been less trouble. Both men had thirty years' more experience than I had, and relations between them were abysmal. They got worse the nearer G came to retirement.

Their enmity had deep roots: for many years Charles had made more rapid career progress than G; he had even once been on a panel that turned G down for a promotion. G had endured a tough war, while Charles had enjoyed a comfortable one; but Charles had to adopt two children while G's were his own flesh and blood. And now Charles was a happily married man while G was a grieving widower. When Tom set up what he termed a *reorganisation committee* to determine the future shape of this new combined sales force, Charles was made its chairman and the other members were G, myself, and my friend David, who had taken over my job as National Accounts Controller. The committee met weekly in the Great Northern Hotel at Kings Cross, and the meetings could be acrimonious. Steam often came out of ears, and sometimes the ears were mine.

My immediate loyalty belonged to G and I always rallied to him when he was in difficulty. Charles naturally resented this, and soon he was itemising all my faults and failures to Tom, while G was relating all my successes and achievements. Although Tom never lost faith in me, it was a difficult time; and at the end of these clashes Charles was going to become my immediate boss. At times it looked a no-win situation. In the office, I felt in the middle of a war zone, and I spent as much time as possible visiting the nine regions and beginning the difficult task of winning the support of their managers.

When I wasn't away travelling, our social life consisted chiefly of entertaining and being entertained by our old friends Reg and Barbara, and by Nick and Vickie, a couple our own age. Nick was a Cambridge scientist who had just taken over his family business and Vickie an amateur actress with a mind as lively as her personality. When Nick began producing plays for the local drama society, and Vickie taking the lead in them, we became their greatest fans. Nick was a rebel in his youth, just as I was, but in later years, when he had grown rich, he became Conservative leader of his county council. High Tory and Radical, we remain friends to this day.

Dawn and I had also become friends with our GP, Tony, and his wife Doreen, who was a partner in his practice. They were a bright and lively couple and, although we didn't share their firm Anglican convictions, we shared numerous other interests. They had four boys under seven and we had three children under six, so that provided a common platform for our friendship. As with Jyant and Penny in Hyderabad, disaster struck this couple when Doreen contracted cancer. It seemed to me that the disease had a special grudge against the medical profession. Tony's faith helped him in his bereavement and he proved an exemplary father, raising his four sons to be happy, successful men. I admired the way that Tony overcame this extreme adversity, and I even envied his faith a little.

Things gradually improved at work: I tried harder to find compromises acceptable to both G and Charles; and Tom also did his best to heal the rift between them before G's retirement. G finally mellowed as the fateful day approached and so did Charles. It was obviously a little tricky for me when Charles took over, but I soon convinced him that he would benefit from the same unswerving loyalty that I had given his rival. Charles had been extremely successful in closing down Domestos, and when he held a series of farewell parties for his van drivers they lionised him. The redundancy terms he had obtained from Unilever were generous and in 1970 a driver could get a new job within twenty-four hours. Charles basked in this success and his new-found popularity.

Charles was only a couple of years from retirement himself and he spent a few weeks each summer on the continent with a caravan behind his large, powerful car, with a dinghy perched on top of it. He began to look forward to the first summer when it could be more than a few weeks. There was still the ongoing business of regular reorganisations and early retirements, but Charles also began to enjoy having a general sales manager to chase sales targets, allocate resources, and settle disputes between the nine regions. By the time he handed over his title of Sales Controller to me he had convinced himself that I was his own choice of candidate. We parted on excellent terms.

Charles died of kidney failure a few years later when I and the whole sales force were marooned on Jersey by fog. Dawn attended the funeral on my behalf and Charles's wife Betsie said that her presence showed Unilever at its best. The two women had much in common, and I suspect that Charles and I were much more alike than I realised at the time. I regretted that we had fought so long before making peace.

In my years as sales controller I was lucky to be working for a chairman with a touch of genius. Len's first book, *Marketing for Profit*, outlined his philosophy and, once in the driving seat, he lived that philosophy. His aim was to maximise Lever's profit share (essentially the ratio of Lever to P&G net profit). Under Len, Lever made much more profit in the late seventies than P&G, so much so that our competitor's head office poured millions into the UK in the 1980s to redress the situation. They were able to do this only because P&G's world profit share was large and rising. Unilever's main board, preoccupied with the collapse of their African business and the low profitability of their North American one, did not appreciate Len's strategy, and they did not match the P&G investment of millions in the 1980s. Eventually Len retired as something of an unsung hero after the first, flawed, introduction of enzymes into *Persil*.

The secret of Len's success in the 1970s rested on a number of factors: they included increasing sales volume (helped by new brands and product improvements) and beating inflation. In the 1970s and '80s British governments of every persuasion failed to control inflation, and it destroyed as many industries as the intransigence of unions or the class hatred of Thatcher. In the seventies there were strict price controls and Lever Brothers became very good at making the case to government for price increases. Without such increases rising costs could cripple a company.

The increasing sales volumes that marked Len's chairmanship were the result of efforts throughout the company but the *coup de grâce* in delivering them belonged to the sales force. As promotion budgets rose so did the complexity of the schemes that the Lever sales force had to sell. One of my tasks was to discourage brand managers from building in unnecessary complexity, and another was to maintain the sales force's enthusiasm for the necessary. The most important, however, was maintaining morale in a situation of entropy: continuous reorganisation and downsizing meant that a shrinking sales force working in a troubled economy had to become as obsessed as their chairman with achieving sales records.

While I needed Tom's, and still more Len's, support, the task of motivation fell mostly on my shoulders. I motivated the sales force in various ways: for the longer term I introduced a new hierarchical layer known as *senior reps*, who had special training responsibilities and a maximum salary 10 per cent higher; for the short term I offered large cash incentives to reps for winning sales competitions, and the perk of overseas holidays (with wives) to managers and reps alike. Sales force wives became as powerful in getting men out of bed in the mornings as they had once been in getting them into it. Taking Dawn on holiday with them helped repay her for my many absences.

My other motivation tools were many: managing the early retirement programme in such a way as to make room for recruiting new sales reps (all graduates, and some women; many of these gained promotion throughout the company). I also met the threat from unions who wanted to recruit sales forces: my sales-force consultation committee met each quarter and enabled one rep elected from each region (usually the bolshiest) to quiz me all day on the company's policies and their own working conditions. Real changes often happened because of this feedback, and not one Lever rep, to my knowledge, joined a union. My final motivation tool was Len, who always appeared for me at the year-end sales conference; after saluting the sales records broken, he told the Lever sales force that it was the best in Britain.

We believed Len. Thus it was that a force consisting mostly of elderly men looking forward to a happy retirement spent their days selling hard and building mass displays. The sales rep's in-store activities were doomed, certain eventually to be taken over by computers and lower-cost labour, but in the 1970s the Lever sales force enjoyed high morale and a good standard of living; and many of them are still hammering the Unilever pension fund today. Thatcher-Blairism blighted the old age of the British worker, and good pensions are now the prerogative of a tiny elite, but the sales force I led and served thought themselves an elite.

As I have argued in earlier chapters, three things make work more fun than play: autonomy, complexity and marginal reward. The British government froze all salaries higher than £8,000 a year in the late 1970s, and so mine, which was considerably higher, remained frozen for some time. When Len and Tom apologised for this I suggested they do a deal with P&G: each would poach the other's GSM for a month at a much higher salary (this was legal) and then poach their original GSM back again. Len and Tom applauded the ingenuity of this, but said I knew too many secrets to be allowed to spend a month in P&G.

I was as lucky in having Tom as my immediate boss as in having Len as my chairman. Tom's wisdom and help were always available, but he allowed me my own way on most things. He had too many other responsibilities to do more than have the last word on the biggest field-sales issues and leave the detail to me. By the late seventies Lever were spending only three million pounds a year on theme advertising but seventeen million on sales promotions. In effect we had two prices for all our goods: the list price to the trade and the actual price charged after promotions. We fought hard to maintain control of consumer price until the trade could discipline its managers better. Our chief weapons were marked packs (such as '3p off') and vigilance by our reps in stores.

Lever Brothers had a big advantage in marked packs because we printed our own cartons: if P&G planned 3p off *Ariel*, by the time it reached the stores the display sites were filled with 4p off *Persil*. Beside my field sales force, Tom was responsible for a promotions department with a seventeen-million-pound budget and a large sales admin department. The field sales force's cost never exceeded four million pounds in one year, so Tom felt able to delegate most decisions to me and concentrate on his other roles. Len's consultative style also meant that Tom had to spend much time at board meetings making the sales force's voice heard on advertising, production, and development issues.

The freeze on higher salaries forced Len to find other ways of rewarding senior managers who delivered for him. These included better cars (I came to run the most luxurious one that France could make), small but expensive Christmas presents (I came to admire Len's taste in Scotch), summers spent studying at US business schools (in my case Northwestern University's), and consultancy work for Unilever companies overseas (in my case France and South Africa). But my biggest perk was taking a sales region on holiday three times a year. I had the backing of a very efficient sales admin manager and his wife so that my only duties were a speech at the opening dinner and responsibility for getting everyone home again. This might have involved long negotiations with foreign police forces and hospitals as well as Unilever Legal Department, but my sales teams enjoyed themselves too much to break law or limb.

My prodigal spending was financed not just by Len's savings on management salaries, but also by my making cost savings from continuous reorganisation and drastic downsizing. In 1970 I took over 600 people, and in 1980 handed over 200. I fired very few, usually for fiddling their expenses, an offence now accepted even among MPs. In 2010 most MPs simply handed back their ill-gotten gains, whereas teenage looters in the riots a year later served eighteen months in jail. Both groups gave the same excuses for their behaviour: it was easy, and everyone else was doing it. With thousands of candidates available at election time it would have been better for 600 MPs to resign from public life: a great cleaning of the Augean stable. But extractive elites don't give up that easily.

Most of the hundreds of people whom I 'let go' went willingly: the early retirement terms I obtained were generous, and Unilever pensions were based on final pay, like those confined to MPs and fat cats today. I attended farewell parties in every region, and I lauded each retiree appropriately and learned his plans for the future. On my side was the fact that men retiring at sixty-five at that time had a life expectancy of only three years, while those who retired at sixty could hope for eleven. Many of my managers and reps lived much longer, which was known as 'hammering the fund'. As managers retired, we reduced the number of regions and areas only slowly, so as to be able to promoted bright younger people, which was good for morale.

Retirement parties, regional Christmas parties, and nights out in London to present forty-years'-service awards meant that I spent a vast amount of time entertaining. A boy who had never been able to afford holidays had become a regular customer of Britain's (and Europe's) best hotels. An establishment that was my personal favourite had also been Oscar Wilde's: the Café Royal, where I often bumped into a drunken George Brown, the second most powerful man in Britain. But there was also much to be said for the Ritz, the Mirabelle, the Ivy, Simpsons, the Savoy, and the White Tower. For forty-years'-service awards I made sure that the venue was always the salesman's wife's choice. In Birmingham, Bristol, Cambridge, Leeds, Newcastle, Cheshire, St Albans, Brighton, and Glasgow it was naturally the RSM's choice, because he paid the bill from his budget.

When Len moved Lever House to Kingston just before my appointment as sales controller, Dawn and I found a house in Woking; it had only four bedrooms, but its three reception rooms and larger garden made up for it. The children had their own playroom, complete with TV, and the garden was divided between badminton court, flower beds, and a mini-playground. Here we entertained grambies regularly, and old friends from all locations: Millie (whose son Ernie had died tragically young from cancer), Soonoo (from Bombay), Nigel and Ruth (from Durban), and Nick, Vickie, Reg, and Barbara (from Bromley). When Dawn began teaching part-time we also became close friends with her headmistress, Helen, and her husband Rowland, who worked for BP. From among our neighbours, one of my retired colleagues and his wife, and a pair of professional musicians numbered among our frequent guests. Our social life was as busy as our working days.

Apart from entertaining, Dawn and I took pleasure from a game of tennis on Sundays; as the children grew more independent she had more time to herself and she gained a degree from the Open University in education before resuming part-time work. My personal time came when I was travelling: I always covered long distances by train or plane and had a book in my briefcase. When I had read most of the work of the English poets I turned to those of France, Spain, Italy, and Portugal, which were available in bilingual editions. While I found modern poetry interesting, I also came to admire the technique of the great medieval masters. I was soon able to read the Romance vernaculars swiftly, seeing the words as local misspellings of Latin.

During those years in Woking I had some success with getting my own verse published by small presses, in poetry magazines and in two slim volumes with obscure titles. Although both volumes received some favourable reviews, their sales were only modest. I did, however, make the acquaintance of many editors and poets and took part in several public poetry readings in London. Three editors, Norman, Howard, and for a while Edwin, became my firm friends. This poetic activity offered a different sort of mental stimulation from that I received at work, and I took care to publish under a *nom de plume* so as not to risk my credibility as a businessman.

In Woking both our working and social lives were very full, but as the 1970s came to a close a number of events took place that clouded our happiness and caused us to think hard about the future, and I need to ponder hard now to reassemble them into a quasi-logical pattern. So I close this chapter at the height of my business career, living a life of luxury that as a child I had never dreamed possible. *Plebs progressus est.*

19

DESCENT

The 1970s weren't all days of wine and roses for our little family: both Dawn and Sarah fell ill, our children's education became a major problem, and the next stage of my Unilever career loomed ominously over us.

In 1975 Dawn developed fibroids and was hospitalised several times for D and C operations, none of which helped. She entered a private hospital in Guildford for a hysterectomy, which was performed so clumsily that she suffered a haemorrhage. Since it was by then Sunday and the nurses were nuns, she was left in pain for hours. When she recovered it was through someone else's god and her own excellent constitution. For a few weeks I drove up and down the A3 with a sick wife at one end and a sick mother at the other. Tom was splendid in the way that he redirected his attention from promotional budgets to standing in for me. Since I was hopeless at looking after the children in these circumstances, I was dependent on the help of our women friends. But at last I had Dawn home again and her good health and high spirits revived.

Sarah was not as fortunate: her cancer returned and her secondary stage was metastatic. She looked unbelievably pale and feeble, and when she became incontinent she no longer wanted to live. Once her doctors had given up hope, they moved her to a hospice in Petersfield, where I watched her shrink away to nothing. Towards the end we could no longer take the children to see her because she looked so awful, and when she was not sedated she insisted that she did not want to be seen. Her drugs gave her delusions and her only pleasure was sucking soft toffees and sipping sherry. I brought both each Sunday and sat holding her hand, mostly in silence. Although the hospice had a very active chaplain, Sarah would have nothing to do with him; the god of her last weeks was morphine, and he was merciful. Her last conscious moments were as I kissed her goodbye; she said only that she hadn't had me for very long; eighteen years of sole possession was nothing in a lifetime of eighty.

Sarah's last years had been spoilt by a quarrel between sisters: Edith had at last left her husband and was living with a new, but rather scruffy, lover. She was also suffering from a brain tumour that made her very moody. When Edith quarrelled with Ann and Sarah she stopped speaking to either of them, and she never once visited Sarah in hospital. Sarah's own wishes were for a funeral with no religious ceremony: she wanted simply to be laid beside her mother. But her other brothers and sisters were offended by this, so only Ann and Harry, Dawn and I went to the graveside in Manor Park cemetery, and cast roses on Sarah's coffin before their common mother earth enveloped the two Sarahs.

And there their bodies lie mouldering, but my mother lives on in my mind, at least until I, too, return to the everything. As I age, I recognise Sarah's expressions on my face, and feel her gestures in my limbs, and I wonder if any of them will appear one day in my children or grandchildren. Edith died a few years later, but her scruffy lover didn't invite her family to the funeral. She was the only one of eight siblings who died childless. The purpose of life is more life, but Edith used its potential for her own pleasure and became alienated from her family. She loved many men, and she married the wrong one; but she also loved me, and when I was small I loved her like a second mother. Her dust lies quiet, at last, in the sandy soil of Hayling Island, where we shared so many laughs.

In the 1970s and 1980s British politicians of all parties competed to see who could close most grammar schools. Thatcher won by a short head: she had been very unhappy at her grammar school, where the girls from the local council estate called her 'Snobby Roberts' and made her life a misery. Her revenge was poetic: she abolished not only grammar schools but also council estates. A Labour government was in power, however, when Woking's grammar schools were closed. It was a great day for rich kids in Surrey's private schools, who would now suffer much less competition. At first I assumed that, if children had good minds, they would do well in any school; and if they didn't, and finished up in manual work, it would be the best thing for them. But Mark's experience in Woking corrected my naive belief.

Although he could play a respectable game of chess at the age of four, his poor eyesight had hindered his progress at junior school. He didn't want to wear glasses and so he read slowly and had to bluff that he could see the blackboard. At Woking boys' comprehensive school he was put in a class where boys who raised their hands in class, or answered the teacher's questions, were beaten up in the playground for it. Lessons were a war between teachers and thugs, and Mark, who liked to be on the winning side, chose to be a thug. This suddenly ended when he was fourteen, because the headmaster didn't trust his teachers to assess their classes and set all fourteen-year-old boys a sort of glorified eleven-plus exam. This told him that Mark had one the highest IQs in the school, so he was promoted to a class that would do lots of O levels. Although he passed them all easily, the school had no sixth form, and the local sixth-form college was a new and untried institution. None of his friends had aspirations to go to university and whether Mark would get there was in real doubt.

There was worse to come: the council was also preparing to close the girls' grammar school because it had acres of playing fields that could be sold to property developers (presumably the ones that funded the local Tory party). By the time my daughters left primary school the local secondary modern school, renamed a comprehensive school, would have to accommodate all the town's girls after the age of eleven. How shortening a school's name was going to increase its capacity had scarcely been considered, and horrendous overcrowding was expected. None of the grammar school's teachers wanted to work in this educational sardine factory, so they were all applying for jobs in the private sector.

The obvious way to solve our educational problem was to follow those teachers and, if necessary, go into debt in order to educate our three privately. Many of my business colleagues were doing just that and packing their children off to boarding schools; but Dawn wanted to raise her own children, and my view of English boarding schools was the French one: they were prisons run by the prisoners, where bullying, sexual abuse, and emotional trauma hardened a ruling class for an empire that had ceased to exist. There were, of course, private day schools in Surrey, but it was too late to give our children the special tuition needed to get into them. Thus it was that our educational problem by 1978 seemed almost insuperable.

A third problem was highlighted by my summer course at Northwestern. I began my visit to the USA with a long weekend in Washington. It is a strange city: I was stopped and interrogated by the police when I tried to explore it on foot, as I had explored New York. White men don't walk in Washington and it took me some time to persuade the officers that I was an eccentric Englishman who wasn't terrified of black people (I had certainly liked the 10,000 whom I met in Chippy). When they released me, reluctantly, I got to see all the sights: I saw memorials to past presidents, and vast secular temples on Capitol Hill, and I touched moon-rock at the space museum.

The most moving sight was the Arlington National Cemetery, where the USA honours its war dead. Some 58,000 young US fighting men had recently died in Indo-China and they were nobly commemorated; but I saw no memorial to the three million Indo-Chinese dead, who were mostly civilians. Back in my hotel a Korean bartender named Duk, a refugee left over from another war, became my only contact with humanity in Washington, and she offered to show me the town. But my stay was a short one and I wasn't a sex tourist.

Northwestern University is in leafy Evanston, in the middle of the North American subcontinent, and when I was given two keys, one to my room and the other to the beach, I thought the receptionist was teasing. But the icy waters of Lake Michigan were at our back door, while the elevated railroad, or *el*, to downtown Chicago was only a few hundred yards away. The mini-MBA class contained five foreigners and nineteen US executives, and the course gave me plenty of time for both reflection – and exercise. The Americans were eager to teach the foreigners volleyball and softball, and I discovered that the history faculty, which ran no summer schools, was nicknamed the tennis faculty, so I could get games of tennis, too.

The classes, however, were a revelation to me: we read and discussed dozens of case studies and tried to derive some principles of business strategy from them. The intellectual level of the debate was low and the case studies were phoney: interpersonal issues within companies were simply airbrushed out, and the amount of calculation required was negligible. All the problems could be solved by simple common sense, but neither the staff nor students could agree what particular piece of common sense was applicable. The thing, however, that gave me time for leisure and reflection was the bulk of the case-study material. The US executives were taking hours to read and absorb all the data, but it was taking me less than half their time.

For intellectual stimulation I wandered over to the computer centre to play my last serious games of chess (after a thirty-year interval). Two of Northwestern's IT staff had just won the world computer-chess championship, and they allowed me a few games with their program, named *Chess 4.6*, which had beaten the Russian machine *Kaissa* to win the title a few months previously. Computers, which can now beat any human, were at that time in their infancy and *Chess 4.6* was working at only six ply. I won two games out of three, and discussed their plans with the two young inventors. I was greatly impressed and felt that these two were in a different league mentally to the businessmen on my course, and to our teachers. The intellectual challenge of the future would surely lie in IT, not in business administration.

The only break from our course's work was on 4 July, when its US members went home to let off fireworks and a German, an Australian, and I visited Canada. We enjoyed Toronto and Niagara Falls, and we hired a car to tour the vast lake district known as the Parry Sound. We saw few people, only the owners of the guest house we stayed in, but we met a bear in the woods: it wasn't defecating, it was devouring the contents of a trash can and ignored us. We also met millions of mosquitoes that didn't ignore us and taught us why caribou migrate. Canada is a beautiful country, but I don't think I would enjoy living there, even in summer.

At the end of the business admin course I took Dawn on holiday to Florence, where we could both relax, and I could ponder my future. The beauties of the past that adorn that city helped me see certain things more clearly. The first was that I had the wrong sort of intelligence for a captain of industry: business leaders do not need great *abstract intelligence*, the ability to analyse deeply plus a facility with numbers and the written word. The intellectual burden of business is not very heavy, and top managers can hire people with all those things. Business leaders need, and will always need, *emotional intelligence* (as it was later termed): self-confidence and the recognition of the effect on other people of everything they do and say. While I trusted my abstract intelligence, I realised that I did not have much of this second type, and so managing people would always be harder for me than for people with more of it.

My abilities, therefore, did not match a high-flying career in Unilever; I was halfway to becoming the chief exec of a Unilever company somewhere in the world (as almost all of my UCMDS cohort did), but I had already achieved my material ambitions and wasn't greedy. At Northwestern our class had been asked how much money they hoped to earn; that is, what sum is *enough*, and my US classmates had all answered from Kenneth Arrow's theory of growth: *there is no such thing as enough*. I had written down my current pre-tax salary and added the words 'after tax'. It was a fraction of what my US classmates were earning, something they blamed on socialism. They thought I wasn't ambitious; I thought they were greedy. But I realised that I did not have the greed that goes with being a real high flyer in business.

The least of my problems was the intellectual deficit I found in a management career, which had many possible remedies. I had tried to remedy it by entering the London poetry scene, but I was not a good enough poet to earn a living by my verse. That scene was like an overcrowded ark: too many would-be poets and too few outlets for their work. Large US corporations were taking over British publishers and closing their poetry lists in favour of less prestigious, but faster-selling genres, like pulp fiction. But poetry offered another type of intellectual challenge. I realised that all my reading of medieval literature could be organised into a thesis for Birkbeck College or, indeed, any university. Rather than persevere as a poet, I could become a scholar. As my fortieth birthday passed I also began to feel that a less physical activity than tennis should be my future hobby. So one small problem was immediately soluble.

By 1978 the family factor and my Unilever career had already clashed. In the course of the 1970s I turned down two opportunities to join the board of Lever Brothers, Nigeria. Unilever Personnel Division suspected that I might have racist motives and in 1980 approved a month-long study visit to South Africa. My friend Nigel, who was

Lever Brothers' CEO there, arranged for Dawn to go with me. We both thought the country incredibly beautiful, but found apartheid repugnant. In fact, our reasons for not wanting to live in Nigeria and South Africa were similar: both were armed camps where men with guns struggled to bring foreign families security. The only advantage of South Africa was the availability of good English-speaking schools. But apartheid and living under a fascist government was an absurd price to pay for this. Back in Britain, Thatcher regarded Nelson Mandela as a terrorist, but to me he was always a hero. Without the threat of violence the Broederbond would have conceded nothing.

Len tried to keep me in the UK by getting me the job of Sales Director with Gibbs, the UK toilet preps company, and its chairman gave me a fake interview. I knew from the grapevine that his boss on the Unilever main board (the man who had once stolen my Indian boss Krishna's wife) had already promised the job to the GSM of Gibbs. This deception seemed to put a curse on the job: his candidate soon became an alcoholic and had to be retired, and for a while the job was combined with that of marketing director. But this led to the company's customers having too direct an influence on marketing policy, and the next two sales directors failed to meet the standards for the job set by their chairmen. Thus it was that I was offered the job twice in my last ten years in Unilever, but by then I was doing one that I enjoyed too much to exchange for two extra job classes.

In 1978 this episode made me realise that my future was in the hands of men that I couldn't necessarily trust. My masters would probably not brook my refusing another overseas posting; old friends of mine in Pakistan and Malaysia were demanding postings in Britain after serving long tours as marketing directors abroad. They rightly coveted my job and I was acting like a dog in a manger. I suspected that if I refused another overseas posting a severance payment and my resignation would be the alternatives. The biggest lure of an overseas posting with Unilever was that the company paid the fees for the manager's children to attend boarding schools in England. But this was the perk Dawn and I least wanted. I could even see the possibility of a situation where I was working in Africa, Asia, or South America, and she was living in England in order to be with the children. This was not a future I wanted.

I realised that if I wanted to leap out of this manger I could do what the youngest and brightest of my RSMs had just done: sell my training and get a job as sales director of a smaller UK company. But there was no company that I wanted to work for other than Lever Brothers. Gradually, I realised that looking outside was my fall-back if a riskier plan I was contemplating failed. So, after careful consultation with Dawn, I decided to take the risk.

Lever had a vacancy for an area sales manager coming up in the South West, my favourite part of England, and I asked Len and Tom to post me to it. I knew that an old colleague of mine named Jim, currently in Malaysia, was the natural candidate for my job as sales controller. Having already served several years overseas as a director, Jim would also be qualified to take over from Tom when he retired. I believed that Jim was far more ambitious than I, and I knew that he had just lost his only son, so his wife was desperate to come home. For their sakes, if not for mine, I was sure that Len and Tom would give my proposal serious thought. My immediate bosses thus became my firm allies in a battle such as had never before been fought in Unilever House.

I was volunteering to take a 50 per cent cut in salary (in today's world, where salary scales are top-heavy, this would be 90 per cent), and to lose seven job classes in an afternoon. But the punitive rate of tax at the time meant that when Dawn fulfilled her ambition to go back to teaching full-time our net income would not fall. Behind my request was the fact that East Devon still had grammar schools, and a couple of family visits to Exeter, plus some tests for my daughters, guaranteed all three children places. The final piece in this rescue jigsaw was that the University of Exeter had made me an offer of a postgraduate place to write a thesis on medieval literature.

Unilever Personnel Division fought my move on the grounds that it would demoralise the sales force, but Len argued it would have the opposite effect: it would prove how worthwhile senior managers thought area sales management, and that at least one senior manager was prepared to make sacrifices to remain with Lever Brothers. Len was right and he won the months of argument. Unilever's last resort was to make me a vague promise: if I stayed in my current post a little longer, the job of Head of Management Recruitment in the UK would soon become vacant, and would be mine.

I was very attracted by this sideways move, which would take me into the world of higher education and allow me to spend a lot of time visiting universities. By the time this promise came, however, we had found a home two miles from the grammar school we wanted our children to attend, and I had accepted Exeter University's offer of postgraduate research. So the die was already cast, and I put my Woking house on the market. When the arrival of Thatcher in Number Ten doubled inflation, trebled unemployment, and caused economic havoc, the best house we had ever lived in took two years to sell. During those two years we lived in Devon by courtesy of a bridging loan from Lever Brothers.

Our children were to attend the King's School in Ottery St Mary, where Coleridge's father had taught, and the bungalow we purchased was in West Hill, an Exeter commuter village two miles away. Our new home was spacious, with four bedrooms and two bathrooms, and its spider-like layout gave it twelve outside walls. It looked down on the tree-lined valley of the River Otter and was called 'Badgers', because those creatures had left footprints in drying concrete when it was being built just two years earlier. 'Badgers' lay between another bungalow and a field full of sheep, one of which had been hand-reared by our predecessors. If you went to the hedge and shouted 'Skippy', all the others would run away and Skippy would come running to you like a dog. This reminded me of my psychotic orange cat, and it seemed a good omen for a loner who had chosen a very different path from the rest of his flock.

'Badgers' had a fairly large garden that needed re-landscaping, and later I bought half a field behind it to prevent further building and our becoming overlooked. We turned the field into an orchard and spent our time protecting the young trees from rabbits and hares. But we lived a rural idyll with a difference: prices in West Hill meant that all its new homes were occupied by young and prosperous local businessmen and their families. So Dawn and I enjoyed a life of entertaining and being entertained, and four years later we knew almost the entire population of West Hill. We had cinemas and theatres in Exeter, nine miles away, but mostly we partied in friends' homes and in summer had a pub-grub-club that aimed to eat in every hostelry in South Devon.

Our children settled reasonably well in the grammar school even though they were grockles with funny accents. We bought a small Japanese car for Mark to drive the three of them to and from school, and it allowed them to enjoy a busy social life. It also enabled Mark to work in a dairy and Roxane in an inn during the summer holidays. Dawn and I learned that teenagers are more demanding than children, and they soon asserted their independence, but we somehow survived this. Exams came and were duly passed, and all three eventually went to university. There was no question, therefore, that the main aim of our gamble had been achieved. Many old friends and relations came to visit us in the summer, and when they saw our home, with its orchard, hillside setting, and three cars parked in the drive, they confessed their envy of our Devon idyll.

We were not so successful in our second aim, restarting Dawn's career, because Thatcher's education cuts at first made it impossible for her to find a permanent job. But, being car-borne, she was able to teach supply in remote villages, and she was also able to travel to a 'Computers in Schools' course on which she did well. The local education authority, however, were very mean about this: Dawn had to lose half a day's pay every week and pay her own fees. The whole of East Devon was in a bad way for employment during the first Thatcher slump: when Mark left school in 1983 his entire class was divided into two: those who went to university and those who went on the dole. Once our children's education was over, the Otter Valley was clearly going to be not the best, but the worst place to be.

In contrast to these problems my work was very much as I had expected. I had designed the area sales manager's job and now I had to see how well I could do it. An old proverb says that the proof of the pudding is in the eating, and few senior managers get to try their own cooking. I had my own calls: the head offices of the South West's largest Co-op and its largest wholesaler, and also those of two small regional grocery chains, plus responsibility for liaising with two Tesco regional directors. I had a study in my home that became my office, and I spent half my time preparing for, and making, my own calls, and doing general admin. This grew as Levers introduced electronic order processing and increased the complexity of its promotions: I now had to master even the tiniest detail before selling each promotion to my own customers and explaining it to my reps.

My team of reps contained six very different characters: Alan, Allen, Bill, David, John, and Tom, and they covered all the sales outlets in Devon, Cornwall, and much of Somerset. They were shrewd and experienced salesmen and when motivated could be very energetic. We got on well, not least because I was younger than five of them and took an active part in display building. And if there was an awkward customer I took him on. They also trusted me to fight their corner within Lever Brothers. I motivated this team only partly by example: my personal customers always got behind all our promotions and gave me plenty of display space. Mostly, however, I did it by money.

Len had always said that his favourite colour was green, the colour of money, and our reps had the chance of winning cash prizes in sales competitions. My team, known as Westward, won more incentive money during my four-year tenure than they had ever won. After all, I had designed the Lever sales incentive system. I spent half my time accompanying them on the road and in their calls, and when I was there we worked as purposefully as if we were emptying a safe. I could only hope that in my absence they had fallen into the habit of believing that they were working for themselves. The other thing I prided myself upon was fairness: I had no favourites and no scapegoats; although I allowed more autonomy to the stronger salesmen and offered more help to the weaker, I tried to give each what he needed.

Regional incentive holidays brought us together with our colleagues in other parts of the West Country and Wales, and through them we got to know each other's wives. Dawn was well liked and that too helped cement the bond with my reps. I got to know the other managers in South West Region well because John, my boss, held monthly management meetings in Bristol. He confessed that the prospect of having a former boss among his subordinates had terrified him, but we got on extremely well from the start. I never tried to run his region or acted as if I were superior to the other area managers. And, most importantly, I cut off all communication on business matters with my old friends at head office. John soon felt secure, and when my team began producing above-average results he showed his appreciation in his annual reports on my work.

As I got to know my team and my customers I found it very easy to meet the intellectual and interpersonal challenges of the area sales manager's job: it became routine, but no more routine than my former round of regional offices and meetings with RSMs or consultation reps. My friends asked if I missed the high life, but the truth was that I didn't: boozy meals in fancy restaurants had only made me fat: I shrank from fifteen to fourteen stone in weight within a few months of alcohol-free lunches. Since I would have had to fire any sales rep who lost his driving licence, this measure of abstemiousness was a necessity. That I found good squash, badminton, and tennis clubs in Ottery no doubt helped with my weight loss, but I took no other steps to diet.

The other element in high life is rubbing shoulders with celebrities. In my previous job I had met and worked with people like Freddie Truman and Mary Peters, from the world of sport, and Roy Kinnear, Tom O'Connor, and Roy Castle, from the world of entertainment. (My role involved a lot of public speaking and comic stage performances; and Len believed in spending generously on entertainers and theme-related celebrities for sales conferences.) I had even been trapped by fog once on Jersey with a troupe of dancing girls; and on another occasion the charming songstress Anita Harris had sat in my lap and crooned me a love song to entertain my troops.

I found that these celebrities were very ordinary people, and most were modest and unassuming. We laughed and drank together and afterwards they collected their fee from my admin manager and went. I did not worship celebrities in the way that many people do today: all those I met had a talent that I admired, but, no, I didn't miss the high life. On the contrary, in Devon I experienced something much more exciting: I became a suspect in a murder case and had my only brush with the Mafia.

My most charismatic customer was a discount-chain owner named Gerald, who was something of a playboy: he drove the fastest foreign car in the region and attracted its fastest ladies. Gerald had grown his business in Devon rapidly and now had Italian connections: joint purchasing agreements and even a merger were rumoured. I usually negotiated with his buying director and was only on nodding terms with Gerald, but each fortnight I visited his home town, where I had another major customer. One afternoon, someone murdered Gerald's wife; when she opened the door he pursued her round the house and killed her. As in all such cases, the first suspect was the husband: another woman and an Italian hit-man immediately leapt to the investigating officer's mind.

Gerald himself, however, had the perfect alibi, and that alibi was me. He had stayed in his office all afternoon, because someone had phoned saying he was from Lever Brothers and needed to see Gerald urgently. The police thought that the killer might have been stupid enough to use the name of his real employer, and everything would fit together if I was really a Mafioso. The police questioned me for hours and went to great lengths to trace my movements that afternoon. I had actually spent the whole day in Weston-super-Mare, but they did not accept the evidence of the rep I was accompanying, they checked with the managers at our afternoon calls. In the end, I bored the police off my case by explaining at length such things as sales cycles, mass display building, and shelf-space allocation. Once their eyes had glazed over I knew I was safe.

The real story of Gerald's tragedy emerged several years later: a psychopath was caught when trying to abduct another rich woman. He asked for Gerald's wife's murder to be taken into consideration in his sentencing, and he gave a detailed description of how he had done it. The murderer obviously didn't want to go down in history as a one-woman psychopath, and he was sentenced to life imprisonment. Normal criminals hate psychopaths and, with any luck, his fellow inmates got their hands on him.

The part of my escape to the country that went most smoothly at first was my academic plan. In the winter before moving to Devon I dined and wined my old prof, Freddie, and learned that Exeter's Italian department was non-existent, and that its French department demanded all theses be written in French. He directed me to the professor of Spanish, a man named Keith who looked like a modern Don Quixote but had a very dry sense of humour. Keith tested me on the passage from the *Cid* that he had set his last finalists and found that because I had read it recently I could translate it on sight. He offered me a postgraduate place on the spot and we discussed the most promising subject.

In the fifteenth century Europe's finest poetry was composed in Spain. England and France were locked in a hundred years war and Italian poets turned their backs on Italian and returned to Latin. But in Castile, Aragon, Valencia, and Lisbon a new generation of aristocratic troubadours poured forth lyrics (*canciones*) and narratives (*decires*). My thesis would focus on one of these poets, the Marquis of Santillana (also the richest man in Spain), and would attempt to assess the relative influence of French and Italian verse on his. All my reading time, always considerable, would now be focused on this project, and I would spend my long motorway journeys learning a large number of poems by heart, before coming to my conclusions and writing up the thesis. For the first year I took a week of my holidays as ten Wednesday afternoons, in which I saw Keith and copied material in the university library. This project went very well, too well in fact: by the beginning of 1983 I had a thesis of about 100,000 words ready for submission.

I then met the problem of Keith's unenviable situation: he was a brilliant scholar whose publications included a paper on the origins of the Tibetan alphabet and another on the pidgin spoken by Filipino workers on building sites (both signs that the University of Hong Kong had no Spanish books in its library when he held a chair there). In the 1980s Keith was appointed Deputy Vice-Chancellor of Exeter University and his pressure of work combined with his chain-smoking to make him seriously ill. As a result he was unable to gain an exception for me to the rules for Exeter theses, which demanded a minimum of one year's full-time study before submitting a PhD thesis, and a maximum length of 80,000 words for an MPhil dissertation. I therefore had to chop the last section off my thesis and submit it for the lower degree. Keith, however, found a solution in his choice of external examiner; Alan held the chair in Spanish at Westfield College, London, and he was keen to boost the number of that college's research students.

Alan believed that my truncated thesis was far above the standard required for an MPhil, and invited me to register for a London PhD under his supervision. All I would need to do was make a few corrections, restore the chopped section, and submit the full thesis. Alan estimated that I would need to go up to London only a few times, and at most my task would take a year. I accepted with enthusiasm and, as always, had my degree certificate sent on by post. Keith died soon after I finished in Devon, and from then on Alan was my guru, and we became close friends. But, as Keith handed over this baton to Alan in 1983, my family's situation in Devon was changing rapidly.

In 1978, when I planned my move, Devon's chief attraction had been educational: grammar schools for my children. In 1983 East Devon council announced that the King's School in Ottery would be converted into a comprehensive. The councillors, who no doubt sent their children to private schools, saw this as a simple issue of saving teachers and money. Fortunately, Mark was already at Nottingham University, and Roxane would just escape the conversion (after which she hoped to gain a place at St Martin's School of Art in London). So, when Ximena and her friends decided to quit King's before it went comprehensive, and find a sixth-form college, our main reason for living where we were vanished. What was more, politics and technology now threatened our family's longer-term future.

Thatcher's decision to de-industrialise in order to crush the unions changed the employment map of Britain. Once it had become a nation of moneylenders, all the good jobs would be in London. By 1983 there were no winter jobs of any sort in Devon, and to make careers our three children would need to live a long way away. Ottery St Mary, which had kept our family together for four years, would now tear it apart. Dawn had by now been placed in a village school with a class of her own, and its children had grown fond of her, but she knew that she would find it easy get a job in London. She also resented the way that the East Devon Education Authority had refused to pay her while she was on her computer course and then exploited what she learned.

Computing was also altering my world. In the1980s a sudden acceleration in IT development meant that grocers were close to the goal I had foreseen in the days of punched cards. Within ten years, I estimated, a light beam at the checkout would send a ripple down the distribution chain to generate orders and deliveries, so there would be no further need for suppliers to play a part in stock control in store. My regular discussions with Tesco's regional directors had made this very clear. While electronic order-generation would not affect my reps, almost all of whom would be retired within ten years, it would certainly affect me. I was now forty-six and might find myself in my mid-fifties looking for my first civilian teaching job – in the employment desert of East Devon. There was really only one rational course of action for me: to get out.

In my 1983 year-end interview I asked my boss John to arrange a visit for me to Lever Brothers' head office in Kingston, and I went to see an old friend there. Another Vic had taken over from Horace as personnel director in the mid-seventies, and this Vic and I had worked together closely on issues like redundancy and heading off the threat from white-collar unions. I told Vic that my children's schooling was now complete, and I pointed out that my sojourn in Devon had saved Unilever a quarter of a million pounds in school fees. I was now available for any job that Unilever chose to offer me. I relied on the goodwill of people like Len and Vic to make this a credible proposition, and also on John's report saying that I had been an exemplary area manager. It was a colossal piece of cheek but, as so many times in my life, I got away with it.

With my shiny new master's degree in Spanish, I suspected Unilever might be able to use me in South America; but Vic had a better idea. Although I did not know it, the job of Head of Management Recruitment in the UK was vacant again. Brian, the scientist who had taken it in 1980, had now been offered a job in Africa and wanted to go to it as soon as a replacement had been found for him. Vic proposed me for this job, but met fierce resistance from Patrick, Unilever's personnel director. Patrick had done his stint in Africa and he regarded my refusal to work there as disloyalty. He was a hunting man who demanded obedience from his horse and his hounds, and he valued the same quality in his subordinates. My choice to go to Devon had unnerved him because he saw it as a threat to the system, and he thought equally badly of my impertinence in seeking to return.

A lucky chance sealed my fate, however: Brian's deputy, Geoffrey, inherited some capital that allowed him to leave Unilever and set up on his own as a head-hunter and management consultant. Patrick grudgingly offered me Geoffrey's job on approval, and left Brian's vacant. The job offered was JC 25 and it paid just enough for me to live in London. It also brought a company move that covered all the expenses of relocation.

I naturally found the opportunity irresistible. When I discussed it with Dawn she immediately recognised such a move as in the family's best interests and the answer to her own ambitions. There were plenty of teaching jobs in London, which was the ideal base for our children's future careers, and London offered the biggest choice of sixth-form colleges. Ximena was looking forward to making new friends and learning in a different type of environment. In West Hill we had provided a car for the three children as a necessity, but it had not brought her older siblings personal or lasting happiness. This was because it attracted the wrong sort of friends: ones who want you for what you can do for them. Ximena, I think, was wise enough to see this and she preferred friends who wanted her for herself. There would be many more of them in London.

Dawn and I celebrated our silver wedding that year and my sales team bought us a beautiful carriage clock. They were shocked by the news of our departure and there were sad farewells. My successor was a young man who looked forward to a few years in the South West before getting back to head office, so there were no clouds on his horizon. I took Dawn and my daughters for a week's holiday in Paris to celebrate the solution of our problems. Then Dawn settled down to selling 'Badgers' (with a few tears in everyone's eyes), while I lived in London hotels and learned the basics of my new job.

In 1984 our whole family joined us for Christmas in a house I had rented in Finchley, and we watched on television as Torville and Dean threw themselves into a volcano to win the world ice-dancing championship.

20

MINDS

I began work in Unilever House soon after it had been refurbished as a sort of art-deco exhibition gallery. Geoffrey worked his two months' notice and did a good job of handing over. We visited university careers services and discussed every stage of the UCMDS recruitment process. Brian was already spending most of his time in his new department, and his final words of advice, spoken over a drink in an airport lounge, pinpointed the chief hazard of my new job: alcoholism. On every selection-board day I would have to lunch in a private room with my masters, and since everyone would be in a high state of anxiety (for reasons I shall discuss later), too much alcohol would be consumed. Since I had ten years' experience of almost full-time entertaining, I knew that alcoholism is a continuum, and I thought I knew where I stood on it, so I was undeterred.

My immediate boss, Trevor, was an ex-colleague of mine: he had been Lever Brothers' distribution manager when I was GSM, and had moved to Sweden when I stayed out of Africa; his work as chairman of our Swedish business had earned him the job of UK National Personnel Manager. He was the buffer between me and Patrick, and Trevor had fought my appointment through on the basis of our previous work together. Trevor was a true son of Wales: he loved his rugby and his god, and he had many strengths as a manager. He was a quiet but firm leader and a good listener; he was also patient and persistent, and he had a strong sense of justice and fairness.

Once Geoffrey had left, my management team consisted of one recruitment manager, named Amanda, and Fiona, a personnel trainee on loan for one season from one of our subsidiaries. Our first task was to recruit 200 final-year undergraduates for Introduction to Management courses to be held in the Christmas vacation, and I was soon supervising the progress of thousands of application forms, interviewing at several universities, writing up interview notes, and supervising the selection of the lucky 200. I also met the four clerical staff, who were supplemented during the recruitment season by four temporary clerks. My next piece of bad news was that Brian's secretary had been promoted to senior clerk and so I had to recruit a new secretary. I found one who had been working at the BBC – for half the market rate, in the hope of being discovered. But I suspect that staff in the media have light workloads, because she lasted only one season in recruitment.

For the first time I saw Unilever as a whole, appreciated its distinctive features, and realised where recruitment and training fitted into the organisation. Billy Lever, who founded the British half of the business in the nineteenth century, grew from being a Bolton grocer to become a tycoon whose decentralised organisation sold everything everywhere. He believed that his most valuable asset was his top managers, and the qualities he valued most in them were loyalty and honesty. In the business world of the twenty-first century these two qualities are rare, and smart operators take what they can from each employer and use it to move on. Hire-and-fire businesses get grab-and-go managers, but Unilever subscribed to a belief in internal management development and lifelong careers. This had the advantage of being cheap: Unilever had always paid much lower salaries than hire-and-fire outfits and it had kept more than enough of its managers for life. Billy Lever was no fool.

Lever's successor, Geoffrey Heyworth, saw the limitations of internal management development: as Unilever grew he needed to find hundreds of company chairmen and internal promotion was producing barely half the number he needed. Since this shortfall also applied to the levels immediately below, Heyworth decided to set up an accelerated management development scheme (the one called UCMDS for which I was to manage recruitment). This gave exceptionally able young people a business education and moved them rapidly from job to job to broaden their skills and knowledge. By 1985 managers developed in this way occupied about 50 per cent of all senior management jobs in Unilever; the remainder had worked their way up within the hierarchy of one of Unilever's subsidiaries.

Between 1945 and 1995 accelerated development schemes (in many countries) produced three out of six chairmen for Unilever Ltd, and an even higher proportion for its Dutch twin, Unilever NV; so Heyworth's thinking seemed sound at that time. The thing that distinguished Unilever from other grow-your-own companies was that its top management were so intimately involved in the recruitment process. This had two advantages: the first was that those managers knew what qualities had helped them succeed, and the second was that choosing the new trainees personally gave them a vested interest in nurturing their careers. Unilever's top managers believed that they were more intelligent, more articulate, and better at motivating people than those they managed (and most of them were), so these became the qualities sought in recruits. They were not very different from the qualities that all business sought at the time. But the close involvement of top managers gave Patrick a problem.

The job of Head of Management Recruitment was a very difficult vacancy to fill; Brian had been a factory manager in Germany who was desperate for a home posting, but he had found it a challenge.

This was because the unique WOSB-type selection boards were the crucial stage of the UCMDS recruiting process. Four senior managers from four different parts of the business had the final decision, which had to be unanimous: any one of them could simply veto a candidate. Obviously, this is the way to minimise the pass rate, and to remedy this the selectors were guided by a board president and two behavioural scientists. These gave professional advice to the selectors in their task and in 1985 this team of advisers consisted of nine psychotherapists and an anthropologist. The job of board president was to reconcile the selectors' views and keep them to the strict timetable. Finally, one of the behavioural scientists would make each candidate's experience less traumatic by giving careful feedback, and a board manager (usually one of my two permanent managers) would steer the candidates through the day.

The selection board ran from 8.30 in the morning to whenever it finished: the selectors usually made their final judgement between 6.30 and 7 p.m., and the president's (and the advisers') objective was to ensure that no candidate who met the scheme's standards was vetoed. When the selectors had left, the board president carried out a process analysis with the advisers and the board manager, who had to write up the results. The president and board manager, who both had to be in the office by eight to prepare, thus worked a thirteen-hour day. But the board manager had a break at lunchtime, while the president entertained the selectors to an elaborate lunch in a private room.

It was easy to see why alcoholism was a danger: the most senior selector was usually capable of making or marring the career of any of the others. The selection board might therefore be more important to the selectors than to the candidates. Nor were the senior selectors used to being exposed to their subordinates in this way, and the president had recruitment targets to meet as well as a consensus to achieve. The advisers also knew that the most senior selectors could bring an end to their lucrative contract, so a more anxious group would have been difficult to imagine. One of my early changes to the system was to change the big set lunch to a buffet that the panel could attend and leave as they wished. Main board members appreciated the chance to look into their offices, and I drank a little less than Brian as a result of this change.

In 1984 Patrick could find nobody who was as well qualified to manage this process as I was, because I knew and was known by so many Unilever senior managers. I also had a top-to-bottom knowledge (remarkably, in that order) of a Unilever company's workings. Patrick only reluctantly agreed to put what he considered a deserter in a key position, and he found a rigorous test of my loyalty and industry: in my first season I was to do both Brian's and Geoffrey's jobs, initially at a salary halfway between Geoffrey's JC 25 and Brian's JC 27. I recognised this test for what it was, but I found the work fascinating and threw myself into it with gusto.

The UCMDS recruitment process was the slowest and most complex in the graduate market. The simplest process was to attract applications, study CVs, and send someone with hiring powers to interview the shortlisted applicants in or near their university. Most university careers services offered interview facilities between January and Easter each year, and the procession of employers who visited and interviewed was known as the *Milk Round*. Unilever's decision to have its top management choose and nurture its graduate trainees made such a simple process impossible. Our process consisted of application form, interview, selection board, and placement interviews at subsidiary companies. During my time in recruitment the number of such companies varied between twenty and thirty (owing to mergers and acquisitions), while the number of vacancies varied, but had for many years averaged about eighty.

The number of vacancies declared depended on the loss of managers during the previous year (which was logical), and the short-term profit situation of the subsidiary (which was not, since trainees are a long-term resource). In 1984 a record number of over 100 vacancies had been declared and most had been filled. For 1985 the number of vacancies increased further, and I realised that I was operating in a market like any other.

The supply of graduates grew slowly in the UK during the 1980s, since when it has expanded rapidly as irresponsible governments began paying universities per student and encouraging young people to borrow wildly. In 1984 new UK graduates represented 14 per cent of their age cohort, but by the twenty-first century it had become 45 per cent. Since the number of jobs requiring graduate-level skills (literacy, numeracy, and analysis) has never reached 25 per cent (and IT will reduce it still further), government higher education policy has created a huge mismatch, which sees many British graduates serving grease-burgers while East Europeans make and mend everything from houses to internal combustion engines. Moreover, no politician can explain how this mismatch would be rectified by Britain's leaving the EU.

By defining its target as the *ablest graduates*, Unilever ensured that their market expanded only with population growth. By *ablest* we meant the brightest and most energetic, but these were the ones that all employers wanted, and they were well able to sell their skills to government, the professions, higher education, and the media. They were thus in short supply and would continue to be so.

The demand for them, however, rocketed in the late 1980s. When the government deregulated the finance industry in what became known as *Big Bang*, the demand for graduates from financial employers increased far more rapidly than the demand from manufacturing industries decreased. In fact, the latter's demand also increased greatly for a while, because financial employers preferred to take young managers from the more numerate disciplines in manufacturing companies than from the untrained new graduate market. And, since finance is always more profitable in the short term than manufacturing, the new finance employers could pay much larger salaries.

Thus it was that Unilever's subsidiaries, which had previously wanted most trainees for their marketing departments, suddenly needed huge numbers for posts in industrial finance and technical management. And, of course, these were exactly the people that finance employers were targeting on the Milk Round. So the biggest challenge of my years in recruitment was to persuade the most numerate graduates attracted to Unilever for its marketing reputation that they would move faster and gain more responsibility if they began their careers in management accounting, distribution-chain management, or (if they were scientists) technical departments.

In my first recruitment season, Trevor, Amanda, and I seemed to be the only people in Unilever who recognised that the graduate market was changing. Trevor accordingly devoted more time to recruitment in the 1984-85 season and Amanda's energy and enthusiasm ensured that we two managers did three jobs between us that winter, rather than my doing two. She worked her socks off and was rewarded by a promotion that gave her two job classes. Amanda became personnel manager of Unilever's research laboratory in Bedfordshire. In return for Amanda in Unilever's transfer market, I received both a new deputy and a new third manager. The first was a very capable young woman named Paula, who had been the previous lab personnel manager, and the other was her fellow Oxonian, a very bright scientist named Nick, who proved himself in a whole series of personnel jobs after he left me. (Research scientists, as a group, had a pretty good record in Unilever, where two of them had become chairmen of the main board.)

Paula was my longest-serving senior recruitment manager and even today she is a consultant working in recruitment and training. I was very lucky in the quality of my deputies: they were all very bright, energetic, and articulate. Like Amanda, Paula, Stephen, Guy, David, and Eva were excellent advertisements for Unilever in final-year undergraduate circles; and my recruitment managers were equally talented, if less experienced: Nick, John, and Kevin. The seasonal loan of a young manager (like Fiona) added to my resources, and Unilever's Internal Audit Department, which declared the highest number of finance vacancies, soon became the chief source of such loans.

As the section's work became more widely recognised within Unilever, I was able to create a fifth management job. Each year we would have strong candidates who wanted to defer starting work in order to travel. As the most international of employers, we did not discourage this, and we made allowance for it in our plans. And every year there would be at least one strong candidate who could not afford the adventure for which he or she yearned. This enabled me to offer the first of them six months' work in recruitment in order to help them build up some savings. Once in the section, they did a sterling job, and every one of them returned from their travels more confident and mature; nor did our companies ever lose a recruit this way.

My reward in 1985 for achieving the second best UCMDS recruiting result of all time, in terms of vacancies filled, was a second season in 1985-86 and a respectable pay rise. At the end of my first season some vacancies in finance were unfilled, and the most vocal of Unilever's finance directors let out a howl that appointing a marketing man as head of recruitment had led to a neglect of their function's needs. Trevor remained resolutely on my side and pointed out that their function had never declared as many vacancies before, nor filled as many before, and that in the face of Big Bang. After a record second season Patrick gave me his full support and began treating my success as his personal triumph; but he retired not long after to devote his time to huntin', shootin', and fishin'.

There followed three more years in which Unilever's UK subsidiaries declared more UCMDS vacancies than ever before and enabled recruitment section to hit records (our highest number of recruits was 140). Then came the second recession of the Tory years: first Lawson caused massive inflation by reducing the top rate of tax from 60 to 40 per cent, and then Lamont drained the UK government's coffers by trying to prove that the pound was as good as the mark. In this recession the loss of Unilever young managers ceased, and some of our companies cut UCMDS recruitment; when the economy gradually recovered they realised that this was a mistake, because if you cut recruitment in 1992 you can't use 1994's new recruits to fill jobs that require two years' experience.

Once I had taken over recruitment section my time was divided between Unilever House in Blackfriars and Britain's fifty universities. Since very few of them were south of London, Dawn and I did not return to live in Woking, which we had chosen for its proximity to Lever Brothers' head office in Kingston. Since Dawn could find a permanent job anywhere she chose, the ideal location for our home was thus no more than an hour from Blackfriars, very near the M25, and on a direct tube line to King's Cross and Euston. The suburb that best answered this description was High Barnet, and we found a home there in 1985. Although it was small, it had four bedrooms, so that our children could live with us, but all three never returned to the nest at the same time.

The house was called 'Jumble Lodge' and it stood in a quiet street not far from the town centre. It was unusual in being surrounded by a palisade of mature trees so that its sprawling garden looked like a clearing in a forest. It reminded us of Devon and later became the ideal place for grandchildren to play games, and for the adults to light bonfires and let off fireworks. Dawn soon filled half the house with plants and pictures, while I filled the other half with books. My salary more than doubled in the next ten years and we could have moved to the sort of roomy, modern house in which we had raised our family, but Dawn grew very attached to 'Jumble Lodge' and I was too busy to make the effort. In the end we stayed there for twenty-two years.

I spent eleven years as Head of Management Recruitment; besides hitting larger targets, the major changes in the course of my regime included advertising investment, the placement of successful candidates, and the proportion of women recruits. The chief change in investment began with cutting down the number of Introduction to Management courses that we ran. In 1985 it was four, all in Oxford colleges, involving 200 students. By 1995 it was one course of fifty students held in one of the UK's first postgraduate business schools (the course was renamed *Four Days at Business School*). Both events attracted around 2,500 applicants, but the cost saving was very significant.

In the early 1980s students who had attended vacation courses had higher-than-average board pass rates and much higher acceptance rates (on average only 30 per cent passed and only 65 per cent accepted our offers). In the late 1980s the gap between these rates for course-attenders and non-attenders closed. This was because we found that students who mobilised their career search early had higher pass rates, rather than those who actually attended courses. By encouraging the applicants for courses who didn't get a place we ensured that most still applied for a job, and they were equally successful. On the other hand, the acceptance rates of course-attenders fell because many other employers soon ran courses: the same candidates shone in a simple 30-minute interview and won places on all these courses, so their Unilever bias was much reduced.

The major benefit of vacation courses was that they enabled us to get on campus early and have candidates for selection boards from as early as January. We also found that running a summer vacation course for students at the end of their penultimate year provided us with good candidates for our first boards. Over those eleven years I managed to increase Unilever's total investment in attracting graduate applications, and part of that was reducing the cost of vacation courses, and spending more on presentations by young managers on campus. And much of the extra money came from the budgets of our subsidiary companies.

The competition for the brightest and most energetic students was very fierce in that period, and this made our final placement stage a potential problem: if our subsidiaries dithered in claiming a successful candidate, a recruit would be lost, and it was the strongest candidates with the most job offers who were lost most quickly. The temptation in placement interviews was for companies to second-guess the selectors and try to offer their jobs only to the strongest selection-board passes. We lost good recruits this way because students often judged Unilever by the speed at which passing a board led to a job offer. In my last presentation of recruiting results to Unilever's UK company chairmen I obtained their assurance that they would stop second-guessing on this final stage, but I do not know whether my successor was able to hold them to this.

The third big change was in gender bias: in 1985 women made up 20 per cent of UCMDS recruits and when I retired in 1995 it was 40 per cent. Had enough women studied science and engineering it would have been more than 50 per cent, and this would have made sense, because women take far more interest in consumer goods than do men. In 1985 most of our subsidiary companies were unwilling to offer too many of their UCMDS vacancies to women because the scheme's fifteen-year retention rate for women was 0 per cent compared with the satisfactory 20+ per cent for men. This changed as British women began to defer starting a family and when Unilever began bribing women managers to return from maternity leave with cash lump sums.

During my years of giving recruitment interviews I spent half an hour at close quarters with more than a thousand different young women. But I was there for their minds and not their bodies, and I left them in no doubt of that. Since no interviewee of mine (of either sex) was ever reduced to tears, there wasn't even the brief physical contact in handing over a tissue. I was interested only in seducing these young people's minds, by making them want to become managers and join Unilever. I never forgot that a job interview is a two-way process: I tried to choose the best candidates and I worked hard to persuade the best to choose Unilever, and the rest to believe that Unilever had given them a fair chance to show their talents.

I interviewed at the majority of the UK's universities at some time or other, but I spent most of my time at Oxford, Cambridge, and London (all about an hour from my home), and Manchester (which boasted the largest concentration of students in Britain). It was necessary to limit my journeys in this way because on four days a week we held selection boards, and I presided at most of them. (My boss Trevor, or a personnel director from one of our largest subsidiaries, presided at the remainder). The recruitment season was winter, so I could not risk getting cut off from tomorrow's board by snow in distant places. (In Manchester it just rains, and this mighty city has always enjoyed the best of Britain's air and rail services to London.)

Oxford and Cambridge yielded larger numbers of UCMDS recruits than London and Manchester. Although the two ancient universities educate only about 1 per cent of Britons they provide well over half of the entrants to key occupations: MPs, diplomats, higher civil servants, judges, merchant bankers, CEOs, publishers, and media people. Yet demographic analysis indicates that Oxford and Cambridge educate fewer than a third of the country's most intelligent people. Oxbridge admissions tutors base their decisions on social factors like self-confidence, which shines in interview, and educational progress, where pupils from ordinary state schools are more than a year behind those from public and privileged state schools. Thus it is that public-school children have a 7 per cent chance of gaining entry to one of these two universities, privileged-school children have a 2 per cent chance, and ordinary-state-school children have 0.1 per cent chance.

This means that nine out of ten of the brightest percentile of children from ordinary state schools go elsewhere for their university education, while Oxbridge places are given to public-school applicants who are barely in the seventh brightest percentile. This is why my eleven years of testing showed that the minimum IQ among Oxbridge students who attended public schools was 110 while that of students who attended ordinary state schools was well over 140. This bias is, of course, splendid news for the country's other universities, but it is bad news for the nation: many top jobs are filled by Oxbridge graduates of modest intelligence when brighter candidates are available. In contrast to the proportions in Britain's top jobs, the UCMDS selection process resulted in around 30 per cent of recruits coming from Oxbridge, a very similar figure to the percentage of the nation's brightest who attend those two universities.

My life as Head of Recruitment was not one that would have suited everyone, but it suited me. At the start of each new season a thrill went down my spine: the 'season' signalled that I would meet thousands of new people and renew contact with hundreds of old friends. My eleven years in the role of section head were very happy, if often frantic ones. In the 1990s there was a lot of talk in business circles about *stress*, but I never suffered from it; stress is only unwanted excitement, and the excitements of the recruiting season were the ones I wanted: new people with new ideas, new targets and the satisfaction of hitting them, new jokes and anecdotes to keep me smiling. And every hectic season was followed by one of quiet reflection.

The recruitment season came to an end at Easter, as finals loomed, and Unilever's recruitment managers spent the summer visiting university careers services and our subsidiary companies' personnel departments. In these meetings all the problems of the year were sorted out and requirements for next year were discussed. The progress of the previous year's recruits was also always on the agenda: we in Unilever's recruitment section wanted feedback, and careers advisers took a strong interest in the early careers of their alumni. The section head's summer included preparing a budget and getting it approved, and writing an annual report for his bosses. Everyone in the Section section also had to fit in four or five weeks' annual holiday. The annual hours of the section's managers were thus unevenly spread. During the season they worked sixty hours a week; in the summer they worked about thirty-five, of which ten were spent travelling. And, if they travelled by air or rail, as I did whenever possible, those ten hours were spent reading. The summer workload also gave me time for reading outside those hours.

Soon after I arrived in London I visited Alan at Westfield College, a haven from London traffic hidden among the tree-lined avenues of Hampstead. It had been founded in 1882 as a women's college: Gilbert called it 'Castle Adamant' in *Princess Ida*, and because women are, on average, much better at languages, it became a centre of excellence in them. In the 1960s men were allowed in, but always formed a minority, which was socially to their advantage. I had been impressed by Alan at my viva in Exeter, and when I began to read his books I became even more so. But Westfield bowled me over: I loved its cool library, its secluded gardens, and its friendly common room, where I was warmly welcomed as a kindred spirit.

Westfield had all the advantages that a residential college with a few hundred students can have over a campus university with thousands: it could become an intellectual home. It was the last privilege of the rich that I managed to steal, and it was as intoxicating as champagne. That its students weren't the children of the rich, however, meant that in the Thatcher era it would be short-lived. Nevertheless, in 1984 the prospect of spending my summers studying with Westfield as my base was very attractive. What made it even more attractive was that I now had to give up racquet games owing to a tennis injury sustained back in Ottery. So I needed a replacement hobby that was sedentary and Westfield offered the best.

I immediately decided to shelve my Exeter thesis: restoring the excluded chapters to gain a London PhD quickly had lost its appeal. And, when I suggested an entirely new subject for my London thesis, Alan immediately offered to supervise it. He persuaded me to polish a couple of chapters of my existing work on fifteenth-century Spain for publication as articles in journals, but my main project was now much wider. I wanted to write a history of Europe's favourite metre (the one Chaucer turned into the iambic pentameter). This had been attempted in French, in 1905, by Walter Thomas, but eighty years of rapid progress in the discipline of linguistics had passed since then. Thomas's book is a good guide to all the European poems that have employed the metre, but it is short on structural analysis. In contrast, my thesis would be a comparative exercise based on the latest research into linguistics. Alan's only proviso on supervising this thesis was that I, unlike Thomas, should restrict it to cover only eight languages (the Western Romance languages and English); and he suggested I add a time limit (from 1020 to 1620) in order to stay within the London University rules on length.

The thesis took me five summers to complete and, when it came in at 20,000 words over the limit, Alan obtained a concession from the University: the over-run (necessitated by the subject's complexity) would be allowed if I indexed the thesis, which took me another year. I was awarded the degree in 1991 and, again, my external examiner Chris (who lectured in language and linguistics at Manchester) became a lifelong friend. As always, I avoided ceremony and had the diploma sent on by post. I decided to use my new title in my business career, because my work was in an academic environment and in Unilever, too, the use of academic titles was the norm. (Unilever employed about 1200 scientists who used the title *Dr*, as did several main-board members similarly qualified.)

There is snobbery in the use of all titles: even *Mr* and *Mrs* are abbreviations of *Master* and *Mistress*, and the titles *Lord* and *Lady* mostly reward accidents of birth or shameless toadying. In contrast, my title of *Dr* was honestly earned, and it signified someone who was qualified to teach adults for 2,000 years before it was stolen by members of the medical profession. They had previously been known as *physicians* and *sawbones*, but most of Britain's medics now use the title *Dr* on an honorary basis (they have only a bachelor's degree and membership of a Royal College). I used my academic title partly because it said something about Unilever in the university environment, and partly because I hoped one day to work in that environment. It also amused me to think that I was a Dr and a pleb at the same time.

Dawn also found intellectual sustenance in London: she got a school right away and soon changed it for a very international primary school. When Big Bang occurred 10,000 Japanese businessmen moved to London, and they all found homes as close as possible to London's only Japanese school (then in Hampstead). So the largest ethnic element in Dawn's class was Japanese, and she took a course in that language so that she could make those children feel at home. Although many of the parents became her close friends, she has not yet managed to get to Kyoto; Unilever, however, has carried us both to China, Thailand, Malaysia, and Singapore, which also provided her class with children. The emergence of Asian countries as world powers is one of the major events of our era and it is certainly time that Europeans learned more about their cultures.

In my eleven years with Unilever's UK Personnel Department I oversaw the recruitment of well over 1,000 trainees, chosen from among 50,000 applicants; to do this I needed to analyse more than 12,000 application forms myself, conduct more than 2,000 interviews personally, and preside over 500 selection boards. These figures will always remain records, because the downsizing of Unilever's human resources and the change in British society have dramatically altered the scale and nature of Unilever's recruitment. It no longer relies on internal management development and lifelong careers, and it has a bought-in Swedish chairman, a bought-in Dutch CEO, and a mostly Indian board of directors, recruited as postgrads from business schools and institutes of technology.

For most of the twentieth century, however, British businesses were managed by amateurs, which is why hardly any have survived. Even the ablest British entrepreneurs coveted amateur status: the second and third generations of Van den Berghs and Jurgens, who founded the Dutch half of Unilever, stayed with the family business, while Billy Lever's heirs became Lord Lieutenants and Masters of Foxhounds. Generally British men claimed the right to manage by owning old school ties and speaking loudly in posh accents. How they progressed from their first job depended on their relatives and old school chums. (Thus the Charge of the Light Brigade was the proud work of a general whose chief qualification was that he was a grandson of the Duke of Beaufort.)

For most of the twentieth century only two lights shone among the benighted hosts of amateur British managers. The first was the accounting profession, which taught vast numbers of businessmen how to count beans, and the second light shone from the management development schemes of a number of big companies, such as Unilever, ICI, BP, Ford, and Marks and Spencer. For eleven years I manned one of these searchlights, identifying talent, and feeding it into a management development programme. It may have been a humble role in a short-term enterprise, but it was intensely exciting at the time. It brought me into contact with thousands of people, and it also brought me affluence beyond my childhood dreams.

As Unilever's spokesman on higher education, I found myself rubbing shoulders with royalty, and being wined and dined in the Houses of Parliament by scheming politicians. I also met some of the nation's best brains, partly through Unilever, and partly in the course of my academic research, and I learned to distinguish high merit from high office. In 1984 I witnessed the start of the fat-cat phenomenon, and I learned that it is based on greed combined with bluff (which politicians are too timid to call). Over the next ten years I saw a decent society (where people often cooperated) transformed into a rotten one (where people can only compete), a society with few winners and many losers. And I realised that I had been lucky in a way that few plebs would be in the future.

In 1994 I accepted early retirement from Unilever on terms so generous that they were as difficult to refuse as the Mafia's. Dawn and I wanted to see more of the world, because five weeks' holiday a year had not been enough to satisfy our wanderlust, and I also wanted yet another career, an academic one. That summer I was made an Honorary Fellow of my college and I saw this as a sign that time was ripe for a change in direction. I wanted to do more research, more reading, and more writing. I also hoped to make myself useful to my friends in academia, who had been so supportive of my efforts.

Besides these positive reasons for my retirement there were also negative ones. The climate of British business was changing: the *personnel* function was about to rebrand itself as *human resources*, adopting the language and morality of the slave trade. In future it seemed that young people would pay for their own business education, which would ensure that only those with rich parents or a willingness to incur massive debts would become tomorrow's top managers.

My suspicions that the days of UCMDS were numbered were increased by the announcement of the next chairman of Unilever Ltd. More than twenty years earlier Niall had failed a UCMDS selection board, because he was too confident of his own judgement and too dismissive of other people's inputs. From my many contacts with him, I felt that the board's observations had been accurate, and also that Niall still resented his rejection. His own career represented the alternative model to schemes like UCMDS: he took a master's degree in business at UC Dublin and then joined an Irish company, which Unilever later acquired. It seemed reasonable to assume that Niall's appointment would eventually lead to the end of internal management development and training in Unilever. I did not know how long Unilever's essential inertia would delay that end, but I knew that I did not want to see it.

So ended my eleven years of doing what I claimed was the best job in Unilever; through all that time I had been happy exploring the world of minds, and I had been fascinated and stimulated by what I found. But in 1995 I looked forward to devoting more time to my own.

21

WORDS

I am what Iris Murdoch called a *word-child*, although I lack the brutality and sadism of her hero, who stole and then killed both the wives of his tutor. Murdoch's hero was also a fake: plebs (of whom she had no experience) do not grow up in caravans with women named Wilhelmina (called 'Auntie Bill'); nor do they travel endlessly around the Circle Line for the want of anything better to do with their pathetic little lives. In contrast to her fiction, I am a genuine pleb; but I am also a word-child, and on retirement from business I wanted to immerse myself in the world of books.

Joining the senior common room at Westfield brought me into the world of British and American Hispanism, which had assumed a special importance during the Franco era. The Generalissimo had appointed Ramón Menéndez Pidal as his cultural enforcer, and even Charlton Heston and Sophia Loren, in the film *El Cid*, had to act out Don Ramón's fascist imagination. This meant that critical and original thinking about Spanish literature and history had to move elsewhere. At Westfield I joined the Association of Hispanists of Great Britain and Ireland and I met many of its members at Alan's Medieval Hispanic Research Seminars in the college. There I heard and discussed papers by scholars from Britain and abroad and I discovered that, providing the speaker spoke slowly, which the most experienced ones always did, I could follow lectures in Spanish.

Since I had been going deaf for five years this was a surprise. I had listened to audio tapes of actors reciting Spanish poetry during those years, but had always had to turn my tape recorder up to full volume. Spanish literature came alive for me in those seminars. In due course I delivered my own papers (since half of those delivered were in English), and I received many helpful suggestions for my own research. Other members of Westfield's staff also gave me a great deal of help, especially two ladies named Jane and one named Leslie, who were Hispanists; Barry, who was a multilingual medieval scholar; Ralph, who was an expert in linguistics; and Peter, who was Professor of French, and an Occitan scholar of great distinction. The Medieval Hispanic Research Seminar and its members were to occupy much of my time in retirement.

My second thesis occupied five summers, including one where I had to do jury duty. For a fortnight I attended court and for most of it was the object of defence counsel's objections, because men in suits are more likely to find the accused guilty. I worked on my thesis solidly through my hours of waiting in the jury room, even though the coffee was disgusting. I actually served on two short trials; the first because the number of men in suits defeated the defence counsel, the second because the defendant was a woman, and the defence counsel focused on removing women in twinsets. Both defendants were guilty, although their counsel's lies hid this until the judge came to sentencing, when the truth emerged. I was sorry for the accused, whose main crimes were being young and poor, and I was glad when they received light sentences.

My second thesis was accepted and the viva became a pleasant social occasion. As it stood, my thesis would find no publisher: it was very long and covered eight languages, and as a book it would not find enough readers to be profitable. So I set it aside for my retirement, when I would have time to turn it into a couple of dozen articles for publication in academic journals. But I continued reading around the subject each summer, in case what I had written became out of date. Soon after, Westfield was forced to merge with Queen Mary College for cost reasons. The Hampstead site was sold for a small fortune for development as a block of apartments for Arab millionaires. But many of the buildings remained empty and decaying for a decade, because the overeager enforcers of the merger hadn't noticed that they were entailed.

These buildings had been gifts from rich Westfield alumni, to whose heirs they would revert if not used for educational purposes. To crown this farce, much of Westfield was used to accommodate students from Kings College, in The Strand, to which they had to commute using three changes of transport. This episode showed that if London was a single (federal) university, it was a dysfunctional one. Meanwhile the new Queen Mary and Westfield College, deep in the East End of London, benefited financially from the sale of the part of Westfield's site that wasn't entailed, and *Westfield* still exists as a street name on the site of London's biggest student village. The federal university's constituent colleges are now universities in their own right.

Queen Mary was the best college with which to merge because it was the smallest: University College swallowed everything, including the University of London itself eventually, and Kings College was little better. The Imperial College of Science and the London School of Economics grew, but their prime commitment was to their original disciplines. So for Westfield's Spanish Department the best fate was to become part of a new School of Modern Languages in Mile End. There ex-Westfield staff played a major role in shaping the future and I was invited to become a member of the senior common room with the title (but no stipend) of Research Fellow. Though the new college's SCR was full of strangers, and therefore less warm and friendly than

Westfield's, the School of Modern Languages retained much of what was best in Hampstead, including Alan, Ralph, one Jane, and the Medieval Research Seminars.

A couple of years later, Graham, the Principal, and Martin, the Chairman of the Council, bestowed upon me the title of Honorary Fellow of the College, which was well worth having because it gave me the rights of a staff member for life. The other fellows were very distinguished public figures, including the college's longer-serving professors emeriti. My elevation to this assembly of the great and the good was, I suspect, due to Graham thinking that I was more important within Unilever than I actually was, and to his need for someone to dress up as Santa Claus.

The new Honorary Fellow had to *process* to the stage for the annual degree ceremony, receive a eulogy, and do a considerable amount of *doffing* of his ermine hat. For the ceremony I had to wear not the plain maroon gown that I had avoided hiring by having my PhD sent on by post, but a splendid scarlet and yellow effort, which looked as if it had been run up from Suffolk regimental ties. I was able to process (something like an inebriated slow march) well enough, but I could not keep up with Graham when he doffed because he had done it many times before. I enjoyed sitting on the stage watching the new graduates, swathed in bible-black gowns, collect their diplomas, until the time came for me to be eulogised.

Who was this man, I thought, that Graham was describing? He had gained the best London first in Latin in 1958 (if Latin was so important, why had the College closed its Classics department?); he had been a successful businessman for more than thirty years (this would have brought jeers from Unilever House); he had written two doctoral theses in his middle age (what was wrong with the first?); he sat on University Appointments Boards (just one), and Government Steering Groups (also one, from which he resigned on a point of principle). If this was what celebrity was made of, then celebrity was bullshit, but Graham was far too nice a man for me to interrupt him. So I did some more doffing and processing and became an Honorary Fellow. I still have a photo somewhere of Graham and Martin dressed in ecclesiastical purple, and me looking like a grinning, beardless Santa Claus.

The government steering group to which Graham referred was on setting up a system for the measurement of quality in higher education, and was chaired by a polytechnic professor with an axe to grind: she was no doubt popular and wanted quality measured by student feedback. The *eminences grises* behind her were aggressive and domineering civil servants, who wanted to boast to their political masters that they had adopted the latest management fads from Japan: Total Quality Management (TQM) and the pursuit of Excellence (meaning whatever delights your customers). Some other members of the steering group were also from industry, but they weren't honest enough to admit that TQM had failed in their companies (some of which folded soon after TQM passed into the assessment of higher education).

My only ally was a chemistry professor who insisted on the obvious: you measure the quality of a department's teaching by comparing its students' competence before and after taking the course. When the civil servants ignored this contribution and my defence of it, and carried on designing feedback forms to test the popularity of lecturers, I resigned, and had I not been busy on other things I would have produced a critical minority report.

I was involved in one other academic ceremony while I was still with Unilever, but it was a very informal affair. For many years I served on the Appointments Board of the University of Manchester, alongside academics, other employers, local VIPs, and student representatives. I had accepted this invitation because that university was a major source of UCMDS recruits, and the board's meetings gave me the opportunity to meet interesting people (ranging from the space-explorers of Jodrell Bank to Britain's first transvestite President of the Students' Union). In 1995 I was made an Honorary Companion of the University, alongside clerks, librarians, porters, and several other people who had done far more for the University of Manchester than I had. I felt it a privilege to be associated with another world-class university, and I enjoyed meeting some of the unsung heroes of British higher education.

My farewell party in Unilever House allowed me to reconnect with many old friends. Trevor retired before me and he was succeeded by Hugh, another of my former colleagues from Lever Brothers. Hugh was aware that a data protection act was about to open the personal files of every employee and he decided to read out extracts from mine. Its entertainment highlights were documents from 1960: a letter from Freddie described me as 'the ablest student he had ever had' (homophobic guffaws); and my UCMDS board report noted my IQ-test result and predicted a meteoric career in Unilever (even louder hoots of laughter). In my speech I confessed the mixed emotions and anxiety that I think everyone feels on retirement, and I spoke of my plans to do some sort of voluntary work at Queen Mary and as much travelling as I could afford. And, of course, I wished everyone present well in the future. Retirement is practice for dying, but being retired need not be practice for being dead.

I retired in October and Dawn retired at Christmas; she enrolled for supply teaching, but in the three years that followed she accepted only work at her old school. She had made some of her closest and dearest friends there, and they did not allow retirement to separate them. I began by exploring what type of help I could give the School of Modern Languages, and I spent some time in Spanish conversation classes taught by a lady from Barcelona. I tried hard to produce exactly the same noises as she did, but my deafness made this difficult. I was also able to attend every medieval seminar for that term.

In January Dawn and I set out on a round-the-world journey, travelling from West to East. We spent three weeks in India and two in Argentina, and in between visited Bali, the Great Barrier Reef, and Auckland. In India we stayed at the best hotels in Delhi, Jaipur,

Bombay, Goa, and Madras, and we filled in some important gaps in our knowledge of the country. We were also reunited with a lot of old friends. We were delighted to see how much the standards of living of the privileged had risen, and dismayed to see how unchanged were the lives of the poor. As on our business visit to China three years earlier, we realised that what these two great countries were selling to the world was poverty. Low standards of living brought low-cost labour and, until Western standards of living fell to Asian levels, manufactured goods would flood from East to West. It was also disturbing to see how much progress religious fascism had made in India.

In Bali we had a beach and sightseeing holiday, which was threatened by monsoon rains that didn't actually fall, and we arrived in Cairns during the annual *Wets,* as the monsoon is termed. (Syllables, like rain, are a luxury in Australia). Snorkelling on the Reef proved fascinating, as did cays and islands and rainforests. We spent our only really wet day at the zoo, marvelling at the continent's unlikely creatures. We saw little of Sydney except the airport, but in New Zealand combined meeting old friends with sightseeing and relaxing on beaches. We flew to Buenos Aires by night and were kept awake for all eleven hours of the journey by excited teenagers whose teachers could not control them. There is a deep lack of respect amongst New Zealanders that makes them the world's best rugby players but the world's worst subordinates.

Our fortnight in Argentina was divided between BA, Iguazu, and Salta (*la Linda*), a delightful town on the edge of the desert. Iguazu Falls are a stunning spectacle, whether seen from Argentina or Brazil (we saw them from both), and visitors can walk across the long ridge of the falls on precarious walkways and jungle paths. Buenos Aires was also a revelation with its magnificent parks and buildings, its brightly coloured Italian quarter and its numerous tango cafés. We resolved to take tango lessons when we returned to the UK, but *tango argentino* never seemed quite the same in a church hall in Kentish Town.

Buenos Aires had a sad air of lost opulence (the average income there was once the same as that in Paris); nostalgia was everywhere. A crowd of old women mourned *los desaparecidos* (their murdered sons) outside the *Casa Rosada*, and a fresh bouquet of flowers appeared every morning on the tomb of Evita in *La Recoleta*, the Washington DC of cemeteries. Argentina's economic woes seemed to be related to the vast wealth gap: on either side of BA's broad highways dog-walkers juggled up to twenty dogs of different breeds for twenty pittances. In contrast, rich *Porteñas* were either overdressed, or undressed, in the most ostentatious way: thus the beauties who lounged beside our hotel's rooftop pool wore bikinis that were topless and tailless, revealing 100 per cent of both breast and buttock. And in BA's best restaurants the diners salivated over steaks every bit as plump and succulent, while in the countryside the poor starved.

In Salta we met an Australian who had visited sixty-three countries, and when we counted we realised we had visited forty, mostly thanks to Unilever. Even though my long legs suffered agonies in the unaccustomed economy class, we added some more in retirement. Yet we were relieved to return to 'Jumble Lodge', deep frozen in winter, to build new lives. We could now spend much more time together, and we spent much of it acting as unpaid servants for our grown-up children. This servitude seemed to be the latest fashion, and in one thing, at least, I was keeping up with the times. Mark had married and lived nearby (but I leave my children to tell their own stories). He persuaded us to take up tennis again, and Dawn and I played two or three times every week for the first ten years of our retirement. She still keeps fit and active this way.

By 1998 tennis racquets were made of feather-light metals and I found that my damaged ligaments had healed sufficiently for me to wield one with the aid of some strapping. Since High Barnet is the Atacama of social life, we joined a club ten miles away in Bushey. Most of the people I played with were middle-aged and, as my mobility grew slowly worse, I was no match for the younger ones. The majority of my partners and opponents were also Jewish, and one couple, who were emigrating, showed me the plans of several flats on the West Bank that they had been offered. Every one had a gas-proof room in case a final solution to the Arab problem were needed on the streets. It struck me that Israel is very much Hitler's legacy, and its five million Arabs are in a similar position today to German Jews in the 1930s.

Such things, however, could not be discussed after tennis; the only Jewish friend with whom I could discuss Israel was Gerry, who had been the lone anthropologist among the team of psychotherapists who aided Unilever on UCMDS selection boards. But, then, an anthropologist is someone to whom *nihil humani* is *alienum*. Gerry's analysis of the hierarchy in kibbutzim was fascinating: he compared it with the enclave of psychotherapists with whom we worked in Blackfriars. His studies of social drinking in Georgia and the black economy in the Soviet Union were also enlightening.

In Queen Mary, as a Fellow and at the same time a voluntary helper, I was outside the hierarchy, which I found refreshing. The College's senior staff were an interesting mixture of scholars and bureaucrats. The former were in the majority, and were always approachable and encouraging; the latter were touchy, status-conscious, and often arrogant. But the bureaucrats were easily avoided once I had discerned that some had the title of professor, while some scholars bore administrative titles.

The first piece of help I gave the School of Modern Languages was with students starting postgraduate courses. Many of these were from overseas, but home students seemed to require just as much help. Their shared problem was that they could write English of the sort found in the *Sun*, but not that found in its sister paper, the (10p) *Times*. London University's MPhil and PhD regulations demanded *Times* English (at least) and examiners penalised students who were sub-literate. I ran a series of seminars entitled *How to Write a Thesis* and gave individual help when requested. The School's various departments accepted that my completion of not one, but two, theses qualified me for this, but my chief aids were the *Modern Humanities Research Association Style Guide* and *The Reader over Your Shoulder* by Robert Graves and Alan Hodge.

I continued to give these seminars for several years, until individual departments began giving them (which made sense because different nations cling to their own typographical conventions). This left me with only the linguistics department's postgraduate students, a very international and interesting bunch. Later I took over the supervision of a couple of PhDs when their supervisors went abroad on sabbatical. From these I learned something about chivalric fiction and the sociolinguistics of Thailand. I combined this limited teaching activity with attending every seminar, symposium, and conference that I could, both in London and elsewhere. Their subjects ranged from medieval heraldry to linguistic approaches to poetry. But most of my time, in the first year or so, I spent turning chapters of my second thesis into papers and articles, and I soon found them increasingly easy to get published.

I continued to pour out articles (around forty in total, published in nine different countries) even when the School recognised me as a long-term resource and found me much more exacting work. This work, like my many articles, was motivated by a change in the way university departments were funded in the 1990s. The simple minds in the civil service had opted for measuring teaching quality by feedback forms, and research quality by the number of books and articles that members of a university department's staff produced. Every one of my articles, like those of the full-time staff, contributed to the Hispanic Studies Department gaining a five-star research rating, and that brought in large sums of government money.

This generous arrangement stopped only when an even more philistine government decided that the only purpose of an education in the humanities was to get a better job, and cut research funding altogether. But in the 1990s great value was placed on the publication of articles and short books, as against longer, deeper pieces of research that might take ten years to complete. This was part of a general dumbing-down in higher education, which also included degree-class inflation, modular courses, and soft degree courses, which required little else but watching TV and copying essays off the internet.

But in 1995 the government money was waiting, and an expansion of academic journals was required to increase competition for it. Britain's oldest journal in my field (*Hispanic Bulletin*) doubled its output by having two versions and editors, one published in Glasgow and the other in Liverpool. *Portuguese Notes* from KCL prospered, and the staff of Queen Mary began to regret that Westfield's *Journal of Hispanic Research* was in limbo. Its founding editor, a very talented man who had now moved to Spain, had made the mistake of allowing its publisher to own the journal's title. This man, named Claude, suffered badly from god, and he was now sitting on a mountain of unpublished material in the Alps waiting for illumination. My colleagues saw this as a major problem that none of them had time to tackle, and they invited me to become Editor-in-Chief of this stalled journal. It was just what I was waiting for.

It gained me an office in college, a computer, and a telephone. I spent roughly two days a week editing the journal for the next four years. The worst part came at the beginning, when I had to squeeze the material in limbo out of Claude, and wrest control of the journal from him. With a heated exchange of correspondence and suitable legal advice, I achieved both of these aims, at the cost of a slight change in title to *Hispanic Research Journal*. In seeking a replacement publisher I was just plain lucky: an excellent firm based in Leeds was collecting academic journals and needed a Spanish one. Our new account director was highly professional, his young account rep very intelligent, and the firm's owner a man of acumen. From then on everything went smoothly.

Editing *HRJ* blasted me out of the Middle Ages and into the wider world of Hispanism, but my colleagues and other British scholars nursed me through this by serving as expert readers. I learned about aspects of Iberian and Latin-American culture that I previously did not know existed. It was an education but, when my colleague Ralph retired and offered to take over, I was pleased to welcome someone with more relevant knowledge. I remained on *HRJ*'s editorial committee for a further four years, and I am happy to say that the journal is still thriving in today's bleaker academic climate.

My second job, which occupied one day a week once I had gained an assistant, benefited from the same government incentive to publish. In 1995 Alan had the idea of publishing a series of monographs by the members of his medieval research seminars. A monograph is a detailed book on a single specialist subject, and most monographs are quite short (100-200 pages). But to the civil servants responsible for the research quality assessment exercise a book is a book (at least they didn't propose measuring quality by the thousand words). The first volume in the series PMHRS (Papers of the Medieval Research Seminar) appeared in 1995, and by 1997 there were eight monographs in print. The research assessment exercise credited each publication to the author's university, but some credit accrued to Queen Mary for publishing the series, and members of our staff figured prominently among the authors.

Approximately half the monographs were in Spanish and half in English, and about 300 copies of each volume were produced (plus review and complimentary copies). Although the books were carefully edited and nicely produced, they sold very slowly. Alan's secretary, who had many other duties, could find time to do little more than wait for orders to come in. When the grant of money the college had provided to kick-start the series ran out, Alan appealed to me for help. I had never marketed books before, but I quickly saw the need for a change in tactics. We had to get a copy of each volume into nearly 200 university libraries (across Spain, Latin America, the USA, and the UK), and we had to get at least ten specialist booksellers in those countries to order a dozen of each title as it came out. This level of sales would ensure that the profit on each volume paid for the printing of the next.

Over nine years I managed to establish contact with the required number of booksellers and universities, and it was very good for my Spanish, which now became a unique mixture of medieval poetic and modern commercial terms. We produced (Alan was production manager) and distributed (I was distribution manager) more than fifty titles in the series. And, like the seminars themselves, PMHRS still continues today in the hands of a new generation of Queen Mary staff.

I contributed two volumes to the PMHRS series: the first was a linguistic study of fifteenth-century Spain's greatest poem, Juan de Mena's *Laberinto de Fortuna*; and the second was a collection of studies on medieval Iberian versification from the earliest times until 1520. Most of my published articles had a comparative slant or covered a single Spanish or English author, but my collection of studies on Iberian poetry gave me the idea for a third book. *A New History of English Metre* was accepted by an Oxford publisher recently taken over by the printers of *Hispanic Research Journal*. Writing that book gave me the perfect excuse for rereading many thousands of lines of English poetry. To parody Plato, I believed that the unexamined line is not worth loving.

My work on Spanish poetry was a substitute for something I missed in retirement: I would dearly have liked to live in Spain for a few years. But, when we were blessed with four grandchildren, Dawn wanted to see them as often as possible. Grandchildren are the pearls in the oyster of old age, and grandparents can love them wholeheartedly because they are not responsible for keeping them on the straight and narrow. My four have been a constant source of delight: the turncoat Bourbon king Henri may have gained Paris by a few masses, but I gladly sacrificed *el sur caliente* for four smiling faces. Our other substitute for living in Spain was exploring it.

In my last ten years with Unilever, Dawn and I had spent most of August exploring France, often with our friends Reg and Barbara. Once we had driven around every *département* we transferred our attention to the Iberian Peninsula, where Murcia became the only province we didn't reach. Initially Reg and Barbara were our hosts in their villa on the *Costa del Sol*, but when they sold it our favourite spot became a little town called Rota near Cádiz. There were few other Brits on the Atlantic coast (the *Costa de la Luz*), which was good for my Spanish, and we stayed for several years running at what had been voted Spain's best hotel. Its food was great and it was flanked by two white, sandy beaches; the hotel front doors opened onto a town square with a castle, a medieval church, and a Moorish lighthouse.

We had discovered Rota when I spoke and joined discussions on a Summer Course at the University of Seville. The audience consisted of teachers and would-be poets and was bilingual (even the French and Catalan professors spoke in English, the latter for political reasons). My chief contribution was to compare the roles of dynamic accent in Spanish and English poetry, but this didn't stop me from joining in on every topic. One result of that visit is that I still sit on the international advisory board of *Rhythmica*, the University of Seville's journal of comparative metrics. As I open each issue I seem to smell orange blossom.

Dawn and I returned to Seville several times and grew to love the city. Its delights include Carmen's cigar factory (now the university), a splendid Moorish palace, a beautiful cathedral, the great river Guadalquivir, the elegant Alameda, the fine parks and impressive modern buildings, and a tower of gold. We usually ended the fragrant evenings in one of the small squares ringed by cafés, tucked well away from the tourist sights. We have many fond memories of the most Moorish part of Spain, *El Andalus*, but, unlike so many Brits who are happy to remain ignorant of the beauties of the Spanish language, we never made our home there.

One of the delights of retirement is meeting old friends under the most relaxed of circumstances and counting over the pleasures of your shared past. Friendship is second only to love as a reason for living. Dawn remains close to her ex-colleagues in her last school: they still lunch or dine together four or five times a year to exchange news and the latest photos of grandchildren. They also take pleasure in one another's cooking and in having a rest from it by eating out. I see the husbands of these ladies on not quite so regular a basis; John is an architect who refuses to retire, Michael an IT specialist who has devoted his retirement to the Arts, and a second John an academic who has become a successful science writer. Dawn has also kept in touch with some of her far-flung pupils and their mothers: occasionally they get to London, and when they can't they send us photographs of beautiful Japanese brides who once sat at Dawn's feet.

Until the last great downsizing I used to enjoy an annual reunion with many old friends from Unilever, but I regret to say that the grim reaper is doing his own downsizing of our generation. Alan, my supervisor and then colleague, died in 2009, to Hispanism's great loss; and Vic, my oldest friend, died in 2014 after suffering a series of strokes and lying almost helpless for ten years. His wife Adrienne remains one of our dearest friends and gives us regular news of their children and grandchildren. Of my Westfield friends, I see Barry and Jane at a reunion lunch each year, and I always try to meet Barry at his august workplace, the British Library, whenever I visit it.

Just two of our Indian friends, Jaspal and Jagdish, still come to the UK frequently, and we look forward eagerly to their visits. They both also spend time in the USA and give us a refreshing international view on everything that happens. I have kept in touch with several of my old colleagues in Unilever Recruitment, but the one I see most often is Gerry, the lone anthropologist among our selection-board advisers. After leaving the group he has enjoyed a very distinguished career in academia and he is still a busy writer and researcher. His insights and observations illuminate my interpretation of events, and we enjoy setting the world to rights over a glass of wine.

Dawn and I are also in regular contact with a few expatriate friends: Alan and Linda, our neighbours in Bombay and co-travellers in South India, remain as gracious hosts in Hampshire as they were in Nairobi. Nigel, who welcomed us to South Africa, lost Ruth, his first wife, many years ago, but he now has a new wife named Joyce, and they live nearby in Chesham. Barbara's brother Derek (who was BAT's chairman in Kenya) and his wife Pam now live in central London, and they share our enthusiasm for the Arts, travel, and grandchildren. The wives of expatriate chairmen do as important a job as their husbands and should be well paid for it: the ones we have known have been exceptionally lively and energetic people. They became highly skilled in entertaining and organising, and experts on the countries in which they lived.

Looking back at our lives, and our friends' lives, makes me realise how random the universe is. Nobody could have predicted when we were young and easy under the palm trees that Ernie, Arup, Jyant, Doreen, Margaret, or Ruth would draw very short straws, or that five grammar-school boys of the 1950s (Vic, Alan, Derek, Nick, Nigel) would have climbed so high in their careers or spent their lives where they did. Like me, they have all enjoyed many lives, and I fear that such social mobility will never be seen again in this country.

To return to my second retirement, however; by 2007 commuting to Mile End had become hard work for me, and I had done it through the ghastly days of *Railtrack*, with its constant delays and fatal crashes on the line that I used. Privatised railways continue to be, and will always be a disaster, like privatised energy generation, from which Britain was rescued by the French government. Perhaps a takeover by SNCF (also owned by the French government) is the answer to Britain's rail problems. In any event I had had enough of standing on crowded trains that were frequently stalled for long periods between slum-like stations.

My swan song at Queen Mary was a public lecture in December. Kate Elder was a bright and vivacious young Westfield student who had been killed in a road accident. Like me, and many more, she had loved the college, and her parents generously sponsored a scholarship in her name and an annual lecture. My lecture was based on a comparison of the free verse of D. H. Lawrence and Federico García Lorca.

The large audience seemed to appreciate my light-hearted approach: I even managed to quote Donald Rumsfeld. His famous phrase, 'The things we don't know we don't know,' is an anapaestic trimeter as well as being a euphemism for 'The falsehoods we promote.' The audience seemed to enjoy the poems by Lawrence and Lorca that I had chosen, and also my extended comparison of free verse with motor cars, both of which appeared around 1887. At the speech's close the audience graciously applauded, perhaps because my ready-read spectacles had broken in the first five minutes and I'd spoken for the allotted hour without looking at my notes. After forty-odd years I had at last learned the essence of public speaking: know exactly what you're going to say before you start.

In 2007 we sold 'Jumble Lodge'; our 100-year-old willow was falling branch by branch and so was I, regularly from ladders, despite paying tree surgeons a fortune for their services. We moved to a maisonette (with a gardener) in the village of Harpenden, which was centrally placed for spending more time with our grandchildren. Before we moved I disposed of 3,500 of my 4,000 books and I said *adios* to many of my Spanish favourites in that downsizing. For the second time I deserted Spanish literature for English, and I kept mostly books on Latin and English poetry, the grammars of twenty languages, and reference works. I have also kept all the volumes that I worked on personally, as author or editor, and the *festschrifts* dedicated to my friends. Many of these friends are now dead, but I can open the pages and visit them. And when I need books not in my few shelves, I use the British Library, only half an hour away at St Pancras.

I continued writing after my second retirement: articles on Eliot, Tennyson, and Chaucer, and a book on the last-named. My particular interest in Chaucer was revived by being invited to examine three Oxford theses on his language and metre, and to peer-review an American book on the performance of his verse. Between 2011 and 2013 I also assisted in the supervision of a thesis for the University of Lisbon (it was on Pessoa's poetry in three languages, Portuguese, English, and French). But I spent much more time reading: works on history, economics, and politics, and literary fiction (defined as fiction that takes language seriously).

I tried my hand at non-academic writing, including these memoirs. My first attempt was at some short stories set in 1960s India. An Indian publisher liked them, but he recommended that I publish in the UK because their atheism would offend Indian sensibilities. A literary agent in Britain, where publishers are inaccessible, told me that the only people in Britain who were interested in India read Urdu. I reflected that perhaps my only subject of common interest with the British public might be pornography and wrote a futuristic fantasy that I sent to another literary agent. Her comments did include the phrase 'well written', but she advised me to leave erotica to young women, who were the only people who understood readers with attention spans of less than twenty minutes. '*Chicklit*,' she warned me, 'is for *litchicks*.' So I left it alone.

And now I sit and read and write, do chores, run errands, and play a little bridge; and Dawn and I watch our grandchildren grow up, and support and encourage them in every way we can. I was surprised by the way that our children turned out to be so unlike us, but now revel in the differences between our grandchildren. I resolved to compensate for my failings as a father by being a better grandfather. I had not been a good father, at least partly because I had never had one; Sarah had raised me to believe that children belong to their mothers and that a father expresses his love by working to support them. I interpreted the role of father in a narrow economic way: my duty was to provide my family with financial security, a nice home, the material possessions my childhood had lacked. This may have been a type of love, but it was a very different love from the passion I felt for their mother. Sarah had held back from being a kiss-and-cuddle parent lest her son become too soft to survive, and I did likewise. I did not consider whether this was the best way to raise daughters, and as a result I became chiefly a discipline figure. The loss was as much mine as theirs.

I wonder what sort of lives our grandchildren will have: will they be as many as ours? Could they possibly be as lucky as I have been? For sure, their lives will be different: their generation has so many mountains to climb and so many barriers to break down. There are many reasons why we should fear for the future of our grandchildren, but there are also good grounds for hope. Among the many reasons for fear are climate change, population growth, and deepening religious hatred. Today's politicians have failed abysmally to tackle all three, but tomorrow's politicians will probably do better – if only because they could scarcely do worse.

The majority of people in the West should also fear globalisation: it enables the owners of capital to cut costs by forcing the living standards in developed countries down to third-world levels. *Tax piracy* (the large scale non-payment of taxes for any reason) is also a major threat to most people: it is capable of bankrupting nations so that they are unable to care for the sick, the handicapped, the very old, and the very young. Individuals and businesses that don't pay tax are at a huge competitive advantage and, if unchecked, they will gradually eliminate tax-paying competitors from every market. Only an all-out war on tax havens, criminalising those who use them, can save the Western world from bankruptcy (either of governments or of the tax-paying masses), which would destroy the infrastructure that we call civilisation.

The chief reason for hope is that the rich may come to their senses and realise that it is in their interests for the masses to have a greater share of the wealth. An affluent population consumes more and this makes economies grow faster, so that the wealthy become even wealthier: elites can extract more if their victims have more. It is also in the interests of the rich to reverse the current downward trend in social mobility. Many plebs (by which I mean all those outside the elite) have exceptional intelligence and energy: if they are able to rise by individual effort they are less likely to use their talents to engineer the overthrow of the ruling class. Social mobility is an insurance policy against civil disorder, sabotage, and the destruction of property. One day the present elite, who own 90 per cent of Britain's property, may realise this and act accordingly.

I regret that I shall not see the outcome of my family's struggles, and I understand why primitive societies believed that the spirits of their ancestors lingered on earth to observe and perhaps to help. But even a word-child must eventually fall silent and be satisfied with having lived so long by words, with words, and for words.